BY SOPHIE PARKIN

THE COLONY ROOM CLUB
1948 - 2008

A HISTORY OF BOHEMIAN SOHO

Contents

Marlborough

Marlborough Fine Art (London) Ltd
6 Albemarle Street, London W1S 4BY
Telephone: +44 (0)20 7629 5161
Telefax: +44 (0)20 7629 6338
e-mail: mfa@marlboroughfineart.com
www.marlboroughfineart.com
Registered in England no. 925765
VAT Registration no. 239 0802 67

Chairman:
The Duke of Beaufort
Directors:
P. Levai, J. Erle-Drax, G. Parton,
A. Bienger, F. Rossi

Dear Sophie Parkin,

I spent far too much time in the Colony Room; between 1956 and 1976, one or two evenings a week.

17th August 2011

Like most of us, I drank too much, talked drivel, had some stimulating conversation — often with Francis Bacon, a few arguments — always with Francis Bacon. Some pick-ups — usually but not always, injudicious.

I was aware of Muriel Belchers moral stature, her courage, her instinctive assessment of people. She was for honesty; for generosity for the vulnerable, against the self-righteous and self protective, the smug and pretentious.

. When she was gone the Colony lost its attraction for me.

yours sincerely

Frank Auerbach

Marlborough Gallery Inc., 40 West 57th Street, New York, N.Y. 10019, U.S.A. Tel: +1 212 541 4900; Telefax: +1 212 541 4948.
Galería Marlborough, S.A., Orfila 5, 28010 Madrid, Spain. Tel: +34 91 319 1414; Telefax: +34 91 308 4345.

In 1982 my father Michael Parkin put on an exhibition at his Belgravia gallery called 'Artists of the Colony Room'. With paintings by Edward Burra, Lucian Freud, Frank Auerbach, Craigie Aitchinson, Francis Bacon, Nina Hamnett and Jankel Adler, the show finally cemented the reputation of the Colony Room Club (or 'Muriel's', as it was always known by its older clientele) outside its own membership. Although legendary, the club was not grand and the Colony lay at the top of one of Soho's seamier stairwells, into which guests were disgorged into an unprepossessing and rather small room. Nonetheless, it had a magic that even one-time Colony denizen Aleister Crowley couldn't quantify.

This book is a commemoration of the Colony and the people drawn to it over its 60 year history. From 1948 when it opened, to its closure in 2008, the club's membership was a Who's Who of the Arts in the post-war period: the ballet brigade, the composers, poets, writers, designers, film directors and producers, the dons, MP's, critics, actors, Lords and journalists. Even the odd spy and gangster looked in then stayed, and political intrigue and sex scandals dashed up and down that dingy staircase for decades. But the Colony always transcended its individual members, and remains more than the sum of its parts.

The Colony Room Club is a story of culture and association in post-war London, all forged in one small green room that allowed autonomy and freedom when so much was outlawed in England. As it grew, it charted the growing confidence in the arts in Britain, and much of the national cultural story in the last six decades has a link to the Colony.

The members of the Colony were often in the avant-garde, most notably Francis Bacon, the most famous denizen of the Dean Street club. Still, Bacon is just one element in the club, which motivated – and possibly destroyed - many other talents. Like other legendary meeting places, such as Les Deux Magots in Paris' Left Bank, and The Cedar Tavern in Abstract Expressionist New York, Dean's bar in pre-war Tangier, the Colony was a place where its guests felt more at home than home, where they mixed with like-minded souls when not at work, where conversation and drinking were the main entertainments.

Soho has always changed, reinventing itself every decade. Some say the best days were the

1950's, others the 70s, 90's or the nought-ies. In a long tradition set by the late Spectator columnist Jeffrey Bernard, Soho is never 'like it used to be, but then it never was.'

Since the Colony opened in 1948 the change in Soho, from sex zone to celebrity media zone has been dramatic. Throughout these years, however, nothing much changed about Muriel's club. The Colony passed from Muriel Belcher on her death in 1979 to Ian Board her barman (reluctantly at first), then when Board died in 1994, to resident barman Michael Wojas. Each one created his own Colony, whilst the essence always stayed constant.

There were, and remain, conflicts about the legacy of the Colony. Arguments over ownership of the club's collection of paintings and sculptures raged. When Michael Wojas became ill and wished the club to end, nobody had realised how important it had become until it was threatened with closure, especially since the threat did not come from predatory outside developments but from within. It became imperative that the Colony remained there, part of Soho's history, squeezed between an Italian restaurant and The Groucho Club. Then again, should it be kept as a kind of museum piece? Or would it have again reinvented itself?

When you put the Colony into the context of 20th century British Art history, it is an obvious loss. As to why it survived for so long as an extraordinary haven of creativity, the answer has to come from Bacon himself: 'You could always be yourself'. The Colony was a place where one could feel uninhibited and unjudged.

That the Colony Room Club continued during the property booms and service industry that changed central London is a remarkable case of survival. Perhaps it is down to the resilience of this club, its extraordinary membership and the charismatic foulmouthed founder Muriel Belcher, who set a new bench mark for club-owner: brutally business-minded, humorously disposed and secretly compassionate. The Colony was a remarkable place, and while the octogenarians and upwards who remembered it remain alive and willing to tell their stories, I felt the club deserves its history to be chronicled in this book.

Chapter 1
The Vintage 40s

This is War

The Colony Room Club opened in December 1948, and instantly became a sanctuary, like Soho itself, for the artists and outsiders in a devastated society. War had unsettled Britain and during the long years of want, many people changed morally and emotionally, wild away from home. As Sylvia Scaffardi founder of The National Council of Liberties in the 1930's told me before she died. Already well into her 90's, she spoke with certainty about freedom, in her smart vowels.

'Sex became an expression and proof of vitality and life. Darling thing, when you are uncertain of whether you were going to die that day, what did the occasional fuck in a doorway with a stranger during black-out matter? It made you feel vital, alive, that was the thing.' And who could see to tell after dark?

Post war, and the lights back on, Britain was a place of shattered dreams. Heroes from that war were lost in a forgotten rebuild, some found it difficult to be relevant in a peace time desperate to build prosperity, family values and normality.

EARLIEST SURVIVING PIC OF LITTLE MISS MU IN HER 'MUSIC BOX' DAYS...

Britain's government had to forge a new way forward and on towards the Festival of Britain 1951, that covered the South Bank and Leslie Martin's modernist tribute of the Festival Hall. Other's sought a different escape.

Muriel's, as The Colony Room Club came to be known by those that frequented it from the early days, for the energy and humour dispensed by the charismatic bisexual from Birmingham, was born of its time. It was the less rowdy, smaller, more homosexually tolerant version of its neighbour, The Gargoyle Club. Across the road in Meard Street, The Gargoyle had been opened by David Tennant in January 1925 with his wife theatre actress Hermione Baddley and was a nightclub in the traditional sense. There was a dining area, a band for dancing and a bar for cocktails and champagne and it had been lavishly decorated with Matisse murals, engraved glass and an elevator to get to and from the fifth storey. And though many of the same people were members of both establishments, they had very different uses. Muriel's was a bar in a room which opened Monday to Saturday from 3pm until 11pm to fill the gap when the licensing laws made all pubs close until 5.30pm. After 11pm members flowed up and through to The Gargoyle to eat and dance and talk and fight until the early hours of the morning. The next day The York Minster pub (which became known as The French House, frequented by the Free French led by Charles De Gaulle during the war) further along towards Shaftsbury Avenue in Dean Street, became the hangover cure from the night before. The York Minster opened its doors at 11am, dispensing Pastis to settle uneasy stomachs and for the necessary cashing of cheques. And if you could afford this merry go round lifestyle, that many artists and writers hopped on and off from, depending on picture, or pulp fiction sales, pre-lunch drinks as they were euphemistically termed (often no lunch was required) turned into oysters and champagne at Wheeler's and once again Muriel's and the Gargoyle.

For the artist Francis Bacon, one of the most famous now, of Muriel's adopted 'son's', this was his comfort zone of habit, but then after some late night gambling, rough sex with a working man and early morning painting until lunch; it was a

3

routine not geared towards sleep. But who lived this kind of life apart from Bacon? Not many.

The rest of the country was stuck with its meagre meat, sweet, shoe and butter rations, listening to the radio and still no fresh or tinned fruit. They lived lives ruled not by pub opening times but clocking into work, making do and mending, trying to lead respectable lives even if that required lies about where they'd been. For many a day out in the West End, a real treat on the bus from Streatham or Dollis Hill, was simply to window shop, to look at the displays and dream. Not all it was knocked up to be. In Noel Coward's Brief Lives, Celia Johnson and Trevor Howard repress their passion in noble sacrifice of doing the right thing for a government that wanted to get the nation back on track but how realistic was it? It later transpired members of the wartime government could be rather more lax, than the rest of their lectured citizens.

4

ST. ANNES, OPPOSITE THE YORK MINSTER, DEAN STREET, SOHO 1940

Too many tightening of belts had ripped corsets free. Marriages were made on leave, after a few weeks or months of knowing someone through letters, no more than one or two nights for a honeymoon, cemented the deal. War was an emotional charge for commitment that acted like night blindness. A famous joke of the time went - I wouldn't buy a suit in the same light I'd find a wife. Waking up at the end of the war, husbands that might not then have been seen for several years, returned as strangers to wives and children, but had they ever been anything else to each other? Everybody relied on keeping up appearances, they couldn't afford anything else.

> **Now Albert's coming back, make yourself a bit smart...**
> **He's been in the army four years, he wants a good time,**
> **And if you don't give it him, there's other's will, I said.**
>
> TS Eliot The Wasteland

Poem: Courtesy Faber

If they wanted to do the maths they knew a child or two, now in the family, could not be theirs but perhaps guilt of their own behaviour, with prostitutes or local girls or boys when stationed far away, stopped them commenting. Morals had to be returned, proper behaviour reinstalled, Family put at the heart, for society to progress. But war had revealed the true nature of some people to themselves as well as others, they didn't want, or couldn't go back. Some people hadn't changed since the roar of the Twenties and didn't see why the hell they should exchange being 'Bright Young Things' for Dowdy Old Has-beens.

The Colony Room Club was a place of freedom and entertaining speech, where traditional morals were left on the doormat and sex was allowed, with whomever. The camp and the comedic Coward style piano, cocktail dress, black humour and champagne, were a quick escape up some backstairs and through a door into a wonderland of bamboo and palm tree décor; smoke and mirrors magicked away the world outside. If the outside world seemed hostile, it was because it was, to gays, artists, free thinking women, people of colour and poets, right through to the eighties and some would say longer. If you felt yourself being criticised for the cut of your jib, but were quick enough with your tongue and easy with your wallet, there was always a home and a party for you at the Colony Room Club, far away from the maddeningly normal crowds outside in London's West End.

Clubland

The Colony Room grew in a city that had witnessed the extraordinary convulsions of war. In 1940, the war had five years left to run, and the Blitz bombs had decimated London. In Soho, St Patrick's Church in Soho Square was hit in 1940 through the roof, causing great damage. St Anne's Church, on Dean Street, can be seen in its bombed state. A tenement on Newport Street near Carnaby Street, the Madrid restaurant on Dean Street and the Chez Fillez restaurant on Frith Street were all bombed on night raids. Somehow Soho continued through this turmoil. The poet Oliver Bernard got his first job at Chez Fillez aged fourteen. The market continued in Berwick Street, while from Piccadilly to Oxford Street working girls sold their wares on the pavements and passages of the district with the typical refrain: 'Fancy a good time love?'.

Meanwhile, the afternoon clubs thrived with a good mixture of classes and professions. Oliver Bernard wrote in his autobiography, 'Getting Over It' about the rich experience of Soho in wartime: 'In those first days in Soho I tried not to be English... As a foreigner, preferably French, I would be able to smoke and drink precociously; even associate with women I hoped... The War had closed the Continent. After Dunkirk, Dean Street and Old Compton Street were suddenly full of Free French. Clubs appeared on unlikely first floors... there seemed to be no more anti-Nazi place in London.' Bernard described how people stood on the pavement and talked outside the Bar Italia and outside Parmigiani's... 'on the corner of Frith and Old Compton Street where there were still yellow horse-drawn Carlo and Gatti ice-carts, traces of straw, nosebags and horse-dung.

THE FRENCH, IN THE FRENCH HOUSE...

At any moment London rain on asphalt and tarmac might give way to Continental sunshine.' Soho promised excitement to young and old. It always had.

Since its beginnings as an urban area of immigrants Soho had become an international zone, home to the Continental restaurants, bars, shops and brothels of Central London that they ran and with them, a sense of tolerance and liberation. The district's first buildings were erected in Soho Fields for Charles II's son, the Duke of Monmouth (who was finally beheaded in 1685 on Tower Hill) - a grand and no longer existing house that stood in what is now Soho Square. Next came Fauconberg House, built for Oliver Cromwell's son in law, and other of his friends including a gentleman builder named Richard Frith who developed the main street that runs between the square and Old Compton Street in 1680.

There were more specific reasons why Soho became international or, to use Bernard's term, 'continental'. In 1791 Monmouth House became the French Embassy and fashionable Soho, by then already raffish, began to be known as the Latin Quarter because of the overwhelming amount of French incomers. St Patrick's Catholic Church with it's extensive catacombs beneath the square, replaced Carlisle House in 1793, where in the mid-18th century, Madame Cornely entertained and became renowned as London's first nightclub queen. For a decade or so the streets were choked with the carriages of nobility and gentry attending her balls and masquerades. In her youth, Madame had been a beautiful conquest of Casanova, with whom she had a daughter who went on to become the Queen's Almoner - the individual in charge of distributing funds to the sick, the aged and poor. Thus were the two parts of Soho set in train: destitution and elegant depravity. Once her party nights became less fashionable, Madame Cornely was reduced to selling asses milk on Knightsbridge Green, pre Harrods and in distributing alms, her daughter forgot her mother, in the race to forget the disgrace of her father, the legendary lover Casanova. Soho people have always been creative in making enough to get by, from Cornely to Canaletto and Marx.

Sexy Soho

As soon as World War II was over in 1945, business reverted to a kind of normality - that is; drinking, prostitution, delicatessens, cafes and racketeering. Food rationing lasted until 1954, but no such austerity existed in the world of sex. Mattresses came out at night to fill the shop floors, to be returned to be collected on carts the next morning, so that the shops could open for service, such was the relentless demand for sex among servicemen and sailors. Pavements were slippery with condoms. The working girls made good business, and a decorum of sorts was upheld. In Patrick Hamilton's semi autobiographical novel 'Twenty Thousand Streets Under the Sky' (1935), which the author had hoped to be an update of George Bernard Shaw's 'Mrs Warren's Profession', he wrote to a friend: 'Lately I've been making the most extraordinary expeditions into Soho... It's always been my ambition to write about harlots... My latest adventures have led me into remarkable sociological observations and enlightenments...' A Soho encounter was described in David Niven's 1971 autobiography, 'The Moon's a Balloon'.

"Nessie, when I first saw her, was 17 years old, honey blonde, pretty rather than beautiful, the owner of a voluptuous but somehow innocent body and a pair of legs that went on forever. She was a Piccadilly whore. I was a 14-year-old heterosexual schoolboy... "All right, it's still early and you're a bit young but come on home and I'll give you a good time".

Back then, the locals tended to sympathise with the girls. Gaston Berlemont, born and brought up in The York Minster or 'French House', which he inherited from his father Victor Berlemont in 1950, told author and journalist Mary Kenny in the 70s. "You know Mary, things aren't the way they used to be, even the tarts these days are really rough. You should have seen the prostitutes that we used to have around here when I was a child, they had such beautiful manners; always in Mass every Sunday." "But they were prostitutes, why would they be at church?", "That was their profession

GOODTIME GIRLS, FEELING SAFE IN THE YORK MINSTER...

Mary, it had nothing to do with their faith. They were always so beautifully turned out. Little white gloves and everything."

In Soho, through the post war period, The Windmill Theatre continued to show the erotic spectacle Mrs Henderson Presents, a near 24-hour a day exhibition of semi-clad models in the 'most artistic of lighting and poses for gentlemen audiences' as it said in the brochure. Anyone who didn't know where the Windmill was could easily spot it from the queue of raincoat-clad men queuing around the corner before the place opened in the morning. As far as the Soho girls were concerned they were simply making a living and helped each other to bring custom to the area.

The York Minster was the Soho pub they went to on nights off and over-friendly customers would be ejected by Victor Berlemont and then later by Gaston whose rejoinder to the unruly was 'One of us has got to leave, and it's not going to be me.' It remained his cry at throwing-out time until the end of his years at the French House.

Opposite The French house was the back of St Anne's Church on Dean Street, reduced to a crater which became a cesspool reservoir afloat with a battalion of phosphorescent prophylactics or 'French Letters' as they came to be known. The British Board of Film censors in Soho Square also got doodle-bugged, but The French with The Berlemonts kindness to prostitutes and sheltering underage drinkers during bombing raids, and the prevalently homosexual pick up joint, The Golden Lion, opposite, had with God's hand been saved. The Lord works in mysterious ways.

A bomb stopped business in Leicester Square on the 8th of March 1941. It dived through the roof of The Rialto cinema, and further below to the famous Café de Paris nightclub where it decapitated Ken 'Snakehips' Johnson and The West Indian Orchestra, the leading top swing band in London, while he sang and swivelled to: 'Oh Johnny, Oh Johnny how you can love'. When the emergency services arrived, the music had clearly stopped and Snakehips had lost his head aged just 26. Still, the guests sat eerily still, as though enjoying the show in their seats. As it turned out, 80 of them were dead and another 80 seriously injured.

War hadn't affected the business of The Music Box, the second business Muriel Belcher had opened after the short-lived Sphinx Club. Few can remember the latter (and it's unlikely that it had anything to do with the advertising industries' Sphinx Club set up in 1904 to make its profession more respectable). Dolly Myer had been Muriel's business partner since 1938 at both The Sphinx and The Music Box when it was still going well, due to its patronage from the leftovers of the 'Bright Young Things': the interwar generation of party-loving cocaine takers immortalised in Evelyn Waugh's 1930 novel, 'Vile Bodies'.

The silent star of GW Pabst's 'Pandora's box', Louise Brooks danced The Charleston in The Cafe de Paris in 1924 for the first time in London (Kathryn Wilson made it famous in the US) before going on to film-stardom. Brooks later wrote about the so-called 'Bright Young Things' she had met during her time in London and described them, apropos of Vile Bodies, as, 'a dreadful, moribund lot. Only a genius could have made a masterpiece out of such glum material.' Later Stephen Fry, a stalwart member of Soho's Groucho Club (but never the Colony, although it was next door), was to turn the same book into a 2003 film called 'Bright Young Things' - an emblem of Soho's great sense of continuity.

Dreadful they may have been, but the 'Bright Young Things' helped to crystallise Soho as a playground for all-night carousing and frequented all the private clubs, supper dance and cabarets that the West End could offer. Entertainment often began at midnight and continued at some venues until dawn, aided by a private party system known simply as 'Bottle Parties' where drinks had to be ordered 24-hours in advance by telephone due to licensing laws that had changed for World War I. The best of these clubs were mentioned in 'Night and Day' magazine, Graham Greene's Spectator-style literary review. As listings in the July 1937 issue announced:

'Four Hundred at Leicester Square, favourite haunt of the rich after 2am. Havana - 6 New Compton Street W.C.2 Cuban band, rumbas cabaret with Edward Cooper. Air Cooled. Breakfast. The Frisco of 17 Frith Street - Where the genuine pulse of Africa migrating via Harlem and Paris now throbs in the Soho 'boite'. This is the real thing.(Dress optional)' - Handy for the naturists.

The Hon. Elvira Barney was a founding member and regular of The Music Box, famed for shooting her homosexual, cocaine dealing lover, known as 'Spider'. She came from a family of influence and managed to be found not guilty. Thereafter, she delighted in bounding into The Music Box with the immortal lines, 'I've shot one bugger and got away with it so don't think I'd hesitate to shoot another.' Four years later she was found dead from a cocaine and alcohol binge while still in her 20s. "I found her enchanting", Muriel later said of her.

During the war The Music Box became known as a 'theatricals' hangout, a fate that The Gargoyle Club run by aristocrat David Tennant in Dean Street was so desperate not to become, that Tennant wouldn't allow Hollywood film star Tallulah Bankhead in as a member, in case it attracted more actors, or perhaps it was her style? When seeing an old lover, an aristocrat who failed to acknowledge Bankhead in the Cafe Royal in Piccadilly, she shouted back across the crowded room, 'what's the matter, don't recognise me with my clothes on?'

Well renowned, The Music Box attracted a type, even the little-known artist Francis Bacon was a member. But Dolly Myer wasn't to last, she argued with Muriel and went to run Romilly's Club. By 1949 Dolly and Muriel were friends again. Dolly married Alf Myer who pushed Dolly fatally down the stairs in the mid 50s after an argument which might have been to do with her relationship with Muriel. Muriel was never one to talk of her relationships with men or women other than to say when asked, "I'm glad to say, plenty of both."

THE FIRST MEMBERSHIP CARD

Telephone GERrard 9179

Colony Room
DEAN STREET W.1

MEMBERSHIP CARD

Member's Signature

DAVID ARCHER, TINKLES THE IVORIES.

The Real History

A small legacy to Muriel Belcher from her mother Ida in September 1948 enabled her to at last open her own place at the age of 40. She bought the lease of a previous club that was decorated in exotic fashion: bamboo, leopardskin bar stools and banquettes. In later years the name and the interior were attributed to Carmel Stuart, Muriel's mixed race girlfriend, because she came from Jamaica, a colony until 1962.

Paul Johnson, the historian and editor, remembered otherwise: "Curiously enough, I think I was taken to the Colony Room before Muriel Belcher took it over, probably 1947 or early '48. I was taken by Teddy and Jimmy Goldsmith. Teddy and I were undergraduates at Magdalen College Oxford. His younger brother Jimmy had won a big accumulator bet on the horses and netted £7,000 or £8,000 which was a hell of a lot of money then, and thought, "What the hell am I doing at Eton when I could be off having a good time?" So he ran away and came to stay with us at Oxford. His mother came to try to persuade him back, but he remained and we used to go to London. I wouldn't swear to it, but the Colony seemed to be a place for people who worked in the Colonies. The chap who took us there was a friend of John Aspinall (later to be the owner of Annabel's nightclub and friend to Lord Lucan): perhaps John Sutro. He said you could get Benzedrine over the bar which was about as wicked as things got in those innocent days. That was pre-Belcher and it was a place where people like district inspectors from Malaya, came to find people like them. Muriel transformed it because she belonged to the artistic and sexual bohemian underground of the time. She knew exactly what she was doing."

The one room above an Italian Trattoria in 41 Dean Street, Soho, up a twisted staircase, became the Colony Room Club on the 15th December 1948. Prior to it being the old Colonial hangout, rumour has it that there had been an Italian social club at this site. Whatever the truth of this, there had definitely a club here since 1924 which at various times may also have been a Cypriot or Maltese knocking shop according to the Soho Society.

Muriel Belcher fitted perfectly into Soho which, post-war, continued in the same vein as it had with the 'Bright Young Thing' generation in the 1920's and 30's. She either proclaimed (or others did it for her) that she was a theatrical Portuguese Jewish lesbian, whose father had owned the Alexandra Theatre in Birmingham. But what makes a legend is not necessarily the truth, although she was born in Birmingham.

The Belchers' were neither Jewish or Portuguese and are one of the oldest-named families in Birmingham and England, post the Norman Conquest according to the The Oxford Dictionary of Names. Her father, Myer, who was at various times a travelling salesman selling stationary prior to acquiring his own shop in Birmingham in 1911 as cited on the National Register, was related through his sister's marriage to one of the Salberg brothers that bought the AlexandraTheatre. He might well have managed front of house at some point, but by 1928 Myer Belcher was dead in Belgravia on the next register. On her mother's side, Ida Amelia née Barnett's, were three-generations born and bred Cardiff Welsh, although it is also likely that there was some Russian, Polish or Dutch on Muriel's mother's side from the 1700's, but no Portuguese or Jewish. To be Jewish the bloodline must run through the females, which in Muriel's family it did not.

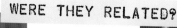

FLOSSIE, MURIEL & IVOR NOVELLO...

WERE THEY RELATED?

Family

Muriel has been quoted as saying how much she hated her father in all of Dan Farson's books from his autobiography to his classic, 'Soho in the Fifties'. She also claimed to have a nanny which seems unlikely with the family's finances but this is not impossible. Fact and fiction are difficult to disassociate from hearsay, but new information from John Hart, a second cousin of Muriel's on her mother's side and part of the Cardiff contingent, that one of Muriel's great uncles who must remain unnamed, was rumoured to have sired Ivor Novello when he was friendly with her mother Clara Novello Davies, a well-known choral conductor. But this is family gossip. Clara was already married to David Ivor Davies, a solicitor's clerk. Whether or not she was known by Muriel, or indeed Ivor, they certainly seem to bear a family resemblance: large noses, deep-set eyes and wide thin-lipped mouths. If this story is true, the Barnett gene was very strong as can be seen between Muriel and her great Aunt, John Hart's mother Flossie. See Pic. Perhaps Muriel's nose was the trigger for the claims that she must be Jewish, at a time of notable anti-Semitic feeling. In 1934 when Anthony Powell's first novel, 'Afternoon Men' was published, a book centred around West End Clubs, there are endless curious racist references. One character says to another. 'He's a Jew and not bad at all'.

What is certain is that Muriel Belcher was born in 1908 in Birmingham and died in London in 1979. If her parents were involved in the Alexandra, they were also involved in a huge success. With plays touring the provinces, and especially with spectacular pantomimes, it attracted big star names and was big business. Belcher rarely mentioned her family and if pushed would say, "I had one nice brother but he died". But she loved her mother Ida, and the three of them moved to Bayswater, London after her father died. According to Jeffrey Bernard she then got a job at Harrods prior to The Music Box. She hated the provinces, hated her father and hated her nanny and governess more. Dan Farson recorded her saying in the 1950's, when he first discovered the Colony Room and became a life-long loyal member, making it his home from home: '...my nanny was a real bastard and the governess would have had more hair on her chin than Che Guevara except that she shaved every day. I loathed my fucking old father...'

Homosexual

From the beginning, people found Muriel charismatic and alluring. She was less pretty, more beautiful in a Hedy Lamarr intelligent way, with a distinctive profile. To some, she was an oppressive figure, maintaining the high-camp humour of the 1930's: sharp, succinct, acid and not to every ones taste. Many found even her gaze frightening. People were often offended by her confident stylised language, while others loved it. It was absolutely camp, from the delivery to the content, but she was always careful to whom she would deliver it. Her private life appeared very public and members all knew she was gay. She would purr at women and bark at men but she loved the pretty boys. Indeed, she was on occasion warned by police friends to up her heterosexual membership when it was becoming too camp. Muriel quarrelled dramatically with Carmel her girlfriend in public, about Carmel's relentless gambling habits, something she had in common with Bacon and Lucian Freud, although Bacon had other ways to make money to squander at Charlie Chester's Casino Club. And she was forever packing Carmel back to Jamaica, then relenting, and allowing her to return again. In the end she resolutely stood by her, by leaving the club lease to her.

Members from the Early Days

Brian Howard, the man that Evelyn Waugh based his character Anthony Blanche in 'Brideshead Revisited' and Ambrose Silk in 'Put Out More Flags', was a wealthy, gay, dilettante, poet, occasional book reviewer and an indiscreet spy during the War. It was Brian who told Francis Bacon that he had heard about a new club opened by the woman who ran The Music Box. He dragged him along in the opening week of December 1948. As Farson reported Bacon saying: "And for some reason I liked it so much I went back the next day and Muriel came over and spoke to me. I don't know, perhaps she thought I knew a lot of rich people, which was untrue, but she knew I hadn't got much money, and she said, "I'll give you £10 a week and you can drink absolutely free here and don't think of it as a salary but just bring people in." I wasn't even a tout. "Just bring in the people you like," she said, and I did." Farson also reported in 'Soho of the Fifties' that Christopher Kininmouth (the well regarded travel writer who had just written Children of Thetis for publisher John Lehmann, editor of Penguin New Writing) said that, "it was so empty that first afternoon, that we played dice along the counter."

Frank Norman, the writer of 'Bang to Rights' and the musical 'Fings Aint What They Used T'be' (music by member Lionel Bart), quotes Muriel in an interview from 'Norman's London' in 1965 about the origins of the club and its success. "In the early days of the club Francis Bacon worked for Muriel as a host. He was paid a commission on drinks consumed by the members at the end of the week. But he always spent his money as soon as he got it." said Muriel. "Of course he was getting far less for his pictures in those days." On another occasion she would say that she'd pay him on a Friday and by the end of the night it was gone. Francis Bacon was well-known then rather than famous, and not wealthy, as he later became. He had had a chequered career, including a cat burglar, a male 'friend' of one of his father's friends for a year in Berlin, a furniture designer, but he went on to prove Muriel right as an astute choice of 'tout'. In the decades to come, he was often the one to be picking up the champagne tabs for anyone in the Colony.

Indeed, she must have sensed that she was making a sound bet for at various times she would allow him to run up bills into many thousands and as Farson noted, when Bacon had no money, the only places he could eat was Wheeler's for oysters and Muriel's for a drink. "Muriel's a very beautiful woman, it's as simple as that," said Francis Bacon, when asked why he had painted her portrait three times from 1959 until 1983. And apparently when Dan Farson went on to ask Francis why he went there so often, he answered: "Because it's different from anywhere else. She has a tremendous ability to create an atmosphere of ease. After all, that's what we all want isn't it? A place to go to where one feels free and easy." This was the lure that attracted a full membership of creative people which then attracted Lords, Ladies, Barons and Earls.

"The club was quite posh," recalled Jeffrey Bernard in 1979, about the Colony's beginnings, in his 'Low Life' column in the Spectator on the death of Muriel. "She never minced words about the fact that she really only wanted rich, famous, successful, titled people as members, but she made an exception as long as those same rich... people spent plenty of their money on us layabouts."

Other Clubs

There were other clubs and pubs but few good ones existed outside of the boundaries of Fitzrovia, Soho and Mayfair. Within those districts, there were places such as The Gargoyle, Mummy's Club, Jack's Club, Ruby's, Club Afrique, le Caves de France, The Mandrake, Byron's, The Rockingham, The Moonlight, The Abalabi and The Kismet. All promised a racier seam to life. Celebrity guitarists like Django Reinhardt from Le Hot Club de France played, dwarfs jitterbugged with big girls to the sounds: 'It must be Jelly 'cos Jam don't shake like dat', as the artist Michael Wishart wrote about in his autobiography 'High Diver'. During and post the War: "I toured the clubs, the Negro Sunset, the Moonglow and the Caribbean. Here Brian Howard was frequently slumped, his old Etonian tie knotted into a bow, incapable of saying anything foolish or pleasant... These clubs were the only places where it was easy to buy marijuana."

If you were gay in 1948, like Howard and Bacon or bisexual like Wishart, to be able to express yourself freely and easily was rare outside of Soho. Homosexuality remained a criminal act until 1967 in Britain. Even in Hampstead and Chelsea, the arty areas, it was difficult to be openly gay. So to be anywhere where you felt 'free and easy' was liberating.

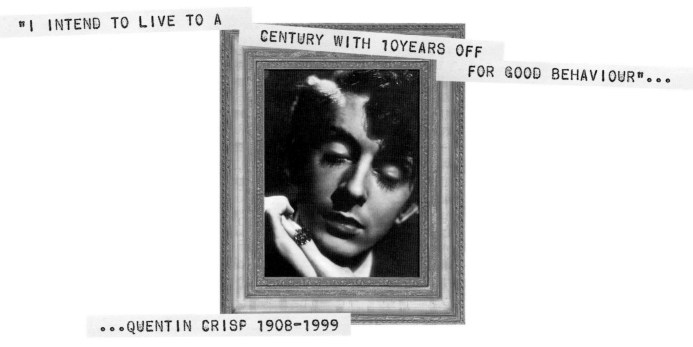

"I INTEND TO LIVE TO A CENTURY WITH 10YEARS OFF FOR GOOD BEHAVIOUR"...

...QUENTIN CRISP 1908-1999

Quentin Crisp, openly and actively homosexual, claimed that he hardly drank because in his visible situation, he had to keep his wits about him. He lived in Chelsea and modelled in art schools, both scenarios thought to be bohemian. Nonetheless he felt threatened for his feminine attire, purple quiff and attitude. It was a dangerous life to be openly queer, as it was then known. Of course, there was plenty of opportunity to be steered by the elbow into an alley but it was hardly a relationship. "I disliked the coarseness of situations in which I found myself," Crisp said. "Courtship consisted of walking along the street, until we came to a dark doorway. 'This'll do' were the only words of tenderness that were uttered to me."

Crisp wished he'd found the Colony earlier, as he later said in a television interview. He must have known about the club as a regular to a café around the corner. The Colony was not for everyone and though the more famous of its habitués at the beginning, from a vomiting Dylan Thomas, Louis MacNiece, the tight-lipped painter Lucian Freud and the young Frank Auerbach were all relatively broke; The supporting cast were wealthy and titled. How else could the place survive? How else would it draw the likes of Noel Coward, Hermione Baddley, EM Forster, Charles Laughton and Tallulah Bankhead, if Baddley's husband, David Tennant hadn't been a member?

Beecham's Mix

Audrey Beecham, the poet and niece of the conductor Sir Thomas Beecham, was a member of the Colony from the beginning and became engaged to another member, Sir Maurice Bowra, a don at Wadham College, Oxford. When challenged in the club about his engagement (he was gay) to 'that plain girl' he replied, "Buggers can't be choosers."

Nor could Audrey. A lover of Anais Nin in Paris, a gun runner in Spain, a martial arts expert and communist; a friend of Antonia White. Audrey believed her grandfather Thomas Beecham, the famous chemist who invented the powders, had poisoned his wife. Nobody believed her. But when Dylan Thomas made unwanted advances to her at the Colony, which he often did to girls, plain or otherwise (the plain ones always being the more grateful), she knocked the unsuspecting Welsh bard out cold.

Among the lists of titled members who under 'Occupation' on their memberships wrote 'Gentlemen' or 'Lady', there was also a mix of guests. One group fed neatly into the other and that was Muriel's great talent. Nobody wants to be just among their own kind. Besides, if you went to where a patron to the arts might be... well, you never know, there might be a sale in that. Or at least a drink. For the young and the pretty, titled and the nobodies, there was always someone to buy a drink. As the photographer Lord Christopher Thynne said, "I almost lived in the Colony", as did the poet Oliver Bernard who although he claimed never to have paid membership and never had money, was never thrown out, probably because he occasionally paid his membership. The Colony was not a charitable institution.

The poet Paul Potts, championed by TS Eliot, George Orwell, Patrick Kavanagh and Sean O'Casey as the 'People's Poet', though 'shamefully unrecognised', as Daniel Farson said. Poet George Barker described his friend Potts as, 'that criminal whose felony is to love everything a bit too much', as well as dreadfully poor, selling his poems for a penny on street corners and often destitute, he was always welcomed by Muriel, despite his smell and rags. The feeling was mutual. "I suppose what makes her so difficult to describe is her originality... a kind of non-ecclesiastical cardinal or perhaps a delinquent saint..." said Potts. "She is as autocratic as the Dalai Lama and as kind as Sophie Tucker (last of the 'Red Hot Mama's' vaudevillian performers, famous for her line "From birth to 18, a girl needs good parents. From 18 to 35 she needs good looks. From 35 to 55, she needs a good personality. From 55 on, she needs good cash.") She is Soho Royalty, an 18th century Duchess would recognise in her a sister." Paul Potts remained an officially welcomed member until his death in 1990 aged 79, although many disliked him including the Bernard brothers, Bruce and Oliver, not just because of his incontinence.

Another Duchess of those early days was Nina Hamnett, as famous for her art as the people she slept with. The original bohemian, Hamnett didn't care what people thought, did or said. She embedded herself into the life of the artists in Paris and London, mixed with the finest company, behaved in a reckless and imaginative fashion, and was painted and adored, written about and immortalised by herself as much as others.

Ruthven Todd, Scottish poet and writer of 'Space Cat', told an anecdote in his unpublished autobiography that while working for fellow Tenbyite Augustus John, Nina came to tell him about losing her virginity at a certain house in Bloomsbury. "One day they will put a plaque on the front of that house saying Nina Hamnett lost her virginity here, on the back, another will say that Rimbaud and Verlaine lived there." The building obviously drew adventure to it but never plaques.

When her first autobiography came out in 1932, called 'The Naked Torso', she became a celebrity in London and New York with her stories of Picasso, Matisse, Modigliani (who was obsessed with her) and Gaudier-Brzeska (for whom she posed for and possibly more), Kees Van Dongen (who asked her to dance around his studio in her underwear, so she removed all her clothes), Sickert (who she worked for) and Augustus John (her old friend), critic Roger Fry (who was madly in love with her). 'The wickedest man in London' Aleister Crowley sued her and lost because the judge agreed with Hamnett. He was the wickedest man in London when the book was published. She had a fast tongue and sharp mind dulled later only by alcohol.

NINA HAMNETT.. "ALL THE NICE GIRLS LOVE A SAILOR!"

"THE BEST TITS IN THE TATE"

In the late 1940's Hamnett was in her 50s and still exhibiting paintings based on her past fame. Always recognisable by her beret and second-hand clothes that had seen better times, she had become a national treasure for some: someone who could recount in a brisk upper class accent the outrageous times she'd enjoyed with famous people, whom she spoke of in first name terms: "Keep up, of course Henri means Matisse". For some she was a bore, as she expected a drink in exchange for these stories that kept on doing the rounds, but Muriel always welcomed her in. "Come on," she'd rally. "Who's going to have a drink with this vision of loveliness? Open up your bead bag Lottie." Then Muriel would instruct with a nod and a wink to her barman, to a new and frightened visitor to pay for the round. Sadly the drink got to Nina and her incontinence meant that every time she sat on a stool it invariably became wet. Muriel had enough. Only strangers dared to sit on the dampened perch that was known as 'Nina's stool'.

YOUNG GAY & BEAUTIFULL 1949

BACON, BELCHER & FRANK THE BARMAN

Cocktail Hours

It is strange that Muriel became such a draw for artists and writers, as she herself admitted. She didn't give a toss for those things. She did however relish the spirit that made the creative more fun to be with rather than the 'boring cunts' that she insisted trump up the funds for the incessant rounds of drinks. Of course, this preference of artists over money was outrageous but as Oliver Bernard said in 2012: "Muriel was alright even in the really early days. I never had any money to speak of and she was always a bit rude and offhand yet she always let me in with 'Oh it's you', as if she didn't like me but she never asked me for a subscription. She was a tigerish headmistress of that place, she was very funny but trying not to be liked too much. She never spoke to me about family or her other clubs." Nonetheless, Bernard did not think much of Muriel's lover Carmel. "I hardly spoke to her and I've got a feeling that if you started to really talk to Carmel, Muriel would have thought that you were trying to get between the two of them. I didn't like her by comparison, she was closed up and rather cold."

Geraldine Norman OBE, Director of The friends of The Hermitage Society, who married the writer Frank Norman in 1971, spoke about her husband's early years going to the club and Belcher's generosity. "I think Frank said he started in Soho sweeping out gambling dens after the war and because he was a Barnardo's child he had nowhere else to go. Eventually at 15 they found him a good job at a tomato nursery. Then a travelling fair came to town and he became a dodgem greaser. The fairs didn't work in winter and so he began his Soho career in the late 40s.'

Quite a few of the Colony queers fancied Frank because he was a tough young burglar. They bought him drinks and welcomed him in, long before he began to write or had anything. Muriel always insisted that somebody buy the rounds but it was somehow made into a bit of fun and the landed gentry who piled in with the celebrities didn't seem to mind. If they did, well, "tat a deary" (roughly translated as fuck off) as she was fond of saying. She made it work. The Colony Room was never intended to be a club for poor artists.

George & Elizabeth
at Scarlet-Sub-Edge, visiting Didy, & looking for a home,
while the children were at the Nursery in Kingsbridge.
On Easter Monday, April 10th 1944

Courtesy Georgina Barker

ELIZABETH SMART LOVED GEORGE BARKER

Sohoitis

Soho was not always the primary place where the artists, writers and bohemians of their time hung out. Before Soho there was Fitzrovia particularly, in the interwar period. Soho was divided from Fitrovia by Oxford Street, north of which ran the narrow strip of Rathbone Place into Charlotte Street. The poet Ruthven Todd, when asked to write in a catalogue for an exhibition at the The Parkin Gallery in 1973, called 'Fitzrovia and the road to York Minster', recalled: 'The name Fitzrovia had nothing to do with either Fitzroy Street or Fitzroy Square but derived simply from the Fitzroy Tavern on the east side of Charlotte Street and Windmill... When first I knew it, nearly 40 years ago, I do not think the habitués had a name for it as The Fitzroy Tavern was usually called Kleinfield's after the landlord. His son in law Charlie Allchild took over in the later 30's, so I think it was from then.' Though JM Tambimuttu (the editor of Poetry London, known as 'Tambi') claimed to have coined the term in the 1940's. He certainly coined the term 'Sohoitis'. The writer Julian MacLaren-Ross wrote about meeting Tambi at The Swiss Pub in Old Compton Street in his book 'Memoirs of the Forties', in a conversation that summarised the times:

"Fitzrovia…It's a dangerous place. You must be careful."

"Fights with knives?"

"No a worse danger, you might get Sohoitis you know."

"No I don't, what is it?"

"If you get Sohoitis, you will stay there day and night and get no work done ever. You have been warned."

"Is this Fitzrovia?"

"No, Old Compton Street Soho. You are safer here.""

But he wasn't. Unfortunately the warning acted more as a fatal attraction for MacLaren-Ross, who was only able to write his 'Memoirs of the Forties' by being paid by the chapter. They remained sadly unfinished but published in 1965 on his death. The Fitzroy Tavern was the place to be and Augustus John compared it to Clapham Common: "Sooner or later everyone has to pass through it". But there was also the Bricklayers Arms, coined as the 'Burgler's Rest' by Nina Hamnett, who'd once seen a crowbar in the middle of the snooker table and of course, The Wheatsheaf and The Marquis of Granby.

CHARLIE ALLCHILD PROPRIETOR OF THE FITZROY TAVERN

Their trips into Soho were prompted by the opening and closing hours of the pubs, which were different depending on which borough of London the pub was in. Charlotte Street was divided in two, one part in Marylebone, the other in Holborn. The Fitzroy Tavern closed at 10.30pm having opened at 5.30pm. If another drink was needed one had to cross into Soho, where the borough of Westminster kept the pubs open until 11pm, after which there were a variety of small restaurants and cafes that could be visited for further sustenance: even a carafe of undrinkable wine. The restaurants in Fitzrovia included Mrs Buhler's café, run by the mother of the artist Robert Buhler, who would allow friends of her son's to eat on tick. For those with money there was the famous Le Tour Eiffel owned by the generous Rudolf Stulik, whose days of popularity and wealth were numbered but who was always supported by the wealthy. Augustus John bailed out his favourite restaurant more than once. John was a mainstay of the area, the elder wealthy statesmen of the bohemian youth that gathered about his coat-tails and his wallet.

The first time Dylan Thomas met Caitlin, later to become his wife, they became so excited at their union that they immediately hired a room with a bed above Stulik's restaurant. Decorated by Wyndham Lewis when he'd been suffering from venereal disease and was hiding out. The Vorticist movement had their launch of their manifesto 'Blast!' as shown in William Roberts painting 'The Vorticists at the Restaurant de la Tour Eiffel - Spring 1915'. Dylan and Caitlin ate and slept for two weeks and signed the bill in Augustus John's name. When the artist got the bill added to his lunch he had with Ruthven Todd, the poet, he assumed it was wrong. "I know you cheat me outrageously Stulik and you know I don't complain much... But £43 for two is a bit steep."

Stulik beamed. "Is not for lunch only. Little Welshman with curly hair" He made a gesture. "He come here. He stay two weeks and eat. He say you pay."

None of them met for three weeks and by the time Dylan told Ruthven, John had obviously forgotten all about it.

Augustus was growing old and was more a fixture of Fitzrovia. He remembered when other artists had lived there, Whistler, Sickert, Duncan Grant, Matthew Smith, Roger Fry and Rex Whistler. But there seems little doubt that Augustus John would have gone to the Colony as his children and grandchildren were members and especially as he was the president of the club opposite, David Tennant's The Gargoyle Club.

Visible from the window of the Colony Room, the Gargoyle was a meeting place for society to mingle, a sort of redistribution of wealth and entertainment to a wide crowd. Sadly the social mixing seldom worked, as the fights at the end of the evening often testified. It was the top three floors above an old printing works, with a narrow entrance in Meard Street, more usually referred to as "Merde Street", off Dean Street. A metal caged lift took guests to the top, where the hall was hung with drawings and mirrors by Henri Matisse and a room designed by Sir Edward Lutyens, with leather engraved curtains.

Whereas the Colony had a rickety old piano, The Gargoyle had Alexander's Band, a wine cellar, banqueting rooms, dining area and dance floor. The successful art world came here Graham Sutherland, photographer John Deakin, artist John Minton, Francis Bacon, John Craxton, Lucian Freud and publisher David Archer who ran The Parton Press in a bookshop of the same name, off Red Lion Square. Parton Press had first published Dylan Thomas' poetry as well as George Barker, WS Graham and David Gascoyne. The company joked about having a Welshman, an Irishman, Scotsman and Englishman. As the 'Parton Street Poets' they were the forerunners of the 'Neo-Romantic' trend. David Archer was both

PAINTING BY JOHN CRAXTON

course and romantic spending his fortune on sustaining and promoting them. He came from a moneyed background but left the earth impecunious in the 1960's. His publishing of young poets meant he wasn't forgotten.

All the bohemians sat on one side of the room at the Gargoyle facing the minor aristocracy, on the other side people like the Cunards, the Coopers, the Sitwells and the Willoughbys. David Tennant was the brother of Lord Glenconner, and like many of his family was said to possess, beauty, intelligence and wit. As a young man he had flown his own plane and as some scathingly remarked, the brandy bottle had soon replaced his joy stick. The Gargoyle was a late night club where dancing, cocktails, dining and flirting went on. As the artist Michael Wishart wrote in his book 'High Diver', 'The adorable Hermione Baddeley taught me to dance the Charleston there. One night I saw Dylan Thomas measuring his cock with a pocket ruler, eagerly watched by some lady poetry lovers.' As a famous actress of film and stage, Baddley who was married to Tennant, was a considerable draw. John Minton would take a selection of sailors in there along with some of his Royal College students, and he would gaily pump them with champagne and sparkle with good humour. If interrupted or deserted, his mood would plummet, fights would invariably break out and the waiters were left pleading with their customers to pay their bills. They often didn't.

GASTON BERLEMONT & PETER THE DOG OUTSIDE THE FRENCH HOUSE

The French

The York Minster was the other place that both Gargoyle and Colony members frequented. Known as the French Pub, it was run by Victor Berlemont and housed at 49 Dean Street. The Berlemonts were a French family who'd bought it off a German landlord, deported in 1914 called Schmidt, and it was previously called The Wine House. Victor stocked all things French from Pastis to Absinthe, Champagne and wine by the glass, to french beer and real coffee. He had a special glass water dispenser for Pastis and Absinthe which in those days still contained the hallucinogen wormwood.

The walls, decorated in autographed photographs of French entertainers passing through London were collected by the Berlemonts through the decades. The photocopied images remain framed in large glass cases, the originals bought by actor Robbie Coltrane in the 1980's. Everyone is there from Maurice de Chevalier to Ann Valery (the French resistance fighter) to Mistanguette (a popular saucy entertainer), Lena Horne, Orson Welles, Charlie Chaplin and Laurel and Hardy. Gaston, who had been born on the premises, took over when his father died in 1950. During World War II, under Victor it became a meeting place for the French in exile. General Charles de Gaulle formed the Free French Forces and was said to have written the speech rallying the French people, 'À tous les Français', in the pub.

But it also drew everyone from streetwalkers to the Allied Forces. De Gaulle even came back after the war to thank the Berlemonts with a presidential visit and exclaimed "Your moustache isn't as big as your father's."

Normal Sex Maniacs

The Colony Room was never intended to be a club for gays. There were enough of those as Daniel Farson noted: The Kismet, the Rockingham Club, The Caves de France and Ruby's of Mayfair. These were full of patrons who were 'intimate with Noel Coward', as they liked to boast. Still, the clientele were often frightened, seeking solace from the suburbs with married men, young lads, old posh blokes and sailors who'd turn you over when they left before the morning. The sailors also had heterosexual affairs and Nina Hamnett liked them best because they always left the next morning. But she did take to posting money back to herself with a second class stamp with the last post in case she lost her funds before the following day arrived. Nor was the Colony ever just a club for the champagne swilling upper classes, although enough of them frequented it, attracting journalists. The club was not a place for the press to solely meet each other. Perhaps the magic of what Muriel had created in the Colony was a cocktail from the chaos of post war London; creaming off the most amusing and remarkable outcasts.

"There was something almost outrageous about her campness," wrote Jeffrey Bernard. "Sometimes she seemed convinced the world was entirely populated by homosexuals." Perhaps she also found it amusing to watch straight men squirm. Certainly she knew that people like Jeffrey and Oliver Bernard were easy game for experienced wealthy gays.

Muriel, always hawk-eyed, was more than capable of kicking out guests as quickly as she charmed in new members. She created a self-sufficient community where the boredom of the upper classes was relieved by the humour and the imagination of the creatives. The journalists had somewhere to hide from their editors in Fleet Street, and somewhere to find gossip away from the usual font, and have a little fun of the racy bohemian sort. As Paul Johnson, the political historian and editor said about the Colony, which he frequented three times a week from the early years, "It was a place where you could pick up a girl. Not a professional, just a naughty bohemian girl with a giggle. Though queers went there, it wasn't a queer joint at all. That's the great mistake. Most of the people there were perfectly normal sexual maniacs. You went to the Colony to have fun and to have jokes in the afternoon, when the rest of the world was working." Who wouldn't want to be a member of a club that behaved like that?

MU, CARMEL, DAVID ARCHER, APRIL GAY, IAN BOARD AND ACTRESS MARTITA HUNT...
LET THE GOOD TIMES ROLL!

Chapter 2
The Repressive 50s

- Famous Farson
- Anti-Establishment Sex
- Youth
- A Bit of Posh
- Foul Mouthed Atmosphere
- The Famous Mural
- Credit
- Gay Chelsea, Homosexual Soho
- Be Bold
- Polotics & Spies
- Le Corp De Colony
- Jazz

Yearly Membership 5/- (25pence)
1950

Famous Farson

'Soho in the Fifties' is the name of Dan Farson's legendary book written in the late 1980's, dedicated 'to Ian Board, and The Members of The Colony and for Muriel Belcher who started it'. It has a thick atmosphere of nostalgia, helped by the black and white photographs by Farson himself as well as Bruce Bernard and John Deakin. Farson had started his career as a talented photographer, added journalism, and went on to become one of the star names of the independent television station Associated Rediffusion. Fronting programmes like 'Out of Step' - also the name of his first autobiography – he addressed the socially excluded in society from naturists to mixed marriages, witchcraft and transvestism. Farson displayed a natural ease with outsiders. As a homosexual and son of one of the world's greatest foreign correspondents and adventurers, Negley Farson. Dan knew how outcasts felt in 1950's Britain and he was drawn to them. His second autobiography is called 'Never a Normal Man', a phrase often said about Negley and dedicated 'To Those Who Don't Belong'. No wonder he loved the Colony Room Club. Farson's first job out of the army was as a Parliamentary reporter, where he was energetically chased through the House of Commons, like so many others, by the infamous MP and Colony member Tom Driberg. Yet Driberg did not introduce Farson to the Colony. That came after a chance encounter in The French pub with the Vogue photographer and spiteful wit John Deakin. When Farson was first led up the Colony's squalid staircase in 1953, a place he'd later consider his home, the bamboo was still in place but the carpet was beginning to look worn, and the leopard skin bar stools had had to be replaced (in part, thanks to Nina Hamnett's incontinence). But mirrors and plastic tropical plants still gave the room a look of faded glamour. There was also a dog and a caged budgerigar, but like Francis Bacon before him, it was Muriel's presence that hooked Farson.

Farson eventually gave up TV presenting to write books and invested his money in the Limehouse music hall pub, The Waterman Arms. The pub was fun for Farson and Bacon's love of rough sex, but bad for his bank balance. Soho, especially in the

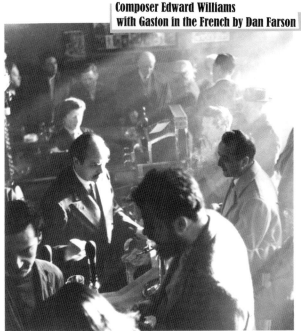

Composer Edward Williams
with Gaston in the French by Dan Farson

Bacon & Farson by Harry Diamond

50s, was a theme he came back to time and again. It was the time that he discovered Soho and it seemed to leave an indelible imprint. Most of all, it was Muriel Belcher and her tight entourage including Francis Bacon, John Minton, Lucian Freud, Lady Caroline Blackwood, Michael Laws, Henrietta Moraes and Carmel Stuart (Muriel's Jamaican girlfriend) that enthralled him.

Soho was exciting and the wider cast of characters, handsome Norman Balon, witty John Deakin, writer Colin McInnes, cheat Gerald Hamilton, genial Gaston Berlemont and composer Edward Williams, helped to leave the grimness of the war years behind. George Melly, a Colony member since the 1940's wrote the foreword to 'Soho in the Fifties', 'This splendid book with its matter of fact title is really about a love affair... Farson's passion for Soho.'

Anti-Establishment Sex

Soho provided an escape valve for non-conformists. Artist and illustrator Barry Evans was taken to the Colony first by wildlife artist Barry Driscol. They were known as the two Barrys, mimicking the two Roberts (Colquhoun and MacBryde) that had also encamped in the Colony. Muriel and Ian nicknamed each; Barry Evans 'Dame Edith' and Driscol 'Doris'. "When I was 15, I'd already left school and got a scholarship to Kingston Art School," Barry told me about his relationship with Soho. "My parents were against me continuing in education, so I had to leave home. I slept in the studio or anywhere. I met David Singleton (another Colony member) and he took me to Soho. We did a bit of black marketing. I met Nina Hamnett on my first trip to The Fitzroy, she was a bit raddled but she was kind and nice, she bought me a drink. Later, I found out she had been the same to Oliver Bernard and to Lucian Freud; I suppose she liked little boys." Actually Nina liked sailors but sex was sex.

Nina with her date...
Peter the Dog by Dan Farson

Sex continued among the young. As soon as Jeffrey Bernard was sure of his impotence, he boasted he was never short of female partners because the worry through the 50s for women was not of sexually transmitted diseases but of becoming pregnant. The poverty of the 40s still crowned Bernard as he worked the building sites and was available arm candy for rich gay men enchanted by his looks and confident witty conversation. The Colony was full of willing subscribers. John Minton was famous for shoring up the poor and pretty of the club having an inheritance and a regular job. As a tutor at the Royal College of Art, when his painting style went out of fashion he became better known for his illustration from Elizabeth David cookbooks to Penguin New Writing covers. Minton was so in demand he often asked his students to do his commissions before signing them, something that artist members would continue to do into the 2000's.

Geraldine Norman OBE, head of The Hermitage Society remembers sitting with Bobby Hunt (a Minton protégé) in the 60s in the Colony with an Elizabeth David cookbook. Bobby was pointing and saying, 'That's one of mine.' Meanwhile, Hunt is remembered for being the butt of jokes. "Muriel, I'm worried I've got to go to a fancy dress party tonight and I can't think what to go as?" he asked. "Why don't you go as yourself, a bald headed cunt?" Tory Stroud retold this to me recently.

A homosexual alcoholic, like so many other members of the Colony, it was Minton who first took the Bernard brothers up the stairs to Muriel's and plied them with drinks, although Jeffrey wouldn't have admitted it. Certainly, other students of Minton's said he was the first to lead them to this 'extraordinary place' and he wasn't the last art tutor to do it. It became a rite of passage for many tutors to see how their students reacted. Aged 16, Minton was taking Bernard to Spain with no objections from Jeffrey's mother about their relationship. By 1957 Minton had committed suicide and when asked by Dan Farson in the 1980's if Minton would have been thrilled at all their Soho successes, Bernard replied, 'He got his kicks from thrusting money on people to show that he was better. He really loathed it if you bought him a drink.' Whether Bernard ever tested this theory is unknown. This was a game that toffs played with their inherited money. Henrietta Moraes and Michael Laws (her director husband prior to her marrying the poet Dom Moraes), always poor and hungry, would wait for a local rich boy Nigel 'rich as Croesus', to beckon them over to keep him company. Sometimes he would ask them along and let them watch him eat, feeding them with just a glass of wine as he sumptuously dined on one course after another. Post war black humour, this was thought to be very funny.

The Bernard brothers, the Laws and Deakin weren't the only leeches off the kindness of strangers that gathered in the club. The journalists, who after a morning of work gathered stories from the bar. One, Sir Peregrine Worsthorne, captured the conflicting views about the club. He thought the place, "Bloody ghastly" and although aged 89 in 2011, had no problem remembering why: "It was an awful place, the Colony. I loathed it and I hated Muriel. Of course we'd be cajoled into going there in the 50s but really, I could never see the point. It was such a squalid room. I shudder with the thought of it, the dirt, both physically and metaphysically.

"It was the sort of place that I like to think I would like, but I didn't. Everyone used to say about Muriel 'isn't she fun and lovely?' But she'd greet you with these awful expletives and make some joke, always at my expense and why should I find that funny? Of course I didn't want to appear a stuffy arse but going there was just a habit all through the 50s. Everyone was always drunk. I'm sure not even I'm terribly amusing drunk. And then all the insinuations and invitations from gays but then I was always a pretty boy. Paul Johnson (his journalist friend) probably didn't have that trouble, but I certainly did."

Bacon wasn't yet the monied beacon he was to become like Minton or David Archer, also homosexual, had inherited money and spent it all on The Archer Bookshop in Parton Street and The Parton Street Press. It famously allowed its poets to retain their copyright. As the deaf poet and editor of magazines Nimbus and X, David Wright wrote: 'The most remarkable figure was David Archer, ex-bookseller, ex-publisher, private and personal patron of poets till he ran out of money, who never read any poetry and certainly never talked it. His Parton Press had published the first books of George Barker, Dylan Thomas and David Gascoyne before the war, and in 1942 that of WS Graham, a record of firsts that compares with the Faber list in its great days.'

According to the writer and another Colony member, Phillip Toynbee. The shop was the prototype of all those left-wing bookshops that came later, 'whose chief object was not to sell poetry but to provide ammunition for the class struggle.' Archer would kick critics who didn't give his friends books good reviews and as the poet Paul Potts put it, would 'look after people who couldn't look after themselves.' By the 50s this had become another generation of poets. In Archer's shop on the Shaftsbury Avenue end of Greek Street, he employed Henrietta Moraes on the till, not the

John Deakin who liked his drink by Dan Farson

wisest thing to do with a Benzedrine addict, and found John Deakin, the Vogue portrait photographer, to live with. Deakin, according to Farson, would humiliate him with his coarse cruelty for an audience, to make everyone squirm. But Harold Chapman in 2012, the renowned photographer of the Beat Poets in Paris, said he found nothing but kindness from him. "I learned from John Deakin in the 1950's. There used to be a rather worn out, dilapidated dump called Caves de France next door to the Colony, a drinking club with jazz music and an electric guitar player grinding out 1930's pop standards. I was standing next to a rather small little man who offered me a drink and asked me what I was doing. I replied pretentiously, Photographing Soho. It turned out that he was John Deakin." Harold then asked for Deakin's professional opinion on his portfolio which he generously commented on pre-empting it with the words, "I shall be very severe." said Deakin. "He looked through all my pictures without saying a word and then said, 'Carry on like this,

take a picture of a guy digging his chick and the hardness of an ashtray. Get up at 5 in the morning and go to photograph markets.' Chapman was impressed. Deakin was the top Vogue portraitist of the time and the reason why so many stars ended up in the Colony; he'd been photographing them beforehand. When Chapman saw Deakin's work on Paris, it was something else. "I went to an exhibition that Deakin had in David Archer's gallery in Soho the first in London that combined a book-shop, a coffee bar and an art gallery. He had an exhibition called 'My Paris'. I had never seen such stark, contrast, rough grainy prints before and thought they were all masterpieces. They inspired me to get off to Paris and do a book called 'My Paris'." The rest was Parisian history and 'The Beat Hotel', published eventually in 1984, is now a collectors' piece and documentary film.

Youth

Soho was being invaded by youth, with its new Italian-style coffee music bars like 21's on Old Compton Street, which started when Achille Gaggia invented the espresso machine in Milan in 1948, imported to Soho by 1952. The Colony, was also attracting a younger crowd, art students from St Martins School of Art around the corner on Charing Cross Road. Among them were the Cumbrian landscape artist Sheila Fell, her boyfriend Clifford Rowan and Frank Auerbach, who would later become her lover. Auerbach, one of Britain's most important artists along with Bacon, had come to Britain on the Kinder transport, escaping the Nazi's. Len Deighton, the spy novelist, was then a student at St Martins when he became a member with his friend Ted Dicks from the Royal College. Dicks was to go on to have hit record success with 'Right Said Fred' and 'A Hole in the Ground', both sung by Bernard Cribbins and produced by George Martin, who later went on to bigger things with The Beatles. Dick also won a Novello award for 'A Mouse in Old Amsterdam' and played piano at the Colony.

Lucian freud and Frank Auerbach discuss the finer points of painting by Harry Diamond

Among the Colony's camp collection of queens, aristocrats and celebrities, there was also a knot of painters. Both Rowan and Fell were part of this informal group, along with Michael Andrews, Leon Kossoff, Tim Behrens, Bacon, Freud and Auerbach. The painter RB Kitaj was later to call this group 'The School of London' but it was a loose alliance and among them were other artists like John Craxton, Keith Vaughan, Eduardo Paolozzi and Jankel Adler. Now in his mid 80's, Rowan recalled, "Johnny Minton and Christopher Isherwood surrounding me at the Colony, suggesting I accompany them home to bed. 'But I'm straight,' I protested. They looked at me, looked at each other and screamed in wide eyed unison: 'You must be bloody mad!'" The sexual changing rooms of Soho put Bloomsbury and its pre-war groups of bohemians to shame.

Cyrill Connolly and Lady Caroline Blackwood waiting for Freud and Bacon outside Wheelers by Dan Farson

A Bit Of Posh

Lucian Freud wasn't homosexual as he endlessly related. He learned to defend himself from older men in the Merchant Navy. But he did shadow Bacon, whom he knew to be the greatest painter in Britain. Freud had escaped to London after burning down his art school in Suffolk and shared a bombed out basement with writer Frank Norman. One Christmas they were so poor they had to share one egg, between three people.

Freud had numerous affairs, famously with Lorna Garman, married to Ernest Wishart of the left wing publishers Lawrence and Wishart, whose first son was Michael Wishart, the artist and writer. Freud then married his lover's niece, Jacob Epstein's daughter in 1948, Kitty Garman who had been born out of wedlock. Freud had two daughters with Kitty; Annie and Annabel. He never liked being told what to do and expected to be in control and for women to be in servitude at home and in the studio. Freud would often say to his wife that he was finishing a painting with Charlie his assistant, then they'd spend an hour or two working and go out to the Colony, the Mandrake or The Gargoyle, gambling en route. When Freud left Kitty in 1952, Jacob Epstein said, "That spiv Freud turned out to be a nasty piece of work."

Freud's unsettling physical presence and habit of staring intensely at people betrayed his shyness. When he fell in love with the Guinness heiress, beauty and intellectual Caroline Blackwood. He was lost, particularly as her money brought him a high-class lifestyle of houses, horses and travel. Caroline described her life with Freud, living in Dean Street and daily in the Colony, as 'a whole kind of Soho life. Going out to Wheeler's, the Colony and The Gargoyle was the thing with that crowd. Francis Bacon, James Pope Hennesey (travel writer and biographer, cousin to art dealer James Birch), Johnny Minton, Cyril Connolly and Philip O'Connor..."

"Caroline was the great love of Lucian's life," said writer Joan Wyndham. "With Caroline he behaved terribly well. Very unusual. He didn't love any of us really..."

Freud slept with all the attractive fashionable girls in town, before, during and after his marriages and even the esteemed art critic David Sylvester in an interview with The British Library Archive accused Freud of being a terrible chaser of titled monied women.

Freud's hero worshipping crush on Bacon also caused trouble. "I had dinner with Francis Bacon nearly every night for more or less the whole of my marriage to Lucian," said Lady Caroline Blackwood. Freud was more established at that time than Bacon and 13 years younger than him but within the inner group of painters known as 'Muriel's Boys' (which also included Andrews, Tim Behrens and Auerbach) Bacon was the undisputed leader of the gang. But apart from the painters, there was a set that grew from them, these were the critics like David Sylvester who cemented Bacon's reputation, the aristocracy and the writers. Brendan Behan wrote this 'Bread and butter note' after a Christmas spent indulging bad behaviour in 1955 at the house Luggala, in Ireland owned by the Guinness heiress, Lady Oonagh Oranmore and Browne and her son Lord Garech Browne.

Lady Oonagh, Garech, Tara
Three bright heads be twice as fair
This time twelve months (and
As hard a curse of mine lies on that stair).
The girl that danced the Blackbird lightly,
Michael Wilding, Harold Lloyd,
Tara's bow to shine as brightly,
Bless Caroline and Lucian Freud.

by Brendan Behan

When Caroline left him in 1957, Freud was near suicidal, according to Bacon. She maintained that she couldn't write in the marriage but other reasons, such as his gambling debts, infidelity and jealousy, were also compelling. Cyril Connolly declared his love to Caroline while both were still married. Freud saw him in Old Compton Street and began relentlessly kicking him in the shins, a punishment of which Freud was fond.

Freud and Brendan Behan by Dan Farson

At some point, Caroline also had a relationship with Alan Ross, editor of The London Magazine and later publisher of Julian Maclaren-Ross', 'Memoirs of The Forties.'

"She was a louche skittish sort of girl," said Ross. "She wasn't easy socially... until drinking suddenly switched her on and then she was very dramatic and over-elaborate in her conversation, but very funny."

Not all of the Bacon gang were Colony members. It wasn't Ian Fleming or Anthony Powell's kind of place, although they would probably have been but East End Jewish photographer Harry Diamond certainly went when he could afford it. A part-time Freud model, Diamond took the much reproduced Freud and Bacon photograph of them on Dean Street near the French pub.

47

Foul Mouthed Atmosphere

Oliver Bernard recalled the atmosphere in the 50s. 'Minton took me in first," he says. "I thought Muriel was quite frightening. Because I wasn't a member, I didn't want to be on anything but friendly terms with her. She was very slow to accept anyone, very slow to accept me. I never did ever become a member although my brothers were. She did let me in all the time because I usually went by myself. Francis Bacon, Minton, Lucian, Henrietta (Moraes), Michael Laws and Edward Williams were there. Everyone was mixed up. Good Lord, it was different from other places. There was obviously more money swishing around than anywhere else but the atmosphere was because of Muriel: camp, decadent, scandalous, foul-mouthed and even the bitchiness was quite amusing. Brendan Behan dipped in and out of Soho, in the pubs more than the Colony, but I may be wrong."

George Melly substantiated what Oliver Bernard said about Muriel and the Colony of the 50s, in the 'Artists of The Colony Room' catalogue for The Parkin Gallery in 1982. 'They found her a witty, foul-mouthed mother figure and a generous one too. The Colony Room was the nearest thing to a Paris cafe this bleak city could offer since

Henrietta Moraes with her first husband Michael Laws "She was clever and she liked toffs" said Joshua Bowler her son.

the great days of The Cafe Royal. She liked her members to be amusing or talented or rich, although she could be very kind to down-and-outs.'

Poet David Wright also noted a Parisian echo in the Colony and suggested it indicated the post-war move away from Paris as the centre of the arts. 'London then had taken over from Paris as the meeting place of the arts or at any rate artists,' he wrote. 'It's literary life was very different from nowadays, and rather than publisher's parties, expense lunches, state-subsidised poetry readings and organised cultural get togethers, what went on was something more spontaneous and organic. If you knew where to go and sooner or later you found out, there was almost no person of interest or achievement, past or potential, whom you did not meet. I sometimes wonder if there will ever again be anything like those casual, unofficial, almost nightly random meetings of mostly young and mostly unlike-minded writers and painters and musicians that took place in certain cafés and pubs round Soho.' Another crucial point made by Melly in the Parkin catalogue: 'The other side to that heavy door sat the enchanting antidote to the empty studio.' For a sometimes lonely creative life, the Colony was a place where artists and writers could find socialising and solace.

From Left to right Anthony Carson, John Davenport, John Deakin and David Wright. The boys around Soho. by Dan Farson

Micheal's Mural for Muriel
© The Estate of Michael Andrews courtesy
James Hyman, London

The Famous Mural

June Andrews, Michael Andrews' widow has said that when Michael was a student at the Slade and a regular attendee at the Colony, he was short of money and one summer in the 1958 Muriel Belcher paid him to decorate the club. Andrews decided that the back wall of the club was bare and using the cheapest possible materials, he then painted the mural, an interpretation of a Bonnard, that was to remain in place until it was finally removed in 2008 by Michael Wojas who sold it at auction following the termination of the club. June Andrews maintains, Andrews painted the mural without any instructions from Muriel Belcher and intended it as a gift to her and denies that it was in lieu of unpaid bar bills and Muriel was delighted with it. There is little chance that it was painted by Andrews as a student, as it is claimed, because by 1958 he was a tutor at the Slade.

Michael Peel found out that a lady in Yorkshire said she commissioned the 'Bonnard' picture and that it wasn't right for her summer house and that Andrew subsequently must have given it to Belcher. It seems likely that this is the truth because why else would it have been painted on canvas? Both writer Ian Dunlop and the patron swore an avadavat when Michael Wojas was trying to sell the mural. Michael Peel wrote in 2012 of the case to try and stop the sale of the clubs assets. "It belonged to the members. Michael Andrew's widow attested that Andrews had given it to Muriel but this was nonsense. She didn't even meet Michael Andrews until the 1960's and this transaction happened in 1958. The bar bill by the way was £850, an enormous sum in those days. We have an affidavit from both the woman in Yorkshire who originally commissioned the painting and from Ian Dunlop, who was a member and was actually present in the Club when Michael Andrews was hanging the mural. Andrews told him quite explicitly that it was to pay off his debt to the Club not to Muriel. Furthermore there are Committee minutes referring to it as an asset of the Club which was believed at one time to be worth in excess of £100,000."

It would eventually sell to Andrews' dealers James Hyman Gallery for £38,400. Andrews first gallery had been Helen Lessores' Beaux Arts gallery at Bruton Place. He was instrumental in getting the young Craigie Aitchinson into a gallery from meeting him in the Colony, Lessore's artists tended to be Colony members. Lessore reputedly favoured Aitchinson over and above her other young artists because of his Mediterranean approach. Leon Kossoff, Frank Auerbach, Sheila Fell, and Michael Andrews, as well as the kitchen-sink school of John Bratby, Derrick Greaves, Edward Middleditch and Jack Smith were all with the Beaux Arts. The gallery flourished through the 50s until 1964.

Credit

Sir Peregrine Worsthorne might not have been so taken by Muriel's ways but his friend Paul Johnson was a fan of her innate business acumen. "The great thing about Muriel was she always sat on the stool at the end of the bar, within reach of whoever came in so when you came in through the door she stretched out her hand and pulled you in, all the better to inspect and see whether you were to be allowed to come in or not. Whether you were a member or not was irrelevant. What she wanted to know was: who were you, had you caused any trouble in the past, or were likely to in the future and did you owe any money at the bar."

According to club regulations credit is illegal. Getting drinks for free was an illusion but one that credit encourages, so Muriel would only allow certain members this privilege. But even successful painters or Lords don't necessarily pay their debts and Muriel was constantly waging battle on her creditors, falling out badly with some of them when there might have been a misunderstanding, '...but I thought it was a gift?'

It was also said by Colony regulars that when you did receive your bill in the cold light of day that a couple of drinks had sometimes been added that you hadn't ordered; indeed, that Muriel might have added her own interest on the unsecured debt. When people are drunk enough to ask for credit they are often not sober enough to realise how many they have drunk and when the end of the evening the cash isn't available (there weren't cash machines or cards in those days) or someone had walked out on their bill, a credit note had to suffice. "Some people were allowed to owe vast sums at the bar," recalled Johnson in 2011. "I remember Bacon at one time had a bar bill of over a thousand pounds but then he was beginning to pull in big money with his daubs but then he only ever drank champagne. I quite liked him but he was a monster. One day in the Colony he said to me, 'I know you don't like my paintings'.

"That's putting it mildly old boy" I replied.

"Well why don't I lend you one and you can hang it up in your house and you'll begin to like it."

I said, "I've got a lot of very good paintings in my house and they might object if one of your daubs was hung among them, so no thanks, old boy. But he was perfectly affable about that."

One wonders how much Bacon might have been pulling Johnson's leg. He wasn't an artist renowned for giving or lending pictures but his tongue in cheek or bitchy humour was famous. Still Paul Johnson was a journalist at the time and remembers the details.

"Writer Anthony Carson, who was originally called Peter Brooks until Peter Brooks the director insisted he changed his name, was a great friend of Maclaren-Ross. I went in one day and Freud was trying to beat up Carson, who was a big man but very beatific. Freud was attacking him, kicking him, biting him, scratching him and Carson just fended him off but eventually I got tired of this and I gave Freud a great kick up the arse and dragged him off down the stairs. What it was about I don't know and Carson didn't know either. Freud was a nasty little man, I never liked him, didn't like his work either. The Colony is the only place I can remember where people went that you'd heard of, artists, writers, politicians. Mary Kenny used to go there and was quite a naughty girl in those days but that was before she rediscovered religion. Now who was the other girl she used to go with, oh hell… The problem is I'm 83 and I just can't remember names... Everybody reinvents their past, she wasn't a very naughty girl but she was quite frisky, she used to like sitting in bars drinking, she certainly doesn't like doing that now and hasn't done for a very long time." said Johnson.

The other place was the Gargoyle Club sold by David Tennant in 1952 post the Burgess and Maclean scandal where it appeared later to have been the exchange place for documents. The Gargoyle swapped from one pair of hands to another until it closed in 1956 after the scandal where photographers managed to snap Oxford Don Raymond Carr and a few Asquiths and Moseleys letting their hair down to

'Rock n Roll'. Scandalous, it wouldn't have happened under Muriel's watch or David Tennant's.

"You know who I used to see at the Colony" said Johnson "Morrea, the wife of Woodrow Wyatt (the maverick Labour MP and journalist). I suppose at that time there were three women one wanted to know, Edna O'Brien, Sonia Orwell and Barbara Skelton who married Cyril Connolly, but we all knew she was trouble." As Cyril Connolly was to discover, along with artist Michael Wishart; neither the easiest of men. As editor of Horizon, and a Bacon patron, you might have expected Connolly to be a Colony member but says Johnson, perhaps it was just too sleazy for him.

Gay Chelsea Homosexual Soho

Too sleazy for Cyril Connolly perhaps, but the paupers did not yet outweigh the titled and wealthy of the club, as can be seen in the membership books of the time. Sir Michael Duff, godfather to Lord Snowdon, was married to Lady Caroline, first daughter of Marquis of Anglesey's from Plas Newydd and sister of Lady Rose

John Minton 'buys a oss'
by CAC member Thompson

McLaren. Both Duffs were bisexual. It was a marriage of convenience, and they had many lovers, artist Rex Whistler and Prime Minister Anthony Eden among beautiful Lady Caroline's known conquests. Their house, Vaynol, was frequented by politicians, royalty and socialites. The private family album was shot by Cecil Beaton and the parties were long weekends featuring all night dancing.

The Moynihan's also were great party givers and were central to London's art and social life. Rodrigo was head of painting at the Royal College of Art and with artist wife Elinor Bellingham-Smith. He left Elinor in 1956 for Michael Wishart's young heiress wife, Ann Dunn, the sister of writer Nell Dunn, Soho's incessant ronde.

Elinor continued to go to the Colony with Ann's ex-lovers Wishart and Freud, while her ex-husband spent more time at The Chelsea Arts Club. Many members crossed over between these two establishments, including Robert Buhler, Ruskin Spear and John Minton. Susan Einzig pictured – another kinder transport child from Berlin, taught by

John Minton with his beard in his lap

Minton, ended up teaching Wally Fawkes, Humphrey Lyttleton and Euan Uglow. Einzig is recorded as saying: "We all used to meet at weekends and draw each other. We went to the cinema and discovered the films of Jean Renoir, René Clair and Marcel Carné. We jived and jitterbugged to Humphrey Lyttelton's jazz band every Monday evening. We also got sucked into the drinking scene in Soho. It was all over within two or three years but in my memory it seems to have been much longer." When not Minton's 'walker', she became a well known illustrator of children's books, her most famous being 'Tom's Midnight Garden' by Philippa Pearce.

At the Colony, Minton could be openly gay and nobody gave a damn but at the Chelsea Arts Club members refused to speak to him when he rolled in with 'the exceptionally good looking' (as Moynihan described him) Norman Bowler. Tom Cross wrote in 'Artists and Bohemians – A History of the Chelsea Arts Club' that there were often unpleasant remarks about Minton. 'I smell buggery here,' was the response of one old gent on seeing Minton and walked straight out again. When Minton bought a sailor friend in everyone complained but as he retorted: 'If he'd have been an Admiral everyone would've been shaking his hand on having such a fine friend'.

It would be years until homosexuals were openly welcome at the Chelsea Arts Club as they were at the lesbian Gateway Club on the nearby King's Road. Francis Bacon had much to do with bringing the flavour of the Colony with him when he was given an honorary membership at Chelsea and as actor-writer Bob Kingdom recalls, "I remember the rare occurrence of Bacon and Hockney at the Chelsea Arts. I heard Bacon shout 'I am not gay! I am homosexual!'"

The term 'Homosexual' for many remained 'a practising pervert', as described in The Wolfenden Report of 1957, which had sprung from the Montagu Case. Daily Mail journalist Peter Wildeblood, along with Lord Montagu of Beaulieu and his cousin, Michael Pitt Rivers were arrested and tried for buggery. In 1954 they were found guilty, the first time since 1895 when Oscar Wilde was tried and sent to Reading Gaol. Wildebood and Pitt Rivers both got 18 months while Lord Montagu, who never admitted anything other than dancing and kissing in his beach hut with an RAF Serviceman, got 12 months.

All three men were Colony members when they were sent to prison. On release, Peter Wildeblood was immediately sacked by the Daily Mail and was the only one of the three who spoke to the Wolfenden Enquiry, exclaiming to a shocked court, 'I am a homosexual'. Wildebood then wrote a book, 'Against the Law' and openly campaigned for Gay Rights. By the late 50s he ran a club in Berwick Street, before enjoying a bright future as a producer and writer in musical theatre. Lord Montagu married and began a car museum while Pitt Rivers also went on to marry Sonia Orwell although the marriage only lasted eight years. He continued to sell off parts of his estate to travel the world, until he settled with one man and rebuilt his famous grandfather's Larmer Tree Gardens on the Rushmore estates in Dorset.

They are now open to the public, as is The Pitt Rivers Museum in Oxford.

Although the report advised the government that homosexuality should be made legal, Anthony Eden's Conservative government feared repercussions as a vote loser. It was not until 1967, ten years after Wolfenden, that Labour's Wilson Government stopped homosexuality being an offence.

For some Colony members like Tom Driberg MP, danger lent excitement to his sexual encounters, especially since his penchant was for the uniformed or working class heterosexual men. But then Driberg liked nothing more, apparently than to have the stickiness of semen still about his mouth as he sat down in a parliamentary committee, chuckling to himself, 'if only they knew', so Colony member Christopher Hitchens recalled of his friend in a review of Francis Wheen's book on Driberg in The Spectator. For most Colony members it made little difference. Entering the room you relaxed into your true self. There is a famous story about Dick West, noted foreign correspondent and Driberg in the Colony in the 50s. When I interviewed West in 2011 he said: "That story about Tom Driberg and me in the Colony wasn't even my story. It was an Australian journalist."

The story goes like this. Dick West (or the Australian) arranged to interview Tom Driberg MP in the 1950's. Driberg says, 'Meet me at my club', something one would then assume to be a gentlemen's club in those days, something like The Reform in Pall Mall. Instead he insisted on the Colony and when Dick got up the stairs he told the lady at the door, who was Muriel, that he was supposed to be meeting Mr Tom Driberg MP and could she please direct him to where he might be. To which the reply came: "Tom Driberg's the one in the corner with his hand round that sailor's cock, dearie."

Just like Driberg, both Farson and Bacon went in for East End rough trade. When he'd gone to St Ives with a boyfriend he'd stolen off Farson, a friend of The Krays known as Ron ('Francis Bacon was a good Freind(sic) of mine,' Ronnie Kray wrote in a letter to Dan Farson). Bacon pretended he had no idea of the artist colony already ensconced by 1958, although he moved into a studio next door to Patrick Heron and wrote of 'the terrible abstract artists living next door'. Roger Hilton, a member of the Colony who lived in St. Just in Cornwall and had as strong a personality as Bacon and said 'Bacon needed a good lesson in painting'. Poet WS Graham (Willie to his friends), artists Peter Lanyon and Bryan Winters. Muriel Belcher and Carmel used to go and stay in Penzance with Winters. I'm not sure what would have been more shocking at that time, Bacon or the black lesbian Carmel in Cornwall. Bacon swanned about wherever he went, from the South of France to the far reaches of Cornwall openly homosexual and masochistic, yet also with a streak of mental sadism; especially where sycophants were concerned.

The artist Robert Buhler was a Chelsea Arts Club member as well as at the Colony. Part of the Moynihan set, he was also an artist and teacher at the RCA and somewhat unusually had grown up in Soho with his mother Lucie, who owned a cafe on 56 Charlotte Street that everyone would go to after a night at the Fitzroy Tavern. When he was a student and his friends were broke, they even got meals on tick, prior to its being bombed in WWII. In 1951, Rodrigo Moynihan was commissioned to paint the teaching staff of the painting school in the staff room. Along with Carel Weight, Ruskin Spear and Buhler, Moynihan put himself at the back, Minton at the front. The staff shifted between Chelsea, Fitzrovia and Soho, the three bohemian parts of London. Chelsea might have been already changing into a place where young rich marrieds wanted to live but there were still many artists' garrets left over from the 1800's. In the 1950's they were still drawn towards pubs like Finch's in the Fulham Road and Sean O'Casey's, The Queen's Elm on Old Church Street. These were places that bohemians could meet and mix outside of the Colony but in pub hours if you happened to have a job.

Working in those days suggested a different set of rules. In professional circles lunches were longer and drinking huge amounts wasn't abnormal. A few cocktails midday was par for the course, although wine was impossible to get in pubs outside of a few gentleman's clubs or The French House. Women rarely entered a public house let alone drank, other than at weddings or Christmas, when a small sherry or a half of light ale would surface. One wonders how anyone managed to function at a job whether painting, teaching or writing.

The novelist Dan Davin recollected in 'Closing Times' in 1975 about his friend Julian Maclaren-Ross. 'It was his habit to write at night. After spending the day in pubs and drinking clubs, he would return to his lair and write all night long, when things got desperate he could work for days and nights at a stretch.' Living on a diet of coffee and cigarettes, and apparently trying to bundle up enough money into a lump sum to settle down and write his novel, drinking and working weren't such easy bedfellows in the end but Maclaren-Ross' novel did eventually get written even if his autobiography was never finished.

Be Bold

Soho, it was often said, was a state of mind rather than a place. It held a reputation of danger and villainy but it was also, as Farson put it, 'blessed with innocence'. Certainly by today's standards, the 50s, as George Melly said, were 'Impecunious and proudly squalid.' Writer Frank Norman, who'd arrived in Soho aged 16 in the late 40s, as an innocent orphan, 'became a Soho addict beyond cure or redemption.' He was also a petty criminal, sharing a bombed-out basement with Lucian Freud, scratching by on a few break ins that only ever got him a sentence. Being 'banged up' gave him a whole new raison d'etre, writing about the underworld in plays, books and musicals such as, 'Fings Aint Wot They Used to be', musical score by Lionel Bart. Ian Board, had also run away from the countryside to Soho. Later to rule the Colony, he was working as a commis waiter in the smart restaurant Jardins de Gourmet in Greek Street, a shy and pretty boy of 15 who did occasional modelling for knitting patterns but wanted more. "Without sounding too corny," Ian said of Muriel, "our eyes met and everything clicked magically." Ian and Muriel's first meeting was in 1947 at Jardin's her favourite restaurant and the most expensive in Soho but it wasn't until later on when Muriel was having lunch with the couturier Otto Lucas of Bond Street that she said to Ian, "I've just opened a new club, anytime you want a job Gal, you come along to me".

Board Valets for Elizabeth Taylor

Isabel Rawsthorne with Ian in the club

Ian waits at Le Gourmet de Jardin

Tries his hand at 'Modelling'

Ian Board with Otto Lucas, Milliner.

Then, Ian's ambitions lay elsewhere. He wanted to be a valet. Muriel suggested there might be a few customers amongst her wealthy clientele who'd be interested in having a personal valet. It was true and Board had lots of work, to the point that it became a little too much for him. He gave valeting up and joined what he thought was a quiet life with Muriel under the title of Bar Manager at the Colony. It was a long haul, though. In reality Board wielded little management power until Muriel became ill in 1976, when he took over. For 21 years he remained under her thumb, as in a way many of her members did too.

As Frank Norman wrote so lucidly in 'Norman's London' in 1969, about Soho clubs and the 12 years he'd been a member of the Colony: 'I have yet to meet someone who is a match for Muriel when it comes to a verbal punch-up. I have seen her render even the toughest of her members helpless under a barrage of abuse, the intensity of which leaves them inarticulate gibbering imbeciles.'

Muriel had a way of speaking that derived from the slang of the hip young things of the 1930's. A lot of 'ies ' and 'ettes' and 'kins' were added to the ends of words, disguising the sharpness of her palette. A drink would become a 'drinkette', dear was always 'dearie', you wore a divine 'dressikins' and the evening was 'blissikins'. Men were always ascribed the female gender: 'Her over there'. Of George Bernard Shaw she said, "What a clever little woman." People were entreated: "Get out your bead bag Lottie"; "Oi Mrs Hitler", troublemakers were stopped with "Why don't you shut your vicious little mouth and buy us all a round of drinks dearie?" When a gangster asked for protection money she turned to him gave her famously imperious look, and said, "Fuck off, cunty." and he did terrified. Apparently a head was later found unattached from its body in Dean Street. She also seemed to manage to share the staircase with the Maltese mafia brothel upstairs with little difficulty. Muriel said she attributed her success to 'a bold tongue dearie': one that she was not frightened to use. Anthony Blond, a member from the early 50s until the 90's who'd gone to school with Lord Montagu and Alan Clark, had hobnobbed with Jimmy and Teddy Goldsmith, John Aspinall and Ken Tynan, pointed out in his autobiography A Jew Made in England, that 'the Zeitgeist in the intellectual, not to say artistic and thespian world was, in those pre-Wolfenden Report times pro-homosexual and incidentally, philosemitic. Everyone used the expression, 'Get you!' when putting someone down, and 'My dear' was the common form of address for the uncommon people we thought we were. Blond was an open bi-sexual and from a high-powered family. His father was married to a Marks & Spencer heiress, and his cousin Baron, the Royal photographer whose assistant was Lord Snowden, was also a Colony member. Jewish people were certainly evident in high-flying circles but as beatnik poet Michael Horovitz said in 2012, he found the literary world in the 50s incredibly anti-semitic and rude. "I was disappointed that the real life versions didn't live up to the wit in books by Waugh or Powell," he recalled. "The people who distressed me in the Colony Club included MacInnes and Bacon, who could be very malicious and cruel. They competed, and Muriel seemed to like that and would stir things up. Philip O'Connor and Paul Potts were always cadging drinks or getting angry and there was a lot of emotional behaviour around."

Colin MacInnes described Muriel accurately as, 'The platinum tough girl with a heart of gold... always glad to see you, "Sweetie! Come and kiss mother! You're a real cup of tea!" For she could be as kind as cruel, and although everything could be made fun of within the room, there were certain lines that couldn't be crossed. If you did, no matter how fond she was of you, you were out for good. This included crippled children, war heroes, and vulnerable people. "She was a brave gal in the Somme"' she said about a retired soldier who never said a word but sat in the corner most days after a day working in the City and always bought a large whiskey. Meanwhile, she bawled out loud mouthed bores. Douglas Sutherland, had won a military cross during the WW11 and was a writer who became such good friends with Muriel that they exchanged jokey postcards from holiday destinations, 'The Duke and Duchess Diana, were very sorry not to get to your party on account of they went to the Algarve... a holiday paradise for whore's maids and used car salesmen...' This postcard to Muriel was undated but looked to be early 60s.

Douglas wrote in 'Portrait of a Decade London life 1945-55' in 1988, about his first encounter after going to a Thursday Club luncheon at Wheeler's in Charlotte Street. The Thursday club was centred around Prince Philip, The Duke of Edinburgh (and occasionally Mountbatten) and invitations came with an unwritten rule that none of the twelve to fourteen guests could leave before the Duke. Thus, afternoons were often lost. On one afternoon the last three to leave were commercial artist Vasco Lazzolo, The Marquis of Milford Haven who had been best man at The Prince's wedding to the Queen, and Sutherland,: "Let me take you," said Vasco, "to a club, where I have only recently and with the greatest difficulty, managed to make myself a member. It is run exclusively for the convenience of whores' maids." This was my first introduction to Muriel's, one of the most outrageous of bohemian drinking clubs... On this occasion Vasco as a new member was still far from being accepted into the inner circle of privilege. He waved us to an unoccupied table and going up to the bar ordered three large brandies. At this point Muriel's beady eye swivelled around and alighted on the two of us. 'Ooo is 'e', she hissed. 'her in the corner?'

"They are friends of mine."

"Ees a copper!' declared Muriel. 'Get him out of 'ere."

'But Muriel! That happens to be the Marquis of Milford Haven.'

"Don't talk shit, e's a copper! Get him out of 'ere."

They had no other choice but to leave but Douglas had obviously been smitten with Muriel and her, 'rod of iron tempered only with a fatal weakness for anyone who might amuse her... they would have the privilege of keeping her glass filled while she regaled them with the most scandalous gossip of who was doing what to whom among the sexually ambivalent members.' And there was enough gossip to keep the conversation well oiled for years. The composer Leonard Bernstein was a Colony member in the 50s and didn't admit his sexual leanings until a couple of years before his death in 1990. Vivienne Leigh would go there with John Buckmaster an actor and close friend, and wherever Leigh went troubled followed as Laurence Olivier and Kenneth Tynan, could vouch.

In any convivial drinking den, gossip is part of the proceedings. A club like the Colony was so exclusive as to throw out people who looked like policemen, could also be relied upon to harbour spies. Donald Maclean and Guy Burgess were both members and spent much time in the Colony before they were extradited to Russia in 1951. It was a progression from Oxford University, after all, where Cyril Connolly, Evelyn Waugh, Brian Howard and Tom Driberg had graduated. So it is unsurprising that they would go to the same clubs in London. Douglas Sutherland knew them both and would later be instrumental in uncovering the fourth spy, Sir Anthony Blunt, keeper of the Queen's pictures. Driberg, originally a Communist like Burgess and Maclean, was voted into the House of Commons as an Independent and labelled a spy posthumously, without evidence. Driberg certainly got himself into trouble with bits of rough that stole his possessions but any blackmail was dealt with by his protector Lord Beaverbrook and the Government, it was thought, because during his lifetime nothing scandalous hardly touched him. The Colony at this time seemed to attract a certain kind, interested in reform or revolution, but also bon viveurs: a way of life later characterised as champagne socialism.

Tom Driberg loved a man in uniform

They would have rubbed shoulders and drank with the people they sought to depose. Baron, the society photographer and Douglas Sutherland would introduce Princess Margaret to the Colony, no doubt alongside Anthony Armstrong Jones, who was Baron's photography assistant on his Royal Portraits and would become Lord Snowdon on marriage to the princess.

Le Corp De Colony

Lady Rose McLaren was Lord Anglesea's fourth daughter and a lifetime Colony member and great friend of Muriel's. She grew up in a rarefied artistic milieu where her father was a keen amateur filmmaker. He made a satirical movie about Sir Oswald Moseley starring Rose called 'Pink Shirts' as opposed to the eponymous black. Rex Whistler decorated their house and Frederick Ashton was a houseguest, whom she fell in

Lady Rose McLaren and Simon Blow

love with and proposed to, Rose had always wanted to be a ballet dancer. He returned her teenage love letters to her, spelling corrected, and said 'Don't be so silly'. "I knew we would have had our own rooms. I was a virgin but not all innocent." She later said.

Lady Rose was not the first or last of the Colony ladies or Royal Ballet dancers to fall for a homosexual. However their relationship survived to the point that when she became part of Vic-Wells (the predecessor to The Royal Ballet) that she was introduced by Ashton to the Colony. Who introduced whom to Muriel's is unclear. We know that stalwart Colony member, Constant Lambert was Ninette de Valois composer and wrote 'Horoscope' for the young Margot Fonteyn, his lover. Erica Bowen, secretary to Madame Rambert company was a member along with Australian ballet dancer, Sir Robert Helpmann. Sir Robert was Margot Fonteyn's first partner and favourite dancer. He became a major film character actor, playing the evil child catcher in Ian Fleming's, Chitty Chitty Bang Bang and Powell and Pressburger's, The Red Shoes.

Prior to establishing the Ballet Rambert, The Royal Ballet and the English National Ballet, Madame Rambert, Dame Ninette de Valois, Dame Alicia Markova and Sir Anton Dolin were all with Diagliev's Company. Prior to this there were no full time ballet companies in Britain. Dancers often relied on performing in burlesque, operas and pantomime. It seems likely that some dancers had probably known Muriel from the early days of the theatrical Music Box.

Artist Patrick Hughes became a member in the late 60s as part of the 'Northern Surreal' artist brigade but had been before as a schoolboy, as this sweet vignette shows: 'In 1957 Erica Bowen was the Secretary of the Rambert Ballet School at the Mercury Theatre in Notting Hill Gate and a member of the Colony Room. Her son Ivor was a schoolboy at Hull Grammar School because he lived with his father during term-time. His father taught economics at Hull University and was divorced from Erica. I was a provincial, working-class, first-generation grammar schoolboy and Ivor's friend. Erica took us several times when staying with her in London to the Colony Room, where Muriel Belcher, seated on her chair this side of the bar, greeted Erica warmly with "Hello Cunty!" and greeted us underage boys too. It was one of several vital introductions that Erica gave me to bohemia, the land where rules are ignored and exciting things are made to happen. Ian Board was behind the bar then. Erica seemed a bit like Muriel, clever, resourceful, unpredictable. I mostly remember knowing John McDonald quite well. He had studied at the Rambert Ballet School

from left to right
Ivor Bowen with wife Jenny,
mother Erica, Alan Wyn
and Robert McBryde

Photo: Ivor Bowen

66

and danced in the West End. His friends the Two Roberts, Colquhoun and McBride, were drunk and obstreperous. Bill Crozier was very thin and had a white mac. Brendan Behan was quiet. There was a wonderful evening there with Erica Bowen and a girlfriend of hers, it must have been in August 1958. They were singing, again and again, Volare, Nel blu di pinto di blu in the Room, they loved it and I was amazed that you could do that.' Domenico Modugno sang it at the 1958 Italian Eurovision Song Contest whereby Dean Martin took it up. It is hard to imagine everyone singing a Eurovision song in the club in later years, without irony.

To Erica Bowen it seemed unconventional. Valda Setterfield, who was to become Merce Cunningham's principle dancer, originally came from Margate, Kent and at 16 in 1950, went to London to audition for the school run by Madame Marie Rambert. She thought she stood a chance because Rambert was known for taking risks. 'First, Erica Bowen, the secretary, had me do two pliés and an arabesque in my street clothes: I held onto the bar, not the ballet barre, but the bar where people drank and did my pliés. Then I was taken to see Rambert. She was shrieking unmercifully at some girl, "...filthy filthy dancer, my God, your filthy, empty sarcophagus feet, I cannot stand to look!" She whipped round to me and hissed, "She will make a marvellous Giselle."

Jazz

The real obsession for young people in the 50s, however, was with jazz. Traditional, bebop or otherwise, it was causing loosened corsets in smoke-filled basements across Soho. It had come over from America in the 1940's and by the early 50s young people, even the improbable likes of Philip Larkin and Kingsley Amis, were going wild for it, as was Colony member Geoffrey Wynn who composed the jazz for Jaques Tati movies as well as writing the story of Alain Roman's WWII espionage.

George 'Bunny Bum' Melly

Map of Bohemian Soho
Commissioned for the Limited Edition Colony book.

George Melly's picture photographed by Michael Woods
Edition of 125 signed and numbered by the artist.

Geoffrey Wynn shows off a first copy to Gaston. He knew a bit about resistance

The clubs were 'temples of New Orleans devoted to cold coffee and hot sex', as John Mortimer remarked. Humphrey Lyttleton's, 'Humph's' at 100 Oxford Street Club had queues on Mondays and Saturdays right through to Soho Square. Although Humphrey was not a Colony member he went often with Wally Fawkes who was in his band. He had the typical Colony mentality: whatever assignment you are offered say 'yes' first and learn about it afterwards, and refuse to be a member of any club that would have you. Thus did Humphrey go from trumpeter to cartoonist to food critic to TV presenter to chairman of radio panel shows. George 'Bunny Bum' Melly, known for his enticing wiggle on stage, was with sidekick John 'trumpet' Chilton, not helping the government cause towards being, 'upright and proper'. They voted with their feet for all night jazz raves. Drugs, dancing and inter-racial friendliness moved onto sweaty all night Calypso parties, leading to physical abandonment between men and men, women and women and men and women of all races and all classes. Cy Laurie, clarinettist, opened a club in Ham Yard. During the day it was Mac's Rehearsal Rooms at 41 Windmill Street, at night the first 'Alnite Raveups' Cy Laurie's Jazz Club featuring Melly on Vocals. They were easy pick-up joints for those that knew how. The puritanical social fabric of early 50s Britain was being destroyed by jazz. In this time of austerity, wrote Melly, 'Soho was the only area in London where the rules didn't apply... tolerance its password, where bad behaviour was cherished.'

'The great thing about Jazz, is that no one, not a soul, cares what your class is, what your race is, what your income is or if you are a boy of a girl or bent or versatile or what you are.' So wrote Colin MacInnes. Permissive thinker and Pre-Raphaelite, Edward Burne Jones was MacInnes great grandfather. MacInnes' cousins were Rudyard Kipling and British prime Minister Stanley Baldwin. Gay and with a penchant for silent dark West Indian men, MacInnes championed the black cause and people who knew him said that he gave money away to people who needed it, taught immigrants the rules and their rights in this new country, well before Citizens Advice had set up its neighbourhood scheme. A Barbadian friend, who shared a flat with him, Michael Hunte, said: 'He thought society was giving us a raw deal, so he bullied us all the time to make more of ourselves.' MacInnes lived at night and imposed upon his white friends. He wrote the novels 'Absolute Beginners' and 'City of Spades' and his homes and book locations were the streets of Soho and Notting Hill, where the ruthless racketeer Rachman ruled and whom MacInnes rallied against. Strange they might have been in the Colony together when Christine Keeler was Rachman's mistress.

A kind of sociologist, predicting trends like the power of the teenager prior to its invention, MacInnes loved Muriel but many other members found him terrifying. He had a way of standing in the corner staring hard and making spiteful comments delivered with a sneer. 'Despite his cantankerousness, Colin could be endearing.' Dan Farson wrote. He was also a perceptive journalist for the literary and cultural magazine Encounter, started by Stephen Spender in 1953 and infamously funded by the CIA.

MacInnes wrote in his book, 'England, Half English', an essay 'See you at Mabel's':

a detailed description of Muriel and club culture during the 50s in Soho and the way that the law had not foreseen these sorts of clubs growing. Legally they were meant to be co-operative Societies, where no profit or loss was made. But in reality they were wholly run, bought, sold and administered by individuals who did profit. Whether Muriel or Brewster Hughes with his own club The Abalabi, The Club Afrique with Ambrose Campbell, Boris Watson of The Mandrake, Mary Douse (known as The Scull) of The Kismet where criminals and coppers mingled, Slim Cattan of The Georgian they all relied heavily on the personality of the manager and the membership they attracted. Of course, Muriel insisted she was far too busy to ever visit other people's clubs but the Colony certainly made a profit for her.

Ruth, Soho by Harold Chapman

Gaston, Brian Rix, wife, actress Elspeth Gray and Cellar Master of the French

Oliver Bernard described Soho as being, a 'members club in itself' and that you joined clubs within that club to get away from tourists and football louts. But wherever you went subscription had to be paid: a half pint in a pub, a cup of tea in a cafe. Nothing was free. Both Bernard and MacInnes point that there were few clubs where you could be certain to meet all your friends and that to go about alone was easiest to fit into a place like the Colony as you didn't have to worry about your friend being entre nous, offended or rejected. For Bernard, the place where most different sorts gathered was The Caves de France, next door to the Colony, where you could expect to meet some of the Colony's banned members, the two Roberts (Colquhoun and McBryde), poet Sydney Graham, critic John Raymond, Peter Brook, Nina Hamnett, writer Frank Norman, Paul Johnson and many others. "It was possible to move from one end to the other and talk with an entirely different collection of people," says Bernard. "To do that in the Colony Room, you had to stay much closer to people and be more intimate."

Gerald Hamilton was always in The Caves and extraordinarily proud to have been the opus for Mr Norris Changes Trains by Christopher Isherwood. He vied with Aleister Crowley for the title of Wickedest Man in Britain. It was said that not only had he avoided conscription during the war by escaping to Ireland dressed as a Mother Superior but had before the war sold forged passports to Jews, informing the Nazis as they approached the border, thus being paid twice. When challenged by Farson: "Is it true that you are the wickedest man in Europe?" he replied:

"Oh that's very kind of you" he chuckled. "Wittiest, well really…"

"No not wittiest, wickedest."

"Well", he replied with outraged innocence. "I'm just a harmless old man and when my time comes I shall face my maker with great confidence."

'I expect he bribed his way in,' writes Farson. I'm sure he was right but as with Crowley, never underestimate the wicked.

Farson's view about it being a more innocent era was perhaps due to his own innocent eyes. The poverty of the time, the buttoned-up behaviour that could be unleashed with a word, the atmosphere of violence hanging like a cloud, waiting to burst. Crowley who had been defeated in a libel action by Nina Hamnett, perhaps had cursed her. By 1956 Nina had had enough, forced to live in Paddington and no longer her beloved Fitzrovia, she threw herself from the window. Her body spiked on the railings 40 feet below. A play written by her friend Bob Pocock about her had been aired on the radio and she hadn't liked what she'd heard. Friends often fall out over portrayals of each other, whether by paintings or words, with egos trampled. At 66 the acknowledged Queen Of Bohemia died. Her last words were, "Why can't they let me die?"

A year later Hamnett's friend Johnny Minton, the life of so many parties, also committed suicide. Norman Bowler his lover, was in love with Henrietta Moraes, and Minton made him choose; Bowler chose her. "My heart fell to my boots," Moraes said. Minton never awoke after taking an overdose .

Like his friend Hamnett, Welsh wild man Dylan Thomas failed to get out of bed one morning at The Chelsea Hotel in New York dying not of alcohol as many thought but of pneumonia (there was little sign of cirrhosis of the liver). He raged against 'the dying of the light' and was only 39 but produced a body of work that defined him as Wales' greatest poet. Hamnett's fellow Tenbyite, Augustus John would die in his 80's in 1961, lorded with Honours and leaving behind a scurrilous reputation and (some estimated) 100 illegitimate children. He had made Fitzrovia his, had been part of The Chelsea Arts Club since the century began and was president of The Gypsy Lore Society as well as The Gargoyle; the old school were dying out.

As Douglas Sutherland wrote about the Colony and Soho in the 1950's: 'You cannot really expect to have such diverse personalities... packed in a small smoked filled room, with the drinks rattling across the counter like bursts of machine gun fire, and maintain the calm of a tea party on the vicarage lawn.' But if you survived, what an education.

Nina with Poet Charles Wrey Gardiner

Chapter 3

The Swinging Soho 60s

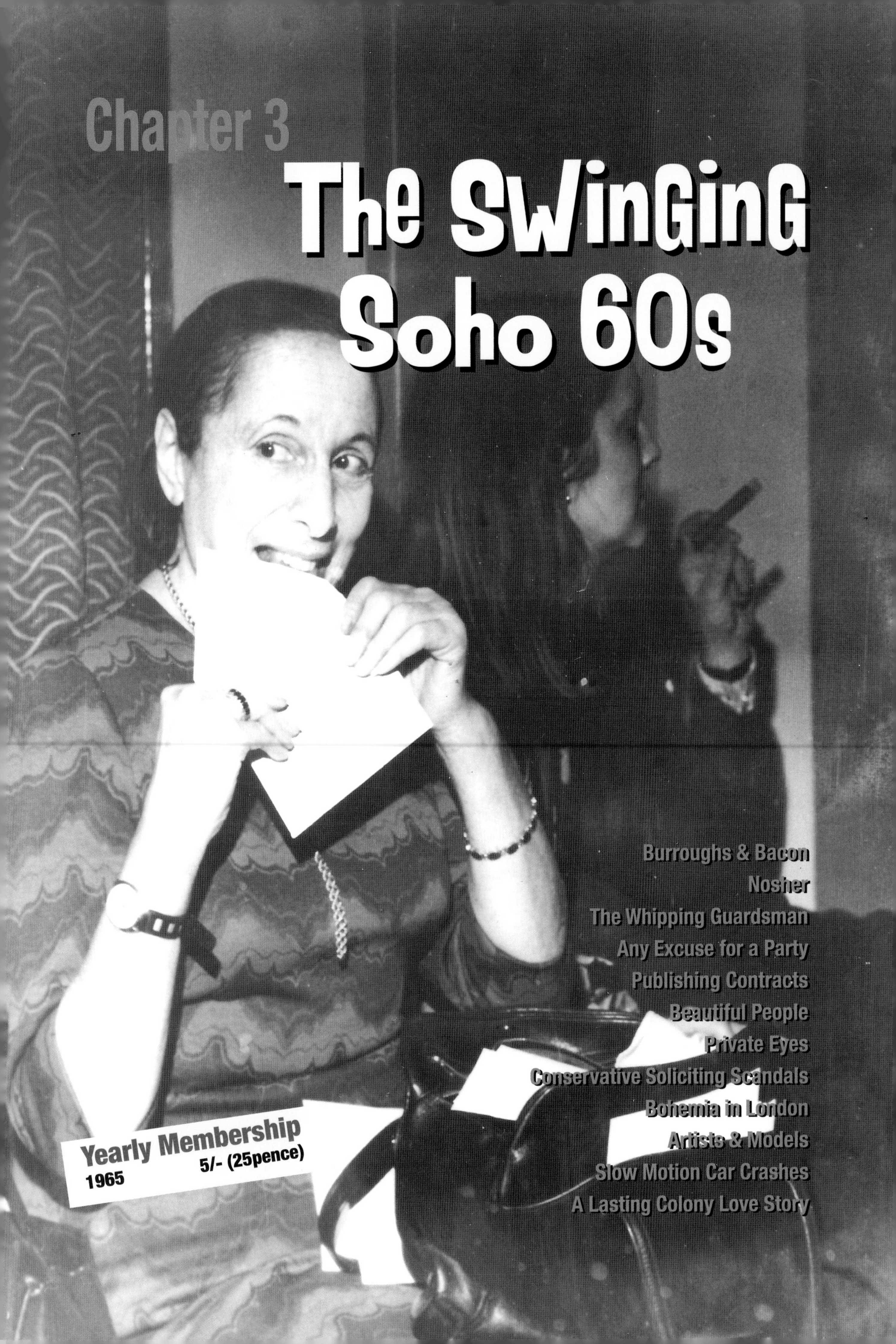
Yearly Membership
1965 5/- (25pence)

Burroughs & Bacon
Nosher
The Whipping Guardsman
Any Excuse for a Party
Publishing Contracts
Beautiful People
Private Eyes
Conservative Soliciting Scandals
Bohemia in London
Artists & Models
Slow Motion Car Crashes
A Lasting Colony Love Story

Burroughs & Bacon

If the 1950's had Soho jumping with rock n' roll and skiffle, emanating from The 21 Coffee Club on Old Compton Street and jazz from Ronnie Scott's and the Club Eleven in Great Windmill St, the 1960's saw Soho becoming psychedelic. Here the drug culture began earlier than most people imagined. Anne Valery, the writer and war time heroine recalled of artist and fellow Colony member and Gargoyle goer, Michael Wishart that in the 50s 'he was always a druggie, you know, out of it'.

At this time, jazz musicians and beatniks from Paris, Tangier and New York bought substances to Soho. Jacques Stern (a fantastically wealthy junkie) remembers visiting the Colony in November 1958 with William Burroughs, who knew Francis Bacon from Tangier when they lived in hotels across the street. "I met Bacon with Burroughs in London," he said. "We went one night off to drink in Soho and I don't know how Burroughs knew Bacon but he did and Bacon was there. Anyway this guy passes Bacon who is not only, as far as I am concerned, maybe the greatest painter of his time and extremely brilliant man who knew everything about everything. I went up there in need of something (heroin) and wouldn't have stayed there more than 10 minutes except Bacon kept on talking and I stayed there for three fucking hours listening to him. This guy was one of the greatest geniuses of our time and also a great painter. Now you compare Bacon to Warhol? Forget it. Bacon was just the stuff... Burroughs and Bacon are like Gods. Oh absolutely. They were friends. I just stood there listening to both of them but mostly Bacon. It was unbelievable. The guy was versed in everything. Gigantic." He said in an interview with Victor Bockris and Stewart Meyer in 2001.

In fact, people had been taking dope in Soho since the 1920's. In the post-war era Benzedrine and heroin came along, then hash and acid made their debut in the 60s. It added to the ever-present river of alcohol, although wine was still an acquired taste and sophisticates stuck to whisky, even with meals.

Denis Hopper who was writing the film Easy Rider at the time with Jack Nicholson and Terry Southern described his adventures in Soho to the film director Billy Wilder who had escaped from Berlin prior to WWII. 'London's the greatest, it's just sensational,' Hopper wrote. 'The art world, the fashion world and the jazz clubs, they were exploding. It was the most creative place I ever saw. I said all this to Billy Wilder and he said, 'Sounds like you're describing Berlin just before the Second World War'.'

The Colony certainly epitomised Berlin in behaviour and dress: alternative rather than hip, bohemian rather than fashionable. For some like Molly Parkin, my mother, who went to the Colony from the 50s through to the 80's, it was character building.

Molly, Sarah and Sophie by Michael Parkin

Mario and Franco. Trattoria Terraza with Gaston. Neighbours in Dean Street

"The Colony was the cream of society; the most dangerous place you could go mentally and a grounding on the rocks for conversation. If you could hold your own there, you could survive anywhere. Muriel was my benchmark of how a woman could be." As Molly said in 2012, the 60s was the time women would begin to shrug off their shrinking violet image and become as bold as Muriel Belcher herself. Indeed, Molly was the first person to swear on television: on Late Night Line Up in 1964. Oddly, this watershed moment is attributed to Kenneth Tynan, fellow Colony member, critic, founder of The National Theatre with Sir Laurence Olivier and renowned spanking fanatic, who later commissioned Parkin to write a segment of his musical, 'Oh! Calcutta!' along with John Lennon, Samuel Beckett and Edna O'Brien. (Now that's what I call a musical). The Colony, where swearing was mandatory, made people unashamed to use language when it was still taboo. For members, it was obvious that the word 'fuck' would just pop out in the heat of the moment. And it was spreading the feeling of freedom through 60s London. So many writers and comedians of the time, all members, had much to do with this; From Marty Feldman, Peter Cook, John Antrobus, Spike Milligan, The Monty Pythons and their producers. The Magic Christian, Peter Sellers' favourite book by satirist Terry Southern, was made into a film starring Sellers, John Cleese, Ringo Starr and Raquel Welsh. The end scene showed a pool of sewage, filled full of money with people rushing off Waterloo Bridge and jumping into the quagmire. The site would later be where The National Theatre was built.

Nosher

London was changing and so was Soho, which
was experiencing a boom in the film, fashion,
music and television industries. But much about
Muriel's remained the same, Nosher the dog
always yapping on her knee. As Molly Parkin
said, "It was full of artists, poets, writers, drinkers,
thinkers and some Lords. I remember going in
there with Donald Baverstock (controller of
BBC1 and married to Enid Blyton's daughter
Gillian) and Ned Sherrin, who were changing
the face of television, but I would also go

STudy foR GoLdfingeR TiTLe
sequence by RobeRT BRownjohn

there with lovers: Robert Brownjohn (the American graphic designer famous for his
Goldfinger and From Russia with Love credit sequences) writer and barrister John
Mortimer, John Bryce, producer of The Avengers and visionary architect Cedric
Price. I was very busy working and with the kids, so I didn't know until later that
Cedric was actually living with Erno Goldfinger's daughter Liz. I didn't ask those
kinds of questions. You'd pop over in the afternoon after lunch at Mario and Franco's
Trattoria Terraza." It was always open from 3-11pm and at 11pm you were bid a
cheery farewell by Mu shouting "Haven't you got a nice little cottage to go to?" This
referred to the homosexual habit of 'cottaging', picking up men in public lavatories.
Muriel was fond of such argot.

Susie B Coworker with Keeler

As the exotic fan dancer Susie Bardolph said, 'There was a little Shiatsu dog that used to sit on the bar yapping and if you came too close to Muriel it would bite you." The dog was called Nosher (1960's slang for someone who performs cunnilingus). Blonde and beautiful, Susie had her own act at The Embassy Club in Bond Street and had her pick of Soho men. She had married in the late 1950's, an actor and onetime understudy for Orson Welles called Bill Mitchell. A Canadian habitué of the Colony until banned by Muriel, from where he sought solace in Norman Balon's pub The Coach and Horses.

By the early 60s they had split up and Susie had their one year old daughter to look after and found sympathy in the Colony. "Muriel was very kind to me. I know she wasn't to everyone, but to me she was," recalls Susie. "One day she asked after Bill, 'What's the bastard been up to?' Bill had started to get a bit of voiceover work but was always in The Coach and Horses spending his money. I told Muriel the truth. 'I'm broke I can't pay the rates' (equivalent to council tax).' Twice she paid my rates for me and never said a word or asked for the money back. Muriel was always kind to me but Carmel could be hard work... There was a couple of members I wasn't so fond of, though. Lucian (Freud) was one of them. Didn't trust him. On one occasion Francis (Bacon) took Lucian and me to Wheeler's. Lucian had this big green Bentley, he was a terrible driver. After dinner Francis suggested that Lucian could give me a lift home, 'Please don't suggest that,' I whispered to Francis. 'I'd rather pay for a cab', and I could ill afford it but rather that than be alone with him. There was something creepy about him. Francis was lovely though, we all had a lot of time for him and he was always so generous, in every way." In fact Bacon could be quite spiteful, and was particularly so to other artists but for those he liked and loved, he could afford to be indulgent, paying off people's debts and hospital bills, quietly slipping £20 notes into handbags, envelopes or pockets; always buying and sharing the champagne. For Muriel and Ian he did even more, paying for them to go on holiday every year. Mombasa was a favourite destination.

On Holiday with Ian and Muriel

The actor Victor Spinetti had come to London in the 1950's and in between his work on the stage he kicked around Soho. In 1959 he was starring in Joan Littlewood's production of 'Fings Ain't What They Used To Be' by Colony members Frank Norman and Lionel Bart. Spinetti described the Colony thus: 'In proportion to its reputation, surprisingly small... the essence of Soho, disreputable but with reputable people in it'. Accurately, he described Muriel 'sitting by the bar, smoking a fag, from her you'd get a raspy, drawly, abusive greeting'.

The Colony Room played an interesting part in his autobiography, 'Up Front' published in 2006. Hard up for money and Christmas growing close, Spinetti met a guardsman in a pub whose second income was from hustling. He agreed to hook Spinetti up with some work but told him he must always drink beer in front of these clients (something he despised) and to never say he was an actor but had just demobbed from the Guards. He was told to rendezvous in the Colony Room Club with the two members, a wealthy Viennese Jewish middle-aged couple, where he had to drink a light ale and make brutish conversation. They told him to come to their house in Hampstead where he was greeted by the man naked but for a dressing gown, the lady in a negligee in a house full of exotic caged birds. He was told by the man that he didn't want to be fucked, 'just whipped' and told to change in the next door room where a SS uniform waited for him from Berman's theatrical outfitters. Being a gentle soul Spinetti had never hit anyone but got into character with his costume and went to work on the naked man, as the woman watched. After ten minutes he was told that was enough. He was told to change was given an envelope and asked to write his address down before leaving. In the envelope there was fifty guineas, a huge sum to spend on presents for his family. When he returned from his Welsh Christmas a red velvet suit with an embroidered waistcoat from Harrods was waiting. It had been sent as a thank you with an invitation to a dinner party. He went to dinner where the couple couldn't have been more charming and explained that the husband had been in a concentration camp and had to re-enact in order to

Paul McCartney & Victor Spinetti.
The man in a uniform

make love to his wife. They had known he wasn't a guardsman. His whipping style, one tap here one tap there, had given him away as an actor; that and his reaction when he'd slipped on a pickled onion on his way in. Spinetti was sad that it couldn't become a regular engagement but at least when asked what his last role had been he could reply to his father, a German officer. When he told the story to Tennessee Williams while wearing the suit, Tennessee had exclaimed 'that's the most beautiful Christmas story I've ever heard, because everyone was happy in the end'. They were probably standing in the Colony at the time.

People often appeared to be reputable in the Colony but appearances were deceiving. There was something of the outsider about all the members, whatever class they were. Later Victor Spinetti would go on to play the sergeant major in Joan Littlewood's West End hit 'Oh What A Lovely War' and worked with the Beatles staring in all their films and writing a play with John Lennon. He told Lennon the story of his SS Officer role. 'What a pity' Lennon said. 'I thought you were set up for life.'

Another friend of Lennon and The Beatles who would become a member of the Colony was John Dunbar. He owned the most happening gallery in London, Indica, and in 1965 married the grooviest girl in town, Marianne Faithful, with whom he had a son, Nicholas. Dunbar is sure the

David Hockney with Madame Stravinsky

Beatles never went to the Colony, as 'it wasn't hip enough'. He did however recall it later. "Going up to the Colony Room Club in the early 80's I realised I'd been there before in 1960 with my Dad (a filmmaker who started The London Film School)," says Dunbar. "I remember going up to that green room and after about ten minutes this lame gay fight started, typically drunken. Muriel said, "Fuck off don't be so silly", but the slapping continued finishing in a sulk. I was young, and thought it was all a bit daft and it was before I was into getting pissed I suppose (perhaps it was the two Roberts: we'll never know). But that summer, I went to my first concert: a jazz festival in the grounds of Beaulieu, Lord Montagu's ancestral home."

Montagu, Pitt Rivers and Wildeblood, all Colony members were sent to prison for homosexual practices in 1954. On release from prison and besieged by reporters Montagu had faced the Press in style, telling them that he found it; "Not much worse than the Guards depot at Caterham, thank-you." Lord Montagu had become a showman to raise the finances of Beaulieu, with his car museum, allowing public access to his stately home. The first in the 60s to have pop concerts, a brave man after the coverage and condemnation he had recieved.

"It was the first time I'd ever heard the chant, 'we want Acker we want Acker...' Over and over. Then Lord Montagu came on stage and said, 'We've now got Muddy Waters or someone but the crowd were screaming, 'Get off you Fairy, queer, poof...' Throwing stuff at him and shouting abuse because of his going to prison. 'We want Acker', and everyone just started going wild. They stormed the stage, turned over and tore a grand piano to pieces, all the stage equipment was pulled down." said John Dunbar.

What did they want? Acker Bilk, the man with the clarinet and goatee beard most famous for 'Stranger on the Shore.' Acker Bilk also frequented the Colony, one student member at the Royal College in the early 70s, the designer Fred Baier remembered playing 'a game of darts played with needles with Acker Bilk... at the time the Colony and the French were hot spots for celebs.' Fred Baier has recently designed the furniture for the Library of The House of Lords.

Barry Miles, the writer and biographer of William Burroughs, John Lennon and Paul McCartney was a friend of Dunbar's and had the bookshop above Indica. Miles was also sure The Beatles didn't go to the Colony. But Cathy McGowan, presenter of the big pop TV show 'Ready Steady Go!', Victor Spinetti and Alun Owen, writer of the Beatles' films, were all members... And then there was Chris Stamp, Terrence's brother who managed The Who and Jimi Hendrix, who Miles often saw in the club. He recounts another Colony evening. "William Burroughs took me there and though we weren't so interested in drinking, Bill did it all," says Miles. "He would acquire from the doctor a liquid cannabis tincture on prescription because his paranoia of being caught by the police taking drugs was making him ill. For three or four years in the 60s, doctors gave it out. Bill would dip his Senior Service cigarettes in it and think nobody realised what he was smoking, apart from the smell and the fact it turned the smokes bright green. Bill introduced me to Francis Bacon there, and they seemed to really get on. They were both homosexual but Bill liked boys, while Francis liked men. The Colony was fun and you didn't notice the décor, except that it was old-fashioned and dated in a 1950's way, particularly noticeable as we were going to all the modern underground clubs like the AdLib. But the company was always great. We always had fun there.' Bacon even took Burroughs to visit Dan Farson at The Waterman Inn, his pub by the Thames in the East End.

Muriel Belcher, Ian Board *invite you to a* Come in a Chapeau Party *on Friday, 1st November, 1968 at Kensington Town Hall from 7 p.m. until 1 a.m. in aid of the Muscular Distrophy Children of Elmfield School*

Tickets 4 guineas. Includes Buffet, Dancing, Cabaret   *Open Licensed Bars*

Hats will be judged for Prizes and Lucky Number Tickets

Charlie Campbell as The devil hides Philippa Potts

Muriel with Lady Rose McClaren, Simon Blow and The Chapeau revellers

Photos: Lord Chrisopher Thynne

Any Excuse for a Party

Four years was a long time in the 60s. As London swung, Muriel ran the Colony but was also organising events for a charity that Dan Farson started for the children of Elmwood School in greater London, suffering from muscular dystrophy and other health problems. 'My clumsy efforts were replaced by a full scale production as members were enlisted to contribute money,' Dan Farson said. The first party was held in the Trattoria below the Colony. The children turned up to find a room full of Colony members who had been told by Muriel to keep off spirits and stick to litres of red wine. Cake, sandwiches and entertainment were provided. Farson remembered a typical repartee between Muriel and the conjurer entertaining the kiddies:

'Decks of cards, I need decks of cards'.

'Speak for yourself Kate, I need Dexedrine.'

It was hard to know who was more shaken at the end, after the children bravely got back on the bus, clutching their presents and waving farewell to the denizens

The Bunny Girls and Annie Ross make sure The Kiddies have a great party

of Soho, as they returned to their homes. Phillipa Potts, remembered, 'Every year Muriel gave a Xmas party for the disabled children at the Home (for want of a better word). I went with Charles Campbell and son Phineas (aged 18 months). As I remember it was in the outer suburbs of London Elstree or somewhere and there were a great many members there." But it showed a less well known aspect of Muriel's make-up, as noted in The Observer's 'Table Talk' in the diary, Pendennis, in 1961: 'Other club managers say Muriel has a genius of getting people to spend money. But she has a charitable side. At present she is trying to find a room big enough for a bingo party to raise money for children with muscular dystrophy. Every Christmas she gives a party for them in the Italian pizzeria downstairs.' Her yearly favourite party 'Come in a Chapeau' was held in other venues. "A couple of times the children's Christmas parties were held at our house in Swiss Cottage with George Melly playing Santa!" Kate Fawkes told me, (daughter of Wally Fawkes jazz man and cartoonist with George Melly) and journalist Sandy Fawkes. The members really did get involved. Later on Muriel organised music events, getting the famous jazz singer of 'Lambert, Hendrix and Ross', Annie Ross and George Melly to sing to the children, comedians to make them laugh and magicians for entertainment. Even Victor Lowndes became involved, providing Bunny Girls from the Playboy Club to administer to the bewildered children. Soho descended in coachloads to the school, with Dan Farson's help and Muriel's organisational skills. By 1968 there was another Come in a Chapeau Ball: 'Lord Christopher Thynne will kindly be taking photographs'. Muriel had a gift for getting members and non-members alike to stump up for charity.

John Deakin was conspicuous by his absence. Farson and Muriel disapproved, especially when it got back to Muriel exactly what Deakin had been saying: 'Don't kid me. Where do you think the money went that was raised from those so-called balls? Straight into Miss Mu's pocket.' Farson reported Deakin saying. 'Muriel would tolerate a great deal and even the charge of embezzlement could be laughed away but the subject of the children was sacred and he was never forgiven'. When Muriel made a decision based on behaviour, she rarely backed down. However, she was forgiving to Farson, who once memorably pulled the telephone off the wall and the next day came in to apologise for behaviour that he couldn't quite recall. 'Know who that was?' Muriel asked. Farson shook his head. "A nice little man who came in his free time to mend the telephone you broke yesterday when I was expecting a call from one of my best-spending customers, and in all my years in the club business I've never known such disgraceful behaviour and do you know? I don't give a fuck. So what are you having to drink, cunty?" She had not paused for breath, her expression had remained steely, but she had forgiven me.'

A more happy party was one of Muriel's birthdays, as artist Barry Evans told me in 2011. They were always an excuse for a party, fill the club up, get the pianist in and celebrate. 'When Muriel had her birthday she was given a cake and it was passed around to everyone. But what we didn't know was that it was a hash cake. I still don't know if she knew. Suddenly, I thought I was looking through the wrong end of the binoculars. Apparently I was behaving appallingly, friends told me later. I'd stormed into Thea Porter's shop on Greek Street where a big address was going on and I attacked the buffet as everyone looked on in horror until I was forcibly ejected. Barry Driscoll appeared and helped me home. I'd never had such a hideous experience in my life. I'd never taken drugs, wasn't into them, certainly wasn't afterwards."

As the 1960's progressed, the Colony continued unfashionably on, regardless. "The Colony just wasn't rock 'n roll," said John Dunbar. "We went to the AdLib where it was cool, with John Lennon, Paul McCartney, Peter Asher (Jane's brother)". The AdLib was upstairs in an anonymous glass building in a lift (it was above The Prince Charles Theatre at 7 Leicester Place). Later the cool people moved to The Scotch of St James (recently reopened), at 13 Masons Yard or The Bag O'Nails at 8 Kingly Street in Soho. The AdLib attracted musicians and also lured writer Frank Norman and Jeffrey Bernard. Bernard watched Norman plunge a bare arm into a tank supposedly full of piranha fish, the latest fashionable accoutrement. When nothing even nibbled his hand, it disappointed him deeply and he mounted the stage and sang, 'Falling in love with love is falling for make believe'. As Dunbar said, "The whole thing exploded in Soho."

Publishing Contracts

Anne Valery now in her late 80's, better known as the writer of Tenko and a very brave woman during the war, was a Colony regular since the beginning. She recalled the changes. "I loved the war, I was seventeen and I could escape from home and live an independent life in Soho where we were part of a set. Lucian, Johnny Craxton, MacLaren Ross, lovely man, sad he was from such a poor family... we once tried to go away for the weekend to Brighton, I think. You know he wrote a short story that weekend, they tell me... He was a bit obsessed." The short story is one of Julian McClaren Ross' great stories, 'The Oxford Manner.' When he began to write his 'Memoirs of The Forties' for Alan Ross, it was the beginning of the 1960's the previous decades had worn him out. Ross paid him by the chapter, he knew that if he'd given him a straight advance there would be no book. Each chapter was written once the money was spent and he needed more for alcohol, cigarettes and coffee; McClaren Ross' writing necessities. He was to die suddenly in the autumn of 1964, manuscript uncompleted. Perhaps the 60s was too much for the old guard. John Heath-Stubbs, a major English poet of the 20th century, was a Colony member. 'I didn't care much for the 1960's.' said Heath-Stubbs, who lamented the decline of literary Soho, 'detested the hideous music of The Beatles and always felt negatively towards Philip Larkin.'

Poet Michael Horovitz went to the Colony at the start of the 60s, became known for his magazine New Departures, his events at the ICA and Poetry Olympics at the Royal Albert Hall. After studying 'the effect on Joyce of William Blake' at Oxford University, Horovitz went to live in Greek Street for four years: "I was a Sohoite, hung out at the French café on Old Compton Street with the older generation bohos like Ironfoot Jack and Foxy Lady, met hustlers, bums and beatniks like Raymond Thorpe, author of the book 'Viper - Confessions of a Drug Addict', King David, Ray Cortenz and Teddy Gordon, also known as Hakim, who smoked a lot of dope and went barefoot everywhere and wore a big afro before loads of folk had afros. He was always stomping around and trying to seduce anything in a skirt. A great dope evangelist, he'd always have bags of grass and hash and vibrant scatting bebop intros.

"There was an art critic called Barry Miller who was a great aficionado of Dean Street and the French Pub. The irony was that the places where we were all converged beat wild and couldn't give a damn, were often run by bourgeois businessmen like Gaston Berlemont and Muriel Belcher, who made an art of taking peoples credit and cashing cheques and so on. Beware anyone who would try to con Gaston and not give the credit on a cheque after a month or two, they'd be barred forever. This was to many people's chagrin because then they couldn't get at their targets for conning and hustling. There were the famous Robert duo, Colquhoun and MacBryde, both permanently pissed and almost permanently banned from the French and the Colony so they'd go to the Caves de France, and possibly get banned from there too."

"Muriel Belcher and the Colony Room had a similar and quite severe admissions and dismissal policy, and when Barry Miller took my girlfriend Anna Lovell and me to the Colony he introduced me to this rather ugly grotesque creature of Hogarthian proportions, who sat on her bar stool saying, 'Who've you brought in cunty, who is this fucking cunt?'

'Oh this is Mike Horovitz he's a great poet and a great guy.'

'Fuck you Barry, you could be banned soon too if you're not careful.'

"Anyway we were grudgingly admitted and either that first, second or third time, I got chatting to Francis Bacon whose paintings I'd discovered for myself and been very taken by their power. I was very susceptible in my early 20's having taken too many drugs and being up all night every night on a mixture of mainly grass, hash but also mescaline and LSD - although Benzedrine inhalers were the nightworld currency of the time."

"When I met Bacon I thought, 'This genial piss head did these terrible images'. I liked chatting with him about New Departures and William Burroughs who'd contributed to it. 'Ah Burroughs, I love Burroughs... Tangier, Dean's Bar. How is the old queer?' So Bacon was very nice to me. It seemed to be his home from home, and had a nice feel to it. I liked the black pianist Todd Matshikiza, he was very genial. And other people I met through the jazz world like Colin McInnes."

"But I didn't like the way Muriel Belcher bust everything up. I never liked the aspect of Soho and bohemia that delights in malicious humour and humiliation, picking on people inevitably from my background - and the kind of racism and cruelty that I detected, perhaps exaggeratedly. The kind of sharpened wit was applauded in the Colony Room. The fixtures in the Colony delighted me when they were either cordial or enthusiastic about art and their art work and rather appalled me when, later in the evening they got pissed and the knives came out. Remarks and epigrams banded out that have since become famous like, 'Champagne for my real friends, real pain for my cham friends'. Repeated endlessly."

Horovitz was part of the Beat hippie crew and the sensibilities of the Colony could sometimes be hard to digest; the cruelty of wit masquerading as humour, the naked ambition of some members.

"Ian had always been an imitation of Muriel. It was very infectious to want to be a part of the supposed elite but possibly not very talented people who wanted to be a member of these bohemian clubs and to be accepted as equal. I was disappointed that the real life version didn't live up to the wit you'd get in a novel."

Bill Hopkins part of Colin Wilson's 'Outsider' Gang

"Sure I'd go there with Bill Hopkins, John Waine, Colin Wilson, We became sort of friends but Wilson was so impossibly conceited that it was hard to stay in his company for more than a few seconds without wanting a sickbag. He and Hopkins 'and Bernard Shaw were the only genius' in the world throughout history'. And then you'd be just about to say 'go fuck yourself' and then they'd disarm you by saying, 'I see you haven't got a drink Mike. A drink here, free drinks on me', and buy his way back into being tolerated, despite his unbelievable egotism. They were all exciting and entertaining people to fall in and out of company with and the Colony was one of the wholly of wholliest places in Soho."

As Maclaren Ross' was coming to end of his publisher's deal, two younger members were forging a new agreement to write spiteful black comedies of more upper class mores. Simon Raven seemed unable to live a productive life in London, gambling, sex, drink and friendships were coming together to form his series of novels titled 'Alms for Oblivion', featuring a few Colony members John Aspinall, Lord William Rees Mogg and Anthony Blond. Blond was the publisher to suggest that Raven should live at least 50 miles from London and he would pay him £15 a week, plus bills and dinner at a local hostelry, his tailor, dentist and wine importer, in advance of royalties. Raven chose Deal in Kent, where his brother worked as a schoolmaster. Occasionally Raven would wing into London and cause havoc, only to shortly return to the seaside where he remained in this unusual arrangement with his old college friend Blond until 1995. It was purely a business arrangement. In that first five years he managed to write five novels, two non-fiction books, six television plays, eight radio plays, a stage play and many reviews and newspaper articles. The sea air obviously agreed with him. Raven and Blond were just two of the high functioning alcoholic members that seemed drawn to play as hard as they worked.

This was not an entirely unusual deal between business and creative types. Indeed it was what the art world of Cork Street had been doing for a long time. A weekly payment to keep an artist producing work was common, although several galleries came unstuck with this arrangement, as did many artists.

Blond commissioned other Colony members to write books but never with the same contract. Molly Parkin's first novel 'Love All' was published by Blond and Briggs in 1969. He also published Jennifer Paterson, who would become one of the 'Two Fat Ladies' with Clarissa Dickson Wright (also a member) but who also cooked for the Private Eye lunches, where Blond was a director. Famously bisexual, 'Who am I to ban half the world from my bed?', Blond believed wives and boyfriends happily coexisted. Private Eye once told of an alleged encounter between Jennifer Paterson and psychotherapist Andrew McCall, one of Blond's more enduring male companions, on holiday in Corfu. "Really Jennifer, you should take yourself in hand, your bum is so wobbly," said McCall, to which Jennifer replied: "While yours of course, dear, is so taut... and who taught it?"

Beautiful People

Some tried to cross the divide between the hip and the bohemian, as the decade progressed. Robert Fraser, the old Etonian and art dealer, was always trying to have a foot in all 'camps', from John Dunbar at The AdLib to Helen Lessore and Victor Musgrave (Bacon's first dealers) and Sir Kenneth Clark (the art historian, author of Civilisation and father to Alan Clark

MP) as well as David Sylvester, Bacon's champion, advisor and critic. Fraser was a fashionable art dealer who had cornered a specialist part of the art market, selling to the new generation of wealthy young people for whom art wasn't about investments or portraits but about being groovy.

The artist Winston Branch, now a professor at Berkeley in the US, was born in 1947 in the West Indies and taught by Craigie Aitchinson at The Slade. Aitchinson had really been a stalwart part of the Colony since the early 50s with artists from The London Group, Tim Behrens, Keith Vaughan and Euan Uglow. It was natural to introduce your students to the clubs you liked. Recently, Winston spoke of the Colony to me. "People walked from the French every day up the road and then they drank until they fell down. It was an odd experience at the Colony, full of odd people of undetermined gender, who all smoked and drank whisky. There were some nice aristocratic ladies there, droopy over drink who bought me drinks and later gave me a good time when I got to know them better. It was a nice social place."

"I loved Soho. It was all so quaint especially when you left Dean Street and went up these stairs into a small room full of a lot of drunk people. I was an unsophisticated wallflower in awe. There were artists, writers and journalists in hot pursuit of ideas, people having real conversations. It was around 1967, I was 21 and it was a hole. There

94

were other clubs around too, but I'll never forget the Colony. One of the overlays of the 60s that along with the pretty beautiful girls and the beautiful people, the people that had the most fun were the ones with undeterminate gender and they were musical and they were gentle and nicer and you found them in the clubs where they could be themselves.'

Styled by Molly Parkin for Nova 66

Photo: Jeanloup Sieff

Christopher Gibb, friend of gallery owner Robert Fraser is a designer and was part of the beautiful set, recalled it too: "My bond with Robert (Fraser) was Eton and going to sleazy clubs. In Soho we went to Muriel's club. We went in one day, Francis Bacon looked up and then to everyone in there said, 'Here come the Belgrave Pansies'. Robert was furious."

Gibb, who now lives in Tangier, "loved the beautiful monumental Queen of caustic badinage and Carmel. I couldn't really cope with Ian. My days and nights at Miss Mu's were 50 years ago with Leonard Blackett (the 'brave little woman at the Somme') at the bar, Francis B, Lucian F, lovely Mike Andrews, Mikey Portman (part of the William Burroughs gang), dreadful little Deakin, blowsy Dan Farson.

The intellectual stimuli chez Ms Mu, and the outing of the timid, made the Colony a more interesting port of call than anywhere else in Soho. Raffish always, but with a certain anchoring elegance, a mix that made me feel at home, it was a lively conjunction of toff and tough, intellectual and buffoon. One got used to being referred to as 'cunty'."

Best of models the latest look outside The Angus Steak House below The Colony

Ned Sherrin CBE broadcaster, Author and Director of Jeffery Bernard is Unwell

Private Eyes

Hanging loose and drug taking wasn't for everyone and even satirical magazine writers had to have somewhere to go. The Colony was full of the Private Eye crowd from the beginning in 1962 when Nicholas Luard and Peter Cook turned it from a school-type comic into a proper magazine. Richard Ingrams, Barry Humphries, Willie Rushton, Ned Sherrin, Marty Feldman, Spike Milligan, John Antrobus (his co-writer). They were all working on Sherrin's 'That Was The Week That Was', a satirical TV show and many had been part of the 'Cambridge Footlights' and 'Beyond the Fringe', which Luard had taken to the Edinburgh Festival and which saw the beginnings of Monty Python's Flying Circus.

Luard and Cook had first opened their own place, The Establishment Club in 1961 at 64 Greek Street as a club presenting new satirical talent. They had live jazz and a restaurant, performances by Lenny Bruce, Barry Humphries, Eleanor Bron, Annie Ross and Dudley Moore and exhibitions by Gerald Scarfe. It was extremely successful for four years and they even opened a place in New York but as Frank

Norman wrote in 1966 in 'Soho Night and Day' (a book where Norman did the writing and Jeffrey Bernard took the photos): 'A room does not automatically become a club by naming it so. A club without a personal touch will not last long in Soho... The members must be made to feel that they are wanted and that the staff and management are pleased to see them... This was not so with The Establishment Club and contributed more than somewhat to its eventual failure.' Frank Norman had a way of saying what needed to be said and he was right. It didn't have a Muriel to be the glue that stuck it together.

By 1961, the Colony Room was 13 years old, 'everybody might have been talking about The Establishment' said The Observer but enquiring how a club survives they sought Muriel's advice. 'If you've had a bad evening never try to make it up after hours. Close and you'll be open again tomorrow.' Also, she said that she rarely bothers the police for extensions unlike some clubs that use any excuse. 'It would be so embarrassing if they turned me down.'

Colin MacInnes observed Muriel's differently. In his essay on Soho clubs, 'See You At Mabel's', he wrote: 'The membership, though in some clubs is mixed and (these are the nicest) is often composed of those who have common interests: professional racial or sexual... In Brecht Street, Soho there are three coloured clubs, in one you will find sleek GI's, in another rumbustious Africans and voluble West Indians in the third.' He was talking about Brewster Hughes who was a member of the Colony and manager of the Abilabi Club, a Yorubian Nigerian Musician for Les Ballets Negroes

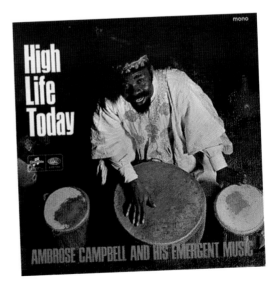

who went on to run the Club Afrique with Ambrose Cambell. In Soho there was no one way to run a club, perhaps the magic formula was that they were all so different.

No matter what went on outside the Colony Room Club, the place always had Muriel as the figurehead and the mother figure. As Toby Roe of The Rockingham Club on Archer

Street said, 'I'm not like Muriel. She's the gimmick at the Colony. Nobody ever comes here to see me.' But it wasn't true, as Norman said people came for a face that would remember there's and The Rockingham attracted the Princess Margaret set at the beginning. Frank Norman interviewed Toby for the book 'Night and Day', 'They were very excited by Toby's club... "Toby darling you really are too brave... it really is the most divine little club but what a sordid district; it's so quaint we really must bring all our friends..." Toby is only too delighted by the fact they did not keep their promise. Blond described it somewhat differently in his autobiography, 'the first queer club in London... he (Toby) used to fling scent at sailors.'

With the law in 1965 withdrawing the special benefit of licensing hours to clubs in the afternoon, many closed. Compared to pubs with cheaper prices, what was the point of going to a club that opened at 11.30am-3pm and 5.30pm-11pm, and cost more? The hundreds of clubs across the city were closing in droves. But Muriel's stayed open which Norman put down to her being so good natured, yet firm with liberty takers. 'Occasionally Muriel manages to get an extension in order to give a party: this she dearly loves to do. A recent card that I had from her read, 'We hope to see you at our reopening party (she had been on holiday) PS. Taking into consideration the visit paid on us by the gentleman from Savile Row (a police station) accusing us of not supplying our members with sufficient supper, we re-open at five-thirty and at eleven you will have to go...'

'It is by no means an easy business running a club', Norman wrote at the time when both he and Bernard were frequently in the Colony and very much on Muriel's side. 'I would say that it is an art.' They are also more intimate places than pubs and emotionally, many get tied into the other worldliness of the club world, the family spirit and cosiness. And maybe that was why the artists and writers, poets and musicians appreciated Muriel. Like them she was dedicated to her art. When the Observer paid her a visit in 1961 it found Todd Matshikiza playing the piano. Todd had composed and wrote the all-black jazz musical King Kong on in the West End in 1961. An artist who was instrumental in spotting both Miriam Makeba and Hugh Masekela's talent and who wrote the major choral pieces which mixed African, classical and jazz, the famous Hamba Kahle. Making London his home when banned from South Africa, he found it difficult fitting into the musical scene and it is typical that Muriel gave him a place and a job. When Farson asked her why so many artists made the Colony their second home, she replied, 'I think it's my charm, deah.' But it was also her kindness. As Farson also noted, 'However turbulent or crowded the Colony became, Muriel observed the scene, apparently with eyes at the back of her head.' She was always working the room and as Paul Potts the poet wrote, 'Drink and conversation are her materials and she brought them together and has caused a huge amount of happiness.'

The art of giving people a good time meant occasional rudeness to strangers that made others laugh. On one occasion someone bought in a white husky and when Deakin bent down to stroke it, she addressed the dog: "Hold onto your sled gal or that one will bum a free ride to Alaska." When the dog looked up with a bemused expression, reports Farson, Muriel turned to us triumphantly: "Glad to see she's got the message!" Muriel's wit often fell upon Deakin.

Ida and Miss Mu share a laugh

Still, there was always another side to Muriel, as Norman wrote: 'You have to be sympathetic and tolerant when people are in trouble... Muriel's customers have troubles at one time or another and some of them seem to be in trouble the whole of the time and never leave off moaning from morning til night... Muriel never seems to get tired listening to their troubles and even if she does, she never shows it.' Indeed, Muriel seems to have had an unusually sympathetic ear, possibly why everyone in the Colony seemed to believe that they were a special case. At the same time, she couldn't tolerate bores moaning on about their troubles, as she had enough of her own. Members knew the routine and alerted their guests. That is, you left your ego on the mat, and were expected to talk in a fluent, fun, witty and clever manner.

This arrangement attracted unusual people like Len Blackett. Described routinely as 'an old queen', he worked in the City and came to the Colony every evening to drink Scotch. In WWI he'd been a Captain and won The Military Cross, and whenever anyone asked Muriel who Blackett was she'd reply: "She was a very brave little woman at the Somme." It was hard to argue with that.

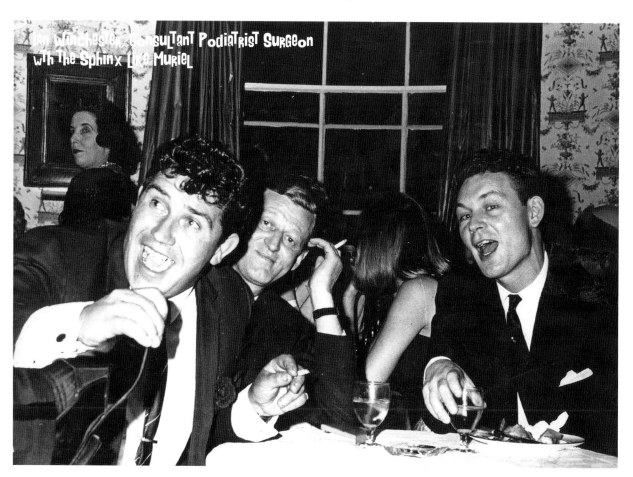

Conservative Soliciting Scandals

As the 1950's became the 60s, the Conservative Government under Harold Macmillan needed to create order and in 1959 bought in the Street Offences Act. This was to stop soliciting on the street, so that the working girls had to become invisible sex machines in run down rooms. Men, of course, complained about being cheated. If they asked, 'Is that a tall slim blonde?' over the phone and were told 'yes', they were disgruntled to be greeted by a short old dumpy brunette and it worked the same for the girls, who wouldn't have propositioned men they sensed to be dangerous and unsavoury on the streets. During that time, 'Mac' had to keep his own ministers on the straight and narrow. The Profumo Affair didn't centre around the Colony but Christine Keeler was (like Stephen Ward) a member and the civil servants who drank there didn't all stop going there just because of the Burgess and Maclean scandal in the 50s.

Soho was Keeler's playground from the early days of coming to London. Her preferred boyfriends were part of the West Indian scene, then chronicled by writer Colin MacInnes, whose novel 'Absolute Beginners' was published in 1959, a year after the Notting Hill race riots. At the beginning of the 60s Keeler was working as a topless showgirl at Murray's Cabaret Club in Soho, where she met the infamous go-between Stephen Ward. A lot of girls ended up in Murray's. "Being a topless showgirl was thought scandalous at the time, now nobody cares about stripping off", says Susie Bardolph, who started at Murray's and knew Keeler and Ward. In July 1961, Ward introduced Keeler to John Profumo, the British Secretary of State for War, at a pool party at Cliveden, the Buckinghamshire Estate owned by Lord Astor, where Stephen Ward rented a cottage. Profumo entered into an affair with Keeler, not realising that she was also sleeping with drug dealers and jazz men, notably 'Lucky' Gordon and Johnny Edgecombe, as well as Yevgeni Ivanov, a naval attaché at the embassy of the Soviet Union. None of it seemed engineered to be politically explosive but it was. The 60s seemed to have ushered in a social mobility that meant that class, age and race became mixed up, yet girls like Keeler were still impressed by the voice, manners and class of Profumo and afraid of Lucky, whose brother was known as Psycho Gordon, and who Johnny Edgecomb fought at the The Flamingo Club in Soho, scarring Lucky with 17 facial stitches. Lippier and luckier was the 19-year-old sidekick Mandy Rice-Davies and her famous retort to the prosecuting counsel when he told her that Lord Astor had denied having slept with her: 'He would, wouldn't he?'

Harold Wilson was elected in 1964 and his Government tightened the licensing laws in 1965, a move that would impose order on the clubs and illegal shebeens that had sprung up all over Soho. Frank Norman also reckoned that councils wanted to make money out of Soho, which had become a lure of sex, food and sleaze. Part of Bernard and Norman's book 'Night and Day' was a rallying cry to stop Soho being taken over by the developers who wanted to bulldozer the old and stack up skyscrapers all over the place; a common 60s folly. They managed in Tottenham Court Road with Centre Point, a building that soon became known as a landmark for junkies and rent boys.

Restaurants had always been part of Soho's draw and the council wanted to exploit this small area by putting up parking meters, painting yellow lines everywhere and policing the post-pub punch ups. The Colony became weaved into Soho's bibulous sphere. Tory Stroud was one of the youngest members of the club, daughter to Allan Hall, bon viveur and editor of The Sunday Times Look Pages. 'being dangled on Muriel's knee as very small children in the early 60s after long lunches at Trattoria Terrazza. As the Colony was a members' only club we were awarded honorary membership.'

Artist Barry Evans, who was part of a crowd, including Barry Driscoll, Len Deighton, Tommy Candler and the 1960's photographer Duffy, who all worked or were otherwise associated with the illustrator ad agency, Artist Associates, were all members. As Barry Evans recalled a place that in some respects, reflected or even presaged the social mobility of the time: "Muriel was always very nice and was always kind to me," he says. "Barry Driscoll introduced me to the place in the 50s and I loved it immediately: a place where you could be yourself, and could meet others to do with art. The thing about Muriel's was that everybody was there: extraordinary people and very ordinary people. There was one, Dick Job was his name, a portly businessman who stood there in a suit being polite and having his drink. It always seemed strange to us as to how he'd landed there."

The rudeness remained part of the Colony. "When I was 41 in the mid 60s, I took Ruth, my girl, into the Colony. I warned her, "I'm afraid you've got to expect to get a mouthful from Ian or Muriel. I introduced her, and Muriel was perfectly charming. Until Ian Mason shouted from the back: 'Who's that waifish cunt you've brought in?'"

Tommy Candler, was a friend of the two Barry's, Driscol and Evans. Working as a photographer and fashion editor at the beginning of the 60s, she was drawn to the Colony. "I was fashion editor of Women's Realm," she recalls. "Those were the days you came to The French for a pre-lunch drink after working for the morning, before lunch at El Paparazzi, or Mario & Franco's Trattoria. They'd leave you with the keys to lock up and pop through the letter box and then we'd go onto the Colony Room for the afternoon and then back to The French and that was the merry go round."

"I ignored where I worked, had a gorgeous time. I designed, styled and had the patterns made up for models Pauline Stone (who married film star Lawrence Harvey) and Sandra Paul. One day we all went to the Colony and Desmond O'Donovan the manager of The Sunday Times had just won £200 on a horse. He took us three girls to Thea Porter's fantastic boutique in Greek Street, which had no dressing rooms. He sat there and watched as we tried on all these dresses and bought us each a dress before we went back for drinks to celebrate our new dresses. (Thea Porter's shop is accurately portrayed in the film of Edna O'Brien's novel Zee and Co, starring Elizabeth Taylor in a ménage a trois with Susannah York and Michael Caine).

"My father had the first of the commercial art studios before the war. He employed loads of great artists including John Minton, Duffy, Felix Topolski and Len Deighton (as well as Evans and Driscol), and they were all Colony members. It employed artists to illustrate adverts for big companies.

"My dad's best friend was called Geoff. He was a serial philanderer, a real arsehole and very good looking and we were going out in the early 60s with his wife, who he always was knocking for being dull and plain. He asked to come with us and we said he wasn't invited. So he gatecrashed and found us at the Colony sitting at the bar with Christine Keeler who was the total star of the times with Mandy Rice-Davies. Geoff of course tried to chat her up but she carried on talking to us and gave him a look, treating him like the scum he was. It was a gorgeous moment."

The place was all about Muriel, recalls Candler. "She made every day into a party. My playmate was a wonderful girl called Marie Scott and we were in the club talking to Muriel one day and bought a round of drinks. When one man finished his and tried to slope off to the cinema, she bawled at him: "Oh no you don't, cunty, you're a very naughty girl! You can't leave without buying these ladies a drink..." She kept a very orderly ship.

"I never once saw her drunk. But how would I know? We must have been all drunk most of the time. One day my daughter was coming to meet me and I said, come and meet me at the Colony. Well she couldn't find it and popped into the French to ask, 'Where's The Coronary?' That's what I must have said, being tipsy."

Paul Johnson also recalled Keeler at the Colony: "It was a really shabby place, the Colony, especially the loo. I went once and the door was locked. A voice from inside said "It's occupied", in a pseudo, prissy upper-class voice. So I sat down on the pipes outside and waited. Suddenly Bacon arrived bursting for a pee. I said, "There's a woman in there, it's occupied." "Oh is it?' he said, and kicked the door. "Come out of there you bitch!" "It's occupied!" she said. He sat down beside me. Eventually the latch was moved, the door was opened and a woman came out with her nose in the air. All she said as she passed us was, "Men!"' A lifetime of bitter experience went into that remark. The year was 1963/4 and it was Christine Keeler. Later I talked to her at the bar and found her very dull. Poor little thing."

Tom Driberg, the Labour MP, was also getting into trouble, but there were always people mysteriously there to help him out. In July 1964, two backbench Conservative MPs reported to their Chief Whip that Driberg and Lord Boothby (a well-known

Conservative peer) had been importuning males at a dog track , probably Walthamstow or Wimbledon, and were involved with gangs of thugs. At parties which Driberg and Boothby attended at the Krays' flat, 'rough but compliant East End lads were served like so many canapés', according to Driberg's biographer Francis Wheen. When one of the pictures was due to appear in a book about the Krays, publisher Geoffrey Wheatcroft, a member of the Colony who'd commissioned it, was phoned by a libel lawyer on Driberg's behalf asking it to be removed. He told the lawyer that it was too late but then had to apologise to Driberg in the club: 'He was very morose complaining that the picture had haunted him and that it had stopped him getting into clubs, though never Muriel's. Later still, I told all this to Muriel, who ended with a recitation: "Well Tom was happy enough with Ronnie Kray's cock in his mouth." Through out the 60s Driberg supplied political gossip to Private Eye, never about himself.

Dublin artist Patrick Swift with wife Oonagh chat to Muriel

Irma Kurtz cuddled by Muriel with Ula 'ex Miss Sweden' behind

Bohemia in London

The writer and Cosmopolitan agony aunt Irma Kurtz found the Colony to be the anchor that kept her in London, not because of the booze, political scandals or dancing around the piano but because of the human interest: "In New York it was The White Horse Tavern in Greenwich Village, in Paris it was the Tonneau on the Left Bank, in Ibiza it was The Domino Bar (now closed) and in Soho it was the Colony Room," she says. "The bohemian bar is the great cocktail: the mix of gay and straight, black and white, male and female, famous and anonymous, rich and poor. I came to visit London in 1968 and within my first week a friend had brought me up the stairs to the Colony and the minute I walked in I knew I could live in London. I used to call Muriel 'what's 'er name'; it was our joke.

"The host/hostess owner of any boho bar has to be bad-tempered or at least puts it on, irascible with a smile behind and a wink, so that when you're not being chastised you feel one of a special group even to be allowed to buy a drink at the bar. Norman at the Coach and Horses, Gaston at The French and Ian Board of the Colony - just like Muriel, they had a secret side, a manqué. I didn't go out a lot, I couldn't afford to but when I did I went to the Colony. I met Jeff Bernard there who was a catalyst for me. I'm so glad we never got married, though.

"I was pregnant and I said to Muriel that I wasn't going to be coming in for a while because I was giving up drinking and smoking. "When you have the kid make sure you bring him round to show me." She was such an old cunty. I pushed him over from Shepherd's Bush in his pram with a friend, who waited outside as I went up to get Muriel who peered in the hood and said, "You done good, gal. You done good." She had a deep maternal side."

Artists & Models

Just as the journalists mixed with the writers and fashion people in the Colony, artists mixed with actors and comedians. Both Johnny Speight who Wrote 'Til Death Do Us Part' and actor Tony Booth, who played Alf Garnett's son in law, hung out there. It has been suggested that Cherie Blair was introduced as a model to Euan Uglow by her head of Chambers, Lord Derry Irvine but it might just as easily have been a conversation in the Colony between Uglow and her father Tony Booth. Both had been members for a long time, perhaps he was trying to get his daughter work experience or at least some pocket money as a student. Cherie posing nude for Euan Uglow at his studio in Turnchapel Mews in Clapham between 1978 and 1980 and is thought to have been paid £3 an hour (this was not below the minimum wage then). She would later, of course, become a barrister QC and wife to Tony Blair, the Labour Prime Minister, who named their first son Euan. Was she fond of the great figure painter?

The artist and model relationship is notoriously suspect but not all the artists who went in the Colony had the reputation of Augustus John or Lucian Freud, who found it impossible to complete a painting unless they possessed their models 'body and soul'. Bacon was different, working mostly from photographs. He would commission John Deakin to take the portraits in a very particular way of his favourite models, such as Isabel Rawsthorne, a painter in her own right and Henrietta Moraes, who famously found Deakin selling prints meant only for Bacon's eyes to sailors for 10 bob a print. "Deakin" I yelled at him, "I don't care really but don't you think you should at least buy me a large drink?". The photographs of Henrietta Moraes taken by Deakin, naked and splayed, were not quite right and Bacon insisted they had to be reshot. Bacon disturbed the final image even more by putting a hypodermic syringe into the arm. 'How did he know?' Moraes later wondered for it would be her future habit.

Henrietta married poet Dom Moraes in 1961, she was 30 and he was 21. 'I was much too neurotic for his delicate nervous system, and we both drank too much', she said. Francis Wyndham, a great friend of Moraes, said that while she was beautiful and adventurous, 'She became a liability. She and her boyfriend burgled a house in Hampstead and then passed out on the Heath with what they'd stolen. When she appeared in court, she came over all Francis Bacon to the judge. "Ooh, I don't like you, dear! I don't fancy you!" Once, on a shoplifting charge from Wallis. she was outraged. "As if anyone would hoist from there." But she had, of course.'

Anne Valery recalls Moraes as one of the most 'extraordinarily naturally beautiful women anywhere.' Audrey Abbott was her real name, by the end of the 60s Moraes had left her first husband Michael Laws, her children and their father Norman Bowler and her second husband Dom Moreas, and was living in a gypsy caravan. Her life exemplifies the ups and downs of bohemia by the end of her life she would be living with the artist Maggi Hambling.

Slow Motion Car Crashes

'To me the club was a place of remote glamour in the 1960's,' recalls the writer Geoffrey Wheatcroft. Sometimes that glamour cracked. Jeffrey Bernard introduced his new wife Jaqueline Sheelagh, a very promising actress in the West End, to the glamour of the Colony in 1963. Great things were expected of her. Bernard was sharing a flat with John Moynihan at the time and working as a stage hand but was mostly living off Jaqui. "I was very found of Jaqui and fancied her like hell... I thought

Jeffrey was a bit shabby to her... it was very stormy," said Moynihan. But Ian Board from behind the bar of the club said it as it was, having seen Jeff's alcoholic black outs and rages. "She was very beautiful... she wasn't a boozer but they got married and it was only a year or so after that she really took to the gin bottle. There was a rapid change in her. She was in a play called 'The Reluctant Debutante' with Wilfred Hyde-White and he said, she was a terribly good actress. If she sticks to it, she'll go places. I think Jeffrey managed to fuck that up beautifully." Ian added in his usual dry manner.

Board and Bernard were never friends and in later decades Board would take particular pleasure in repeatedly banning Bernard from the club. Jeffrey wasn't completely unreflective. In a Spectator Low Life column in 1978 he wrote his own mock obituary: 'He drifted from job to job and between jobs he spent months at a time accepting small sums of money from homosexuals or friends who were working. He began to develop a greed for unearned money and the growing conviction that he was cut out for better things... to Soho, got married, and split up from his wife a few weeks later. He leaves two unwritten books and a circle of detached acquaintances.'

The phrase 'detached acquaintances', adequately describes the very fibre of Soho life. The two Robert's knew more of this than many with the constant battle against Sohoitis. In 1962 Robert MacBryde would die aged 48 in London of alcoholism, his early success as a painter, forgotten, except by his lover and friend Robert Colquhoun who followed four years later when sharing a house with the poet Patrick Kavanagh in Dublin, whom he'd met at the Colony. He was singing and dancing down the road when a car hit him.

One of the benefits of being a barman is you can see lives and careers being ruined

The Two Roberts MacBryde and Colquhoun

in slow motion, arguments and tensions rising from nothing and ballooning and if bored you encourage them. Muriel and Ian had to join in daily and be part of the party although it was essential to remain in charge. Political arguments must have occurred when Simon Watson Taylor, the translator of 'Pere Ubu' drank with writer Germane Lombardi (who founded Group 63 with Umberto Eco), Baron Ravensdale, otherwise known as Nicholas Mosely, and 'Cathy Come Home' creator Jeremy Sandford with heiress Nell Dunn. Then there were the journalists: Dick West, Philip Toynbee, Paul Johnson, Peter Jenkins. Add polemical artists Jeff Nuttal and Anthony Earnshaw, and a few actors, and it's amazing there wasn't more fighting. That was when Lucian Freud appeared.

Sandford and Dunn married in 1958, and at the beginning of the 60s sold their fashionable Chelsea home and went to live in working class Battersea to watch and learn how the other half lived. Sandford wrote 'Cathy Come Home' which was made into the film, while Dunn wrote 'Up the Junction' and had an affair with a Battersea car dealer, before writing, 'Poor Cow'.

The fashionable crowd as ever were drawn to this mix, Molly Parkin, in full Ossie Clark, was dating the producer of 'The Avengers' TV series John Bryce and they would ride into the Thames from the embankment in his aqua car and sail down the river beating the traffic. In those days you could drive straight up from the river near the House of Commons from Battersea. Suna Portman, the beauty and uncrowned head of The Chelsea set, was a member during this period as was boutique owner Michael Rainey of 'Hung on You' and married to Jane Ormsby-Gore, Lord Harlech's sister. Cathy MacGowan, famous face for presenting first pop tv show 'Ready Steady Go!' Commentator Peter York recalls it as, "louche, arty, old fashioned and dark green and that in a nice way the people you'd expect to be members, were.' Many of the poseurs were to be found at Gerry's basement bar in Shaftesbury Avenue but as Molly Parkin said, "nobody talked to each other as they did at the Colony. There wasn't the witty repartee of the Colony. How could there be? Gerry's was full of actors used to interpreting others words. The Colony was full of writers who had written them."

A Lasting Colony Love Story

Geraldine Norman OBE, now head of The Hermitage Society, was married to Frank Norman. He had played out the 1950's and 60s in Soho and met Geraldine at the end of the decade. It was a rare Colony love story of the rough and the smooth finding harmony and happiness which lasted until his premature death.

"I first met Frank on April Fool's day 1969," says Geraldine. "I was with Barry Miller (friend of Michael Horovitz), the art dealer, and we were celebrating because he'd just sold a Francis Bacon to Victor Lowndes, head of British Playboy. I was the auction room correspondent for The Times and it was the first time I'd been to the Colony and I thought it was pretty wonderful. Frank was standing where he always stood I was to discover, by the standing stork ashtray and I was there finding him most amusing. Barry and I left the Colony and went to the Dumpling Inn Chinese restaurant in Gerard Street. Frank came stumbling in with Francis Bacon: "Give us a fag", he shouted over to me. I was swept off my feet by his charm, and then we all, Francis, Barry, Frank and I went onto Victor Lowndes. We went up to his suite in an ermine-lined lift and giggled our way through his apartment full of erotica and Frank and I never looked back."

The end of the 60s also heralded Muriel Belcher's 60th birthday. For most women this time of life heralded a pension. For Muriel, 1968 brought a party of unbelievable proportions organised by Allan Hall, who was then supposed to be writing a book in celebration of the Colony Room Club such was its fame or notoriety by this point. Sadly, he never delivered as Tory Stroud, his daughter recounted. "I don't know what happened to the manuscript if there ever was one, but I think it was Peter Owen who commissioned father to write a biography of Muriel, in 1968. I remember lots of research was done by mainly propping up the bar whether words were committed to paper, I doubt. Allan did organise Muriel's 60th birthday party in the cellars at The Cafe Royal but stupidly didn't get money upfront from the guests and ended up with the bailiffs knocking on the door for the £17,500 bill. That night, a very pretty young male assistant to the cellar master John Elliot had finished introducing the

Heartbreaker 2008   by Molly Parkin
Commissioned for the Limited Edition Colony book.   Edition of 125 signed and numbered by the artist.

port and had asked "Are there any questions?" David Edwards, friend of Muriel's and Bacon, brother to John Edwards, stood up and shouted, "yeah, wot are yer doin la'er, darling?"

In 1968 the Colony was also celebrating 20 years and John Mortimer who was covering for Colony member Kenneth Tynan at The Observer, was sent to report: 'I found myself last week in the Colony Room, the last outpost of the old literary and revolutionary Soho in an age of strip clubs and dirty bookshops...' he wrote. 'Muriel Belcher sits sipping vodka and soda out of a green glass goblet and talks ceaselessly, "I remember Dylan Thomas of course, dear," she says. "A little man who couldn't get a word in edgeways. His wife was someone whom I had a few differences of opinion."

By the end of the 60s Muriel was immortalised by Daniel Farson in a piece about clubs for Queen Magazine, a piece he would write many times, over the years for newspapers and magazines. 'Muriel is a legend in the club world. Many cities boast a small club that exists around the personality of the owner, Harry's Bar in Venice, Bricktops in Rome, in London, Muriel's.' Farson also tells the Olga Deterding story. Olga was a socialite who inherited £50m and was engaged to journalist Alan Whicker, as well as Colony member Jonathan Routh of Candid Camera. One day she left the Colony and Farson asked Muriel, 'Do you know who that was?' 'Do you mean the drab little number in the raincoat?' 'Yes, that was Olga Deterding.' This meant nothing to her but once it was explained that she was the richest woman in the world, "her complexioned softened, her eyes grew radiant, her hair took on a new lustre...' before she said, "a very glamorous little lady that Miss Deterding".'

Miss Deterding sadly died on New Years Eve 1978, champagne in hand, choking on a sandwich in a nightclub in London. It was not the Colony which did not serve sandwiches.

In the book 'London After Dark' by Geoffrey Fletcher 1968. Muriel is in a sketch with her dog Nosher. Fletcher was a member who produced hardback books about London filled with his thoughts and quick sketches of the quirky parts of the city.

Allan Hall researches his biography of Muriel and 'the Clolony'

It is hard to believe that the price of one of his books was three years membership of the Colony Room. He mentions that the Colony was in 'The Millionaires Diary', the must have diary of the day for a who's who of what's in or out (the Colony was in 1968 along with Boodles and Whites) and that it is the most famous and best run of all the Soho drinking clubs as well as being a place full of Royalty, Peers of the Realm, film executives, top writers and painters, adding that 'the members are far more interesting than this seems to suggest'. Membership, he wrote, is essential if you want the 'lowdown on what's going on' and that ' Mu's Nosher must be the best informed dog in town, indeed could become a gossip columnist.'

Fletcher can be forgiven for his dreadful sketch, for he sums up Muriel's in the 60s. The edict had been maintained, Fletcher writes 'The atmosphere is that of a successful party where the people get on with each other, where things are said that are worth saying and where bores are not.' The 70s would bring new challenges.

Sketch by Geoffery Fletcher

The Laidback 70s

Yearly Membership

1970	10/-6 (52pence)	
1973		£2.50
1979		£10

During the 1970's the membership of the Colony Room Club became calmer than its previous decades. There wasn't one single political scandal, as far as can be detected. This is remarkable as in the 1950's and 60s the Colony had been up to its neck in outrage.

Daniel Farson noted that Muriel's Boys, the artists that became known as the 'School of London', including Andrews, Kossoff, Freud and Bacon, no longer went as much. Even John Deakin was absent. In 1972 he died in The Ship Hotel in Brighton, where Bacon had paid for him to convalesce after cancer. According to Farson, this was Deakin's last mean trick to make Bacon 'next of kin' and forced him to identify the body in Brighton. Farson quoted Bacon as saying, 'They lifted up the sheet and there she was. Her trap shut for the first time in her life.'

Though younger students from the Slade were still enjoying Muriel's particular brand of hospitality, another art grouping, 'The London Group', had adopted the Colony along with artists from Helen Lessors Beaux Art Gallery and also, Angela Flowers Gallery situated then in Soho. But Farson knew little about them and in the early 70s, Michael Parkinson, the Saturday night chat show host commented at a party that he wouldn't go to the Colony because it was 'full of failures', as if it was a contagious disease.

Did this mean that the Colony was falling out of fashion with the trendsetters of the time, or that the Dexedrine rush had been replaced with a cannabis languor? Not necessarily. The 'official' club photograph of 1973, marking 25 years of the Colony, was taken by Lord Litchfield for The Sunday Telegraph in a piece written by Quentin Crewe. In the picture, fashion designer Jean Muir is front centre next to fashion designer, Thea Porter. These two women were some of the most important trendsetters in fashion of that decade, Muir in particular, who was known because of her diminutive stature as Britain's Coco Chanel and was inextricably linked with silk jersey for sophisticated, sexy, women.

Thea Porter, meanwhile, was renowned for her expensive dressing up box of Far Eastern promise - flowing vintage kaftans, embroidered silks and chiffons. The daughter of Morris Seale and sister to Patrick Seale, both Middle Eastern experts: Porter's sister-in-law, Lamorna Heath had an affair with Martin Amis in 1972, resulting in a child, Delilah, who discovered her father was Amis at 18 after Lamorna committed suicide. Porter liked Muriel and the club: 'The Colony Room is a deep dark green pool of a party... I adore her... The timeless hieratic face, the strong kind real person; I love Ian too.'

Front Row: Thea Porter, Jean Muir, Anthony Blond, Earl Cawdor

Second Row: Isabel Rawsthorne, Alan Hayes, Hubert Dalwood, Lady McClaren

Third Row: Lord May, Muriel Belcher, Peter Jones, Robert Carrier, Annie Ross, Denis Vance, Tom Driberg

Back Row: Ian Board, Adam the pianist, Ian Winchester, Francis Bacon

In the front sits the publisher of Simon Raven, Molly Parkin, Spike Milligan, Henry Robbins, The Carpertbaggers and The Exorcist, Anthony Blond. He wrote about how strong Muriel was when faced with Soho adversity. "I was in the Colony Club one afternoon and nobody else much was about," he says. "Muriel was blasting off at me for how badly I was behaving to my wife, when a heavy man came in and tried to sell her a one-armed bandit (a slot machine), but he didn't get far. Muriel moved her eyes a little in his direction said, 'piss off'. And he did." Blond also went on to publish in 1983 'Who's Really Who: Who are the people who really set the social scene?' by Compton Miller, gossip columnist, many Colony members are mentioned but not Francis Bacon.

Another man in the picture is Hugh John Vaughan Campbell, The Earl of Cawdor. He became the 6th Earl and 25th Thane of Cawdor in 1970 and died in 1993. He lived for several years at Golden Grove, Llandeilo, one of the family's several estates and his daughter Liza Campbell has written an illuminating account in her book 'Title Deeds' about growing up in Macbeth's Castle and of her sexually philandering, money squandering father, whom everyone adored at the Colony.

Also in the photograph was Lord May, inheritor of the match fortune and beautiful Lady Rose McLaren. Robert Carrier is there and at the height of his fame as the first person to invent boxes of wipe clean cooking cards for Harpers magazine, and for writing the cookery book 'Great Dishes of The World' which sold 11million copies. By 1971 he owned Hintlesham Hall, a two Michelin starred restaurant and hotel in Suffolk. A note from Michael Wojas, attached to his membership, noted that 'Carrierbag', as he was known, opened Hintlesham with life insurance money after academic, Oliver Lawson Dick died from alcoholism and that both Belcher and Board had lied to the insurance assessors about writer Lawson Dick's drinking. Though Carrier never married, Lawson Dick, the famous and brilliant editor of 'Aubrey's Brief Lives' was his close companion for many years.

The celebrity chef's Michelin restaurant, Carrier's in Islington, where Princess Margaret, Lisa Minelli and Ava Gardner were seen dining, wowed diners into the

1980s. Carrier also branched out into television post Fanny Cradock and pre Nigella Lawson, delighting housewives with his camp American performance, French savoir faire and dishes like Guinea fowl en croute with truffles on his weekly programme Carrier's Kitchen; Little surprise that his roots lay in musical theatre.

Alongside Carrier is Dennis Vance, television director (the Avengers) and inventor of Armchair Theatre. Beside him is Tom Driberg MP, still standing having just won his seat back in Barking, Essex in 1970 despite Harold Wilson losing to Edward Heath.

Driberg had been in opposition to Wilson on several political issues and was unashamedly to the left in the Labour Party and the epitome of the gay Champagne Socialist, with homosexuality, CND, Vietnam, church affairs, racial discrimination, and pro the common market (Europe), the televising of parliament and the lowering of the voting age to 18. Next to Driberg is Orthopaedic surgeon Ian Winchester who spoke about the club in a startling way: "The club means so much to me as a place where distinguished people go, where I meet people of the highest grade of intellect, to whom I can talk in a civilised way." And next to him was Francis Bacon, who acclaimed the club as "An oasis where the inhibitions of sex and class are dissolved. I think of Muriel as a woman full of compassion but also someone who belongs to a very ancient world. A world before Christianity had dragged in its hideous paraphernalia of petty morals and spite."

Beside Bacon sits his muse, artist Isabelle Rawsthorne who had been married to Constant Lambert, stepmother of member Kit Lambert, manager of The Who, in those first years at the Colony when poets and composers frequented the club. Next to Isabelle is Annie Ross, from the 1950's mixed race trio Lambert (no relation), Hendrix and Ross, who said of the Colony, "It's not like a club, it's more like a womb", and the sculptor star of the 1960's and 70s, Hubert 'Nibs' Dalwood who in 1973 made the bronze commemorative 25 year Colony Club Ashtray, 'made to be stolen' and consisting of two balls to rest a cigar between, and a 'clitoris' for cigarettes .

Adam Stevenson, the club pianist stands at the back with Michael Dillon, owner of Gerry's Club in Dean Street, Stevenson was going off to run a hotel in Marrakesh; He went to manage the exclusive Gazelle D'or.

Michael Winner wrote in 1999 in The Sunday Times on a freebie to the luxury hotel, 'The king of this domain is Stevenson, a slim Englishman who was barman and pianist at the Colony Club in Soho. This was also known as Muriel's Club because of the celebrated owner, Muriel Belcher... The 1970's live on in Adam's persona and demeanour.' Not quite. Adam was only ever the pianist, according to the painter Michael Clark and Michael Dillon.

Ben Tranin was the barmen prior to Wojas' arrival in 1983. Ben was the son of member Moyna Pearmaine who'd started going to the Colony in the late 1960's. She stayed with Ian Board for a while. Ben was very fond of Ian, as was Will Self, who wrote to me, "Ben I loved very much. As for Ian Board, as I said obliquely in the story, it depended on whether or not he liked you and he hated me with a passion. I see no need to gussy up the reality of rather sordid alcoholic lives." Time spent at the Colony was rarely forgotten.

Moyna and Ben would say that Ian was his father, Ian looked after Ben during a mental illness. Ben sadly died and Cathy, Ben's sister introduced Michael Wojas to the club. They had lived together in France and split up, Wojas went onto Amsterdam but found it difficult to survive there and returned to London.

Morocco was a destination for many club members' holidays and second homes, especially Tangier. It encapsulated all the things they loved about the Colony. The Parade bar and Dean's Bar were home from homes, where Bacon's sadomasochistic relationship with ex fighter pilot, Peter Lacy had been played out.

Lacy destroyed Bacon's canvases by stabbing them, prior to throwing them off the hotel balcony. Before drinking himself to death he played the piano in Dean's bar (founded by Joseph Dean in in 1937 and said to be the inspiration for the movie. Casablanca) until 1962. Bacon had drifted back and forth between Tangier and the South of France where his mentor Graham Sutherland lived, and London, as unimpressed by the American beat poets as Dean: 'Romantically poor with their American Express cards', he said.

Still, Bacon's friend William Burroughs was to write The Naked Lunch in Tangier and Allen Ginsberg and Gregory Corso were all set to end up in the Colony but in Tangier they went to The Parade. The Parade Bar was run by a small vibrant French woman much in the mould of Muriel Belcher called Lily Wickham, who ran it until the 1980's with a foul mouthed parrot at the bar's entrance. The squawking bird could be heard swearing before you even got in through the door, not unlike Ian Board in later years, and coincidentally, Muriel had kept a Mynah bird at her Shelton Street home although it didn't utter oaths but a sweeter, 'Who's a pretty boy then?'

Trips and club outings had always been part of the fun of the Colony Room, whether raising money for disabled children or going to members exhibitions. There seemed an illicit naughtiness to take what was so unusual about the place, it's mores, and mix it into normal life. In 1957 Bacon had an exhibition at The Hanover Gallery when desperate for money because of £5000 worth of gambling debts. The paintings not fully dry and the place crowded with friends, more of a party than a private view, many might well have emerged with Bacon's on their backs as David Sylvester did, getting a half-naked man on his suit jacket. Bacon left the pictures as they were.

Muriel and Ian always went on holiday together, to India or Kenya, a favourite resort was the Mombassa Beach Hotel for a months holiday in August courtesy of Francis Bacon; for much needed liver rest from pure alcohol. Because of the heat they would be forced to drink beer during this break. Muriel would lie there doing nothing, Ian would go off for the occasional search for local willing men. Muriel would never go in the pool other than a quick descent into the water for a minute or two, and one day the hotel manager came up to her and asked deferentially why she would not go for a full swim, was there something wrong with the pool?

"Don't be a cunt dear, I only go in for a piss."

However they always maintained, "the best way to be sure to get good service was to tip the 'help' when you arrived, not to wait till you left. And tip generously!" Parties were regularly held at Elizabeth Smart's place in the country where the two Roberts Colquhoun and MacBryde house kept and nannied her children by poet George Barker, while she earned their keep in London working in advertising and on magazines. The house in Essex had originally been poet Ruthven Todd's. Geraldine Norman remembered one party in the early 70s after the two Roberts had died: 'Elizabeth Smart had a wonderful house in the country. She got fashionably interested in gardening and she made this wonderful quarry. She invited all her friends and had a tremendous party and I remember she put little cushioned beds all around among the shrubs so that people could get up to tricks or sleep until morning; very considerate. We had actually booked into the local pub so we were very superior."

Other 70s away-days included cricket at the Oval with Jeffery Bernard playing umpire and staying with David Edwards in Suffolk where Allan Hall, who invented the Beaujolias race was to retire to work at Edward's wine shop in Long Melford; not necessarily the best job for a man who enjoyed the product so much. One picture taken by Paul and Suzie Bardolph shows the jolly spirit of the occasion. Muriel in a spring frock tripping the light fantastic with Ian Board across the grass.

In 1973, for Muriel's 65th birthday, Francis Bacon gave a party at Robert Carrier's country hotel Hintlesham Hall, taking over the whole hotel for the weekend. Unfortunately not all members could be invited but Muriel was happiest at home, as the uncrowned queen of Soho. 'Muriel,' said George Melly. 'On her stool, a glass in her hand and a gleam in her eye, her tongue wrapping itself around joyfully obscene epitaphs has something of the presence of an Archetype.'

Richard Whittington, the food writer and co-author of many cookbooks was a member from the early 70s and indeed even shared Board's flat which led to a vivid description of the then still sexually active Board: 'My sleep would be interrupted by terrible shrieks and whipcracks'. He also described Belcher: 'Muriel's wit came from so much more than her words. The delivery, the body language, the coarse juxtaposition... a sense of shared absurdity... interspersed with lines of Ortonesque

originality.' Whittington illustrated the point by quoting Muriel's words about a woman with whom he was having a passionate affair. "You'd better have a word with that nice doctor Neil Perrett about some penicillin. If they joined all the cock she'd had together you could make a handrail across the Alps." And of Peter O'Toole, "If she was any prettier dear, they'd have had to call it, Florence of Arabia."

TIP TOE THROUGH THE TULIPS

'Gerry's was full of actors - Mark Boxer's camp, self-obsessed monomaniacs,' as Geoffrey Wheatcroft wrote in his essay on Muriel Belcher from his book 'Absent Friends', about the 1970's. Many members were happy to jump between Gerry's and the Colony, just as members of the Colony were also members of the gentleman clubs of St James like The Athenaeum, Buck's and Brook's. Wheatcroft wrote of the holy trinity of the Colony, Gerry's and The French, 'the camaraderie of Dean Street was always partly homosexual, as well as wholly alcoholic'. By then The Gargoyle, Le Caves De France ('true Bohemia', wrote Farson) and The Mandrake had closed but the Kismet, home to a sweet mix of police and criminals and journalists, kept going until the early 1970's. Popularly known as 'The Iron Lung' or 'Death in The Afternoon', in a damp basement on Little Newport St, Edwina McPherson, Sugg's mother from the band Madness, was barmaid. None of them would last as long as the Colony or Gerry's in Dean Street, now run by Michael Dillon who bought the bar from actor Bunny May.

"I first came into the Colony and I thought, Fucking hell, it's the most amazing place," said Dillon "It must have been 1970 and I went with a friend, Paddy Saville on a Saturday. Muriel was sitting on her usual perch: 'So what's your name?' I was smoking a cigarette and replied, My name's Michael Dillon. She pulled the cigarette out of my mouth, pulling at my lower lip. 'Don't talk to me with a cigarette in your mouth, cunty.' Fuck you, I thought and went to the other end of the bar and pulled a bottle of champagne out of a bucket and said to the barman, Ian, Ask that charming lady if she'd like a glass of champagne. She apologised and said, 'come over here'. We had a chat and became friends almost immediately. I liked her very much, she was good fun. A lot of people found her frightening. I didn't. I got on well with her. 'When is your birthday,' she asked me once. In June, 'what's your birth sign?' I'm Cancerian. 'Well, so am I'. Very strange thing. Few days from me."

Gerry's had employed some of the more remarkable barmen to be seen in Soho, actor Dudley Sutton, poet Roger McGough and Jeffrey Bernard all at the bar at the same time. By spring of 1974, Jeffrey Bernard now writing a column for The

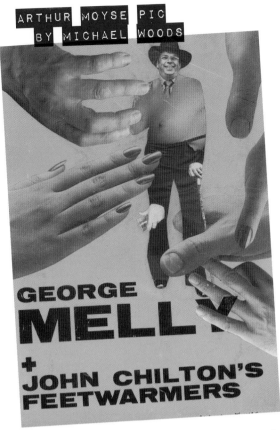

GEORGE
MELLY
+ JOHN CHILTON'S
FEETWARMERS

Spectator and being paid a considerable £40 a piece, persuaded Bunny May to employ him as a non-drinking barman, to stiffen his resolve against the drink. It had been his drunken exchange of whacking Edwina McPherson in the face with a telephone at The Coach and Horses that had convinced Bernard to give up the booze. With an alcoholic like Bernard on the wagon, he became censorious and rude about people getting pissed, disapproving of affairs, patronising and bitchy. He was also commissioned during this time to write his autobiography and so wrote a letter to The Spectator asking for information: 'I would be grateful to any of your readers who could tell me what I was doing between 1960 and 1974.' A reply came from Mike Molloy, editor of The Daily Mirror, 'In September 1969 you rang my mother to inform her that you were going to murder her only son... I can put you in touch with many people who've enjoyed similar experiences.' Around this time Geoffrey Wheatcroft assistant Editor on The Spectator, suggested Bernard as the television critic. The Colony seemed to work as an anarchic version of the old school network and Bernard could be very funny writing every week about Melvyn Bragg's book programme, until an inevitable apology had to be printed. No wonder Melvyn Bragg never became a Colony Room Club member.

Bring some colour to your cheeks.

When in 1975 Francis Bacon took Bernard out to lunch and asked what he was going to do now he'd lost his looks. It might have rattled his cage, because like Bacon, Melly, Carrier and Parkin, a peacock complex seemed part and parcel of the Colony Room's membership; whether male or female. Parkin in her hats and gold lame, Melly in his pinstripe suits and big cigars, Bacon in his black leather

Photos: Jorge Lewinski Courtesy David Edwards

and Carrier in his pinny not forgetting Peter Langan in his easily stained white suits.

It could have been Bacon's comments that made Bernard drink again but in reality it was being dumped by a 28 year old PR girl. Bernard admitted to Farson that he'd 'never met such boring people as my friends when I was sober and never been so miserable or so lonely.' He had also become diabetic. By the end of 1976 Jeffrey Bernard had flung himself off the wagon. His friends Eva Johannsen, Frank Norman and actor Tom Baker helped him to drink through the following decade.

The artist Maggie Hambling had a premonition of the destruction that the Colony could cause and made a decision in the 1970's. "I remember being with Craigie Aitchinson when I first went up the stairs, and I remember that we all went back to a party in Marsh Dunbar's house in Canonbury Square. I can't remember very much else, except the next morning waking up and going down into the basement and finding Craigie making tea before we went back to South London. That was my initiation if you like, and then I went rather bravely back on my own the following week. I wasn't a member but Muriel seemed to take to me and I had some drinks

but began to think that I wasn't going to be able to drink all night and as a very early riser and workaholic, I could see it becoming an addiction. So I didn't go for many years after that." Hambling did become close to a number of Colony members, painting and drawing people from Melly to Sebastian Horsley and she would end up looking after Henrietta Moraes until she died.

Marsh Dunbar was a beauty and wit, as Geraldine Norman said, "really significant to the Colony." The girlfriend to Bobby Hunt, a trumpeter and painter with Johnny Minton, they went on holiday and one day, Bobby got up late to find Marsh had already formed a

IAN BOARD AND BOBBY HUNT OUT WITH THE BOYS IN THE ITALIAN DOWNSTAIRS

relationship with book designer Peter Dunbar, typical of the way that people swapped partners. At the same time, it was still a chauvinistic era. "I think I was always looked upon as Frank's appendage," says Geraldine Norman, "I think Muriel quite liked me, 'Hello, cunty', she'd say, fondly. And she came to our wedding party."

Norman recalls that as a couple, all their friends were members of the Colony. "The pattern of Frank's week was to work from Monday to Thursday writing on his typewriter and then on Friday morning he'd put his suit and tie and go down to Soho for opening time at The French. Then it would be a good lunch and then up to The Colony, then down back to the French at opening time because drinks were cheaper there. At about 7pm I'd arrive from The Times on my bicycle and have two double whiskeys to catch up and then it would be drinking right through and onto Gerry's." It was what Jeffrey Bernard dubbed a "Soho masterclass."

It took all weekend to get over the hangover and sometimes a lunch would be on a Tuesday and the whole week might be lost. "'Sohoitis' comes with heavy drinking and not cracking on with work," says Geraldine Norman. "I suppose I gave him structure."

Still, at least the Colony allowed women, in a time when some fustier institutions barred them. "I never really looked on the Colony as a club," says Geraldine Norman. "It was just a place to go and drink with your friends, as was the French, and it wasn't like The Garrick or The Wig and Pen where women were not being allowed to drink at the bar only at tables.

Geraldine Norman also remembered the reason why she and Frank had been banned from the Colony. The correspondence is reproduced with her permission below. It shows the style of the committee and Frank Norman's enormous humour and how easy it was to fall out when communication was left to letter alone.

c/o *The Saloon Bar*
The York Minster
Soho W. 1

F Adams Esq
Committee Chairman,
Colony Room,
41 Dean Street,
Soho W.1.

11th June 1975

F.Adams dear,

In the 17 or 18 years that I have been getting drunk in the Colony Room my popularity has waxed and waned like the silvery moon. Indeed I have often been able to calculate how much money I have in my little bead bag from the warmth of my welcome as I make my entrance.

Now out of the blue comes your camply worded letter which for some reason, is unsigned and dated 14th June. But never mind I do assure you that its unpleasant tone and veiled threat comes over as clear as crystal never mind that either, let us get to grips with what you so charmingly call the 'the problem'. Plumbing the depths of my memory the picture that emerges from the murky past, concerning this money you say I have owed to adorable Miss Belcher for 12 years is entirely different to what you say it is. But then tempus does tend to fugit, doesn't it love? Which of us can swear to anything that happened two or three hundred crates of whiskey ago?

But here revered committee chairman is my own glamorous version of the story. How true it is that I went skint when my second stage play was not the glittering success that Fing's' had been a few years earlier and how true it also is that big hearted Muriel slipped me £25 quid one heaven-sent day, with the enchanting phrase, 'here you are c*ntie stick that in yuh bead bag!' you can just imagine my amazement, can't you love? I had not asked her for a loan, you see, so natures gentleman that I am, I took it as a beautiful gesture of unparalleled generosity towards a favoured 'punter' whose bar bills, but a short year before were never less than £50 a month and sometimes as much as a £100.

Page 2

My memory of the £34,16s bar bill, you mention, is a lot less clear as this figure has at no time been mentioned to me. But I vaguely recall that there might have been a bit owing. But I also remember it being agreed that whatever I owed was scrubbed and I would not have anymore tick till I wrote another smash hit. Alas, my talent has not turned anything up since and I've paid in cash as I've gone along ever since. There it is. The honour of which you speak has not been entirely neglected, for Muriel and I have not mentioned the matter again.

Having said all that, if Muriel needs a few quid for her operation or a bottle of brandy, I would love to help and enclose a tiny donation of £30 from my dear wife, a mere slip of a girl, who has only been a member for a couple of years. I do hope you aren't going to get bitchy because it isn't more, it would be if it could be.

Goodness this is a long letter, isn't it ducky. I do hope you are enjoying it so far. Nearly finished though.

I'd just like to wish you joy in gathering all the old debts in. The last time I caught a tiny glimpse of the bills they were a foot thick and yellow with age. As a long standing member of the club might I make a small suggestion? Thank you. For goodness sake don't write to everyone in such a nasty tone or the roads out of London will be crammed with wheel chairs as an army of alcoholic ageing queens make good their escape and seek sanctuary in the peace and quiet of the country side. On the other hand, old thing, an ungenerous thought crosses my mind that perhaps you have picked me out with your tiny pin because I am one of the very few old faces still around.

Do please give Muriel our undying love, we wish her better goodness knows.

Yours (still a big spender at heart) ever,

Frank Norman.

The reply came back dated two days later...

The Colony Room Club
Dean Street, Soho W1

Dear Mr. Norman,

Thank you for your recent letter which shocked Miss Belcher, myself and the rest of the committee very much. We also thank you for your wife's cheque for £30 which has been used to repay a £25 personal loan; the remaining £5 has been set against your outstanding bar bill.

You mentioned in your letter that your, 'dear wife' had only been a member for two or three years. On looking through our membership Book we find that she is not and never has been a member. In the circumstances, and to avoid any embarrassment to Miss Belcher, you must realise that you will no longer be welcomed at the club, and your name as from today will be removed from the List.

We trust that you will also have the decency not to enter the Club premises with any member as a guest, as this will only necessitate Miss Belcher or Mr. Board having to insist that you leave to the embarrassment of the member concerned and other members who may be present at the time.

A copy of this letter is being sent to the relevant authorities.

Yours Sincerely,

F. Adams
(On Behalf of the Committee)

P.S We regret that our original letter was undated and unsigned due to clerical errors.

Norman's banishment from the club after almost 20 years is predictably angry:

c/o *The Saloon Bar*
The York Minster
Soho W.1

Dear Mr Adams,

Re your letter of 17th July. I wish you to know that I think your behaviour in this matter has been reprehensible from the outset. The distasteful nature of your correspondence has prompted me to look into the legalities of the claim you make against me in connection with an alleged bar bill of £34.16s dating back more than 10yrs and an unsolicited personal gift of £25 given to me by Muriel Belcher. I discover without surprise, that both these debts (although in the circumstances I admit to neither) are 'Statute Barred' in that no claim, in writing or otherwise, has been made within the statutory period of seven years. I suspect you were well aware of this from the outset, in which case I would have thought you would have had the decency to approach me in a far more polite and civilised manner.

In view of the above I now formally reject all claims that you have made including the deduction of my wife's gift to Muriel Belcher from the amounts mentioned. If she is prepared to accept this money in the spirit in which it was intended she is welcome to keep it otherwise she is at liberty to return it.

As you may be aware I have written to Muriel Belcher personally about this matter. It was therefore entirely unnecessary of you to threaten me yet again; even if you did have second thoughts about it and made an effort to strike out: 'A copy of this letter is being sent to the relevant authorities'. Whoever they may be. Neither of us would dream of visiting the Colony Room again. I might add that if you fondly believe that you have the support of the other members of the club in this matter, you are very much mistaken. There is not a single one with whom I have discussed your actions who is not as appalled as I am – This includes many of The Colony Room's oldest members.

Yours Sincerely,

Frank Norman

To Muriel he wrote privately and more than a little aggrieved from his home address

23rd July 1975

Dear Muriel,

How on earth did you expect me to react when for no good reason your accountant writes me an unpleasant letter about some ancient bill of which I have no certain knowledge and doesn't even bother to sign it!
My first thought was that it was some kind of joke. Surely a more diplomatic approach would have been a better way of going about it.

Now in his second letter dated 17th July he takes the opportunity of taking a dig at Geraldine as well, why if 'she is not and never has been a member' was she sent a request to renew her subscription several weeks ago?

It is a shame that this matter could not have been settled without so much unpleasantness, but there it is. You may be sure that you will see neither of us ever again.

Yours Sincerely,

Frank Norman

Dan Farson who also employed the very same accountant as Muriel and the Colony, Fred Adams(who was also Chairman of the club), wrote of F.Adams: 'a pinstriped, plump and pompous homosexual who is yet to come out'. On Queenie Watts advice he became my accountant… It took me a long time to realise he was crooked'. But perhaps the words of Anthony Blond are more appropriate. 'A good upper class ploy is to shelter behind a professional when wanting to behave badly'. All remained members of the Colony.

By 1976 Craig Brown, columnist and humourist, was introduced to the Colony. In 1990, when it seemed it was in danger of closing from the developers, he remembered the club fondly in an article in The Times. 'It was the first club I joined and easily the best... It was about 3.45 in the afternoon on a bright summer's day. We walked along Dean Street in Soho, turned right through a dingy black door and ascended some dingier, blacker stairs. My companion, a member, pushed open the thin door and we walked into a room little bigger than a billiard table. The curtains were pulled together, banishing all sunlight, perhaps so as to make the racing from Kempton Park on the television all the more vivid. There was smoke everywhere, and everyone wore the intent, calm expressions of the seriously drunk. As I entered, a pretty woman with long, fair hair dipped into her handbag and began to throw all the money it contained coins, notes and a chequebook on the floor in my direction. "I don't want it, I don't need it, It's no good. Go on take it. TAKE IT." The membership was extraordinarily varied. I was once introduced to an attractive, rather smartly dressed woman with the words, "Have you met Christine Keeler?" Each afternoon was like a bizarre cocktail party, hosted by Jean Genet and Albert Steptoe, an extraordinarily and inseparable mix of the exotic and the down-at-heel. Even the burglars were of a better class, and given to hauteur: one of them (Brian the burglar) had, as I remember, just done over Mrs Thatcher's house in Chelsea and delighted in expressing himself flabbergasted at her reported insurance claim.' In 2012 Brown recalled writing the story and added that, 'as reported in the papers, the jewellery claimed was far more than the jewels were worth. But this was deemed libellous of Mrs Thatcher, so I had to change it.'

Gyles Brandreth, the ex politician, writer, performer and media mogul also went to the Colony in the early 1970's. Renowned for his taste in snazzy jumpers, Brandreth had along with Cliff Richard been chosen as Lord Longford's idea of regular youth when setting up his anti-pornography campaign. "It was Irene Josephy (the literary agent) who introduced me to The Colony Room, or Muriel's as she and we always called it. This was the very end of the 60s and the beginning of the 70s. I was in my early 20's and had never known anything like it. I wasn't a member but I was young and welcome entirely on that account, and because I came with Irene. We would go there after lunch at either Bianchi's or the Gay Hussar: that's why everyone seemed to be there, for drinking after lunch. Francis Bacon was the star attraction. I did see him fall off his stool. Going there was the way one was "blooded" into Soho life. It's like the famous Bacon meets Michael Heath story (Ken Thompson PR for Channel 4 also told me in 2012). Michael Heath was introduced to Bacon who asked him what he does. Heath muttered that he was a cartoonist. Bacon responded grandiloquently: "A cartoonist? You are the chronicler of our age. Yours is the art that counts. Yours is the line that defines our world. Yours is art made history! I salute you." Heath's head swelled with pride and pleasure and as he moved along the bar, he heard Bacon mutter, "Who was that cunt?" I think Bacon was there every time I went. You felt he was there, even when he wasn't." Heath gave up drinking for a long while and remarried, stayed sober and opened up a chain of decorative cupcake shops while still cartoon editor for The Spectator and Private Eye. By 2012 he got divorced.

"Dan Farson was the other regular I remember well." Brandreth recalled. "His speciality was selling the same project to several publishers at the same time. I remember going to meet Dan at Muriel's at his invitation and then him sleeping throughout the encounter. I can picture the bar, the narrow stairs, the louche and illicit atmosphere, the sense of being admitted to the orchard where the forbidden fruit is grown..."

The filmmaker and artist John Maybury was another young man introduced into the Colony at this time by one of the original bad boy members, Michael Wishart. Maybury would later go on and direct and write about Francis Bacon in the film Love is The Devil with Tilda Swinton as Muriel Belcher. "Muriel, however ill, seemed always to be there propped up in the corner and we were very conscious of her presence," says Maybury. "When we were researching the film, we got footage of Muriel but we could never find any audio of her and yet people say that Tilda sounded just like her, and she was pregnant with twins at the time."

Maybury was also able to recall the Colony from that time as a place to go after the 'Cork Street crawl', the days when galleries combined to have their private views on Tuesday night. "He (Wishart) was forever trying to get a show but he had become a complete anathema because he was such a drunk and a major drug fiend which is why he connected with (Colony member) Kenneth Anger." says Maybury. "Anger put a spell on Wishart round the time High Diver (his autobiography) came out in 1977, writing with green or purple ink with little bundles of herbs, with instructions to burn them. Anger was incredibly good looking and came to England because he was a major follower of Aleister Crowley and had gone to The Temple in Cefalu (Sicily). He would have been of great interest to the queenie element, and he'd been with Cocteau in Paris. He was a little bit of an underground star but I'm surprised to see his (Anger's) name there as a Colony member. But then a good looking face was an entry point for many."

Another surprising member through the 70s and a friend of Kenneth Anger was Sir Francis Rose, an artist championed by Edith Sitwell, Gertrude Stein and Alice B Toklas: he illustrated their cookbook and Gertrude Stein bought his paintings for her esteemed collection of art now owned by Yale University. He had started his professional life with Diaghliev, designing backdrops for the Ballets Russes and Rose's affairs included artist Christopher Wood. In 1972 He appeared in Kenneth Anger's film Lucifer Rising: perhaps they too met at the Colony.

A fluid approach to sexuality, finding a wider audience in the 1970's, had long been cultivated at the Colony. "All the Bernard boys were good lookers and handsome lads that Muriel had as her boys," says Maybury. "In the pre-Aids years, all those straight boys would 'put out' if drunk enough, for the right person at the right time. It was much looser and freer." The camp language "get you!" that Anthony Blond wrote about as being the smart way to talk for the star Oxford University grads of 1948 was 'part of being subversive, clever and part of the deal. It was underground and remained underground, that was the point of the Colony.'

Jay Landesman, the publisher, dealt like Anthony Blond with Colony writers and had Pam Hardyment working for him. She was one of the many strikingly good looking females in the club: a writer, journalist and publisher's mistress to Landesman. Muriel was still at the helm when Hardyment joined but like so many before her, she soon realised that it hadn't been her first collision with the club. "Although 1977 was when I started to go, I had been there once before as a teenager," she says. "It was the late 50s, I'd gone up there to meet a crim friend. I can't say who he was as he's still alive and he was married, and I was well under age and it wasn't 'Mad' Frankie Fraser, although he was there too. He told me to meet him at 'his club', and I came home from school to change into my red plastic stilettos. I went up the stairs and was so nervous, I sat down. Someone said: Ooh that's Muriel's chair. I said, Who the fuck's Muriel? A little woman appeared and said. 'I'm Muriel and I like you. What are you drinking?' She was theatrically posh, terrifyingly for me as a north London cockney schoolgirl. Blimey! I thought. All these people! I thought I must come back here, this is my kind of place I was in heaven but I didn't because I went off to have babies.

When I stood up from the stool, she was tiny, like a child but I'm 5 feet 10 and I had these enormous red plastic heels on. She bought me a few drinks when the bloke never turned up and then I had to get home on the bus, but as I staggered through Soho I thought, I'm going back there one day."

It might have taken 20 years but Hardyment got there, and her description of gangsters is reiterated by writer Quentin Crewe in his acute observation: 'Some of Soho's rough life has inevitably intruded occasionally into the sentimental bohemianism of Muriel's Club...

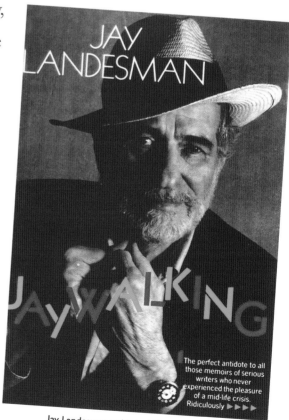

Jay Landesman published Elizabeth Smart's
At Grand Central Station I sat Down and Wept 1977

136

a well known gangster came in and made it clear in a very polite but determined manner that a little protection money would not be out of place. In the event it proved unnecessary, the gangster was found dead further up the street the next day. 'Nothing to do with us', Ian Board claimed.'

By 1974 they couldn't get insurance on any part of the property other than if they fell down the stairs and broke a leg. There had been apparently five break-ins, a fatal stabbing on the door step and the upstairs room used as a knocking shop. "When I came back in '77 it all came back." Pam Hardyment told me. The décor had changed and been painted bright green but the atmosphere was the same and before you knew it, you were in there day after day getting pissed and ringing up the kids and telling them to go and get fish and chips for tea because you're going to be late home again. If they came into town with me, I used to give them a fiver to go to The Family Fun arcade on Old Compton Street. It was different in those days. My kids learnt self-reliance. Different times."

Orlando Campbell also learned self-reliance among the Soho slot machines. A son to Colony member Charlie Campbell, front man of Sir Terence Conran's Neal Street Restaurant (Conran loved that Campbell drew Bacon, Aitchison and other Colony celebrities to his place) Orlando was 'blooded in Soho' from an early age and would progress onto running clubs; The Globe in Notting Hill, Green Street in Mayfair and The Westbourne Hotel. "I was first carried into the Colony in a carrycot and dumped on the banqette," says Orlando. Muriel Belcher would put vodka on her thumb and shove it into his mouth when teething, and he later became a regular. "I was seduced and doomed from then on," he recalls. "We moved to Newcastle but in the holidays we always ended up at the Colony and if we went to see a film or play, we'd nip in there at the interval. I remember meeting John Le Mesurier (Sergeant Wilson from TV show Dad's Army) who was another regular at the Colony. It was heaven. We were given as much Coca Cola as we wanted and Muriel would tell Ian Board to open the till and give us two pounds so that we could go to the amusement arcade on Old Compton Street. This was a lot of money in those days.'

In 1976, nobody thought when Muriel first went into hospital, leaving Ian Board her loyal barman to look after the place, that it was anything other than a small stay. Or, that Ian would blossom (as did his nose) into a club host, or hostess in her away time to hospital. Some likened Board to a parrot squawking on his high stool at the end of the bar, others thought him a bore and incapable of stepping into Muriel's grand shoes and nobody thought Ian as clever or as witty as Muriel. As Quentin Crewe wrote: 'While Muriel sits outside the bar Ian works behind it, his tongue nearly as quick as hers, but softer'. But like Cinderella escaping to the ball, Ian Board often known as Ida, which was also Muriel's mother's name came to inhabit his own special persona on the other side of the bar. He even acquired his own barmen to taunt: David Marion (aka Maid Marion) and Ben Tranin. Members used to the rapier wit of Muriel found that Ian, unleashed, was as subtle as a caveman's club and more foul-mouthed and cruel than even Muriel, whose pet names tended to stick for a long time and were given new life by Board. As Michael Peel recounts, who gained his pet name in 1979: 'I didn't know Muriel, having only met her once on the last time she was in the club. But when I went up there to meet Allan Hall, unaccompanied at first, Muriel looked up at me off the perch and said: "Hello, you fat cunt, who are you? Twiggy?" Ida was behind the bar and despite being addled, had a very good memory. So the next time I went in he immediately said: "It's that fat cunt Twiggy." Indeed very few in Soho knew my real name until later on.'

As Ida, Ian could be very funny. As Dan Farson noted, he was 'never averse to shouting his mind and insulted a number of important members who vowed never to return because he went for the jugular by defaming those they loved: Auberon Waugh's father, Evelyn; Geraldine Norman's husband, Frank, and Robert Carrier's recipes. After returning to the Colony after several years, Carrier was to sweep away furiously, shouting: 'I haven't been here for ten years and won't be going back for another ten'. As he left, Board's invective followed him down the stairs: 'And you stole all your best stuff from Elizabeth David.'

What others thought, Ida said out loud. But just like Muriel he could be surprisingly kind to those that required his tact. He never loaned money but gave it, banishing the recipient's shame by shoving it into their pockets: 'What would an old man like me have to spend it on anyway?' or 'You've got to pay your rent and bus fare, now off with you.' But the bile remained there bubbling away. Michael Dillon remembered being on the Committee. "I was voted onto it, when Allan Hall was on the wine committee (Hall was an editor on The Sunday Times and ran its Wine Club). Bruce Bernard and I went off to check out some wines and we made up a list. I said to Bruce, You must be careful how you approach Ian. He thought it best to go and approach Ian at about 6pm after he had been on the brandy all day. Not a good idea. "We've got this list of wines," said Bruce. Ian picked it up, tore it up and shouted: "If the wine was good enough for Muriel, it's good enough for me. Now fuck off."

Not everybody appreciated Ian or Muriel's wit. Performer Hanja Kochansky met Michael Horovitz there in the early 1970's also present were Barry Miles, William Burroughs and Gregory Corso and like Horovitz, didn't always appreciate the atmosphere. "We met at Muriel's Colony, a drinking club in the heart of Soho. It was an inferno of cynical humour, drunken slobbering lust, cruelty, degeneracy, and brilliant conversation. If one was lucky one might cop a glass of champagne (more often than not accompanied by an insult) from Francis Bacon; hobnob with a reputable publisher, or at least get a good racing tip. Balding, unpleasant, grotesque, sharp nosed Muriel, perched, like a moulting parrot, all night on her stool in the left-hand corner of the bar, where she neurotically caressed her small dog while chain drinking vodka which eventually made her splutter, drool and curse. It was best to keep on her good side lest one got thrashed by the rough edge of her tongue, and Muriel could get extremely nasty if she didn't like you. "Fuck off lovey, I don't want you in my club," was the mildest abuse she'd spit out at the humiliated undesirable."

Phillipa Beale, the one-time president of The London Group of Artists, from 1964-72, remembered that Muriel was often nastiest to young women. "We lived on Shaftesbury Avenue and used the Colony as our local. I used to go with Hubert 'Nibs'

Dalwood and Neville Boden, sometimes with my husband (David Koos Troostwyk). I used to crawl home dead drunk but still work the following day. Francis Bacon was always there and usually drunk. The conversation was mainly camp and spiteful but fun for all that. Muriel was always nice to me although she was generally horrible to young women; I think she was gay and I looked boyish and went around with sculptors and was creating quite a stir at the time showing in the West End."

Molly Parkin went to New York during the mid to late 70s before deciding to move there permanently in 1979. On that trip with her then husband, artist Patrick Hughes, she went to Elaine's Restaurant. Run by Elaine Kaufman who asked her if she knew her 'good friend' Muriel of the Colony. When Parkin screeched in recognition, the friendship was sealed. Elaine told Molly that when friends were going to London she always told them to visit Muriel at the Colony and say Elaine sent them. Elaine was in some respects the Muriel of New York, and reigned for 45 years: "I introduce people... I create the atmosphere for people to talk to each other." Exactly like Muriel.

Hubert 'Nibs' Dalwood's girlfriend Ros Archer, remembered things with extra spice but then she was still a teenager. "She was certainly an intimidating presence, perched on her high stool just inside the door," Ros said. "Her head was so sculpted, her features and dark hair barely softened the shape of her skull. She was like a bird of prey, long face, long nose, long fingers, dark eyes circled by her large sockets. As you know she didn't hold back, calling everyone "cunty" or "Mary". She turned to Ian saying something like, "Look what this cunt's dragged in", cocking a long thumb in my direction. Ian, also haughtily intimidating, gave me a good looking over and made some remark about our age difference. Thank goodness, they thought

LADY MARCIA FAULKENDER, IAN BOARD AND HEATHCOTE WILLIAMS

FRANCIS BACON AND HUBERT DALWOOD

I was good enough to stay and after asking me some preliminary questions which I mumbled as smart replies as I could, she ordered someone else at the bar to buy me, and Nibs, champagne. I seem to remember a pretty packed room: Lucian Freud, Francis Bacon, Jeffrey Bernard's brother, Bruce, who we used to call 'the spy' as he was always in his unwashed raincoat."

Nibs, who ran the Sculpture department at Hornsey School of Art, liked Ros to dress up and act out scenarios. "Nibs had me dress up as a school girl and bought the uniform tunic, white shirt, striped tie, white socks and flat Mary Janes and talked an American friend into joining us for tea at Fortnum's where he pretended to be my uncle, while sexually 'assaulting' me under the table and kissing me in public as tea and sandwiches were served. The American was bemused, wondering what part he was supposed to play. Later we retired to the Colony, where Muriel laughed and thought it was an amusing turn. Plying a St Trinian's dressed student with Pernod in the Colony didn't pack the same punch as 'outside', since we were in the company of a bunch of degenerates. My relationship with Muriel and Ian solidified and we became very close after Nibs died in 76. I spent any number of lunch times with them at Wheeler's, over whitebait and white wine. They were both extremely generous and kind to me, so whenever I was having difficulties of various kinds, amorous, financial or whatever, I would turn up and chat with Muriel and Ian. It changed when Muriel died. Before, when the old cunt sat at her sentry post, the place was a club, fairly quiet. Although members felt relaxed, they were with friends and didn't have 'outsiders' to deal with. The rules were that you didn't bother anyone else and did what Muriel told you to do. In the afternoon, at 3.00 when it opened, there might be one or two people there and you could just chat quietly on the seats under the window or by the piano or shuffle up to the bar and chat with Ian & Muriel, both down to earth people until they got to the other side of a champagne bottle or two."

"Muriel was a stable person, and controlled everything, Ian included. After Muriel died, Board went further down the line into drugs and alcohol and began to feel he was part of the 'scene', which really was not what the place had been about before. I remember going out with him and others after closing the Colony early and having dinner at the Neal Street Restaurant, where Ian was insufferable, ordering everyone about, when they were dying on their feet and were already doing a favour for us by letting us eat so late. Muriel would never have done that. It was good behaviour, lots of fun, laced with the foulest language. She went home to her girlfriend, Carmel, who would on occasion come into the club. So for me it was a different Colony after Ian became the doyen: camp, noisy and lots of sightseers, not the same vibe at all. It was the centre of my universe for a good ten years. Then after Muriel died it started to tail off and I moved to the US.'

Muriel knew how to sort the wheat from the chaff, but in hospital and unable to keep an eye on the business, she became worried and began to recall her debts, which created problems with regulars like the Normans and also made trouble between Carmel and Ian Board after the funeral. Perhaps she didn't enjoy always having to rely on asking Francis Bacon for money, who always shelled out for Mu.

Barry Evans a Surrealist painter now in his late eighties told me, "When Muriel died in 1979 there was a lot of people at the funeral that I'd never seen before. It was very cold. There were no tears and afterwards we all went back to the club and had a jolly time as if it were a normal afternoon, except of course Muriel wasn't there. She was the queen and while she and Ian worked as a team, it was quite apparent he was her underling; subservient to her. But she had such a huge personality that it was hard for Ian, but he did it. After that I always kissed Ian on the cheek on my way out: only ever Ian. One day Bacon came in as I was kissing Ian and exclaimed, "Ooh you kiss men do you?" "I'll give you a kiss too," I said to Bacon and I did. "A straight man giving kisses to gays: well I never!" he replied."

Many people didn't get Bacon or Belcher's wit. David Edwards did. A friend of Muriel and Ian, he was brother to John Edwards, Bacon's friend, who would eventually be left his estate. Once again, accountant and Chairman of the club, Fred Adams was the connection, when David met Muriel in the early 70s. "I used to have the Swan at Stratford, a pub," he says. "Fred rang me up one Sunday morning and said, Would you take my friend to the country? (Edwards had a place in Suffolk). Her name's Muriel, she lives in the West End and she's got a black girlfriend. When I picked her up she tried to give me a tenner, as she thought I was a taxi driver. Of course there was a big bust up, I said 'Fuck off', she said, 'Fuck off' and eventually she said, 'Well, let me take you out to lunch in Lavenham.' So we got drunk, had a great 24hrs and I had to stay the night.

"The next day she said she wanted to meet me in London. I knew nothing of the Colony. She said, 'David I'll introduce you to people who will change your life' and

Ouroboros
Commissioned for the Limited Edition Colony book.

by Patrick Hughes
Edition of 125 signed and numbered by the artist.

144

that night she introduced me and my friend John Tanner to Francis Bacon. I didn't know who he was and all he tried to do was impress us all evening. We were the only two life members made by Muriel, which was wonderful because no matter how drunk we got we were never told, 'You haven't paid your membership'. It was a great place."

Ian had a tough time deciding to continue with the club. In 1979 Muriel and Ian met up for a not entirely agreeable meeting with the club accountant, who was still Fred Adams. In a letter from Muriel to Ian she began in gratitude, 'for all his effort and hard work' in keeping the Colony going during her illness but set out some points to discuss when she was fit to return:

i) That you had no intention of ever working behind the bar again.

ii) That if I would not accept this then you would claim redundancy payment.

iii) That you objected to me being accompanied by Carmel when I came into the club.

You are of course employed as a barman by the members, not by me. If you are not prepared to carry out your duties, the committee no doubt will make the appropriate decision... I am concerned that overheads have been increased without reference to the committee'.

Muriel was alluding to the fact that through Fred Adams, Board had employed Adams' boyfriend 'Maid' Marian. She also said that club rules didn't allow credit to members and said that that any debts from credit were now due. Muriel was obviously trying to get things in order prior to her death, but as she concluded. 'My only and sincere desire is to see the club return to normal.' They made peace, of sorts, and Board figured that after 27 years working in Dean Street where else would he go? He was 50 when he took that momentous decision that would see the club stagger through to Soho's big renewal in the 1980s when more surprises awaited him.

Artist Michael Clark, who would draw and paint Muriel on her deathbed wrote to me: 'Ian told me there were only two magical people he had met in his life. "One was Muriel, who rescued me from the gutter, and the other was Francis Bacon."

One afternoon in 1979 I was with Francis and Ian, who told us how ill Muriel was. Francis wept. It was the only time I ever saw him cry. At Francis's studio one morning he showed me some photographs of Muriel. "She had an extraordinary beauty," he said.' Muriel died on Halloween, 31 October and was buried on Guy Fawkes day, 5 November 1979.

MURIEL BELTCHER ILL IN BED BY MICHAEL CLARK 1978

Photograph by: Prudence Cuming Associates

chapter 5

THE EXCESSIVE 80s

Kinder Society
The Committee
John Hurt. Did He?
The Jewish Piano
The Polish Sausage
Birch & Bacon to Russia with Love
Keith Allen Goes to Jail
Masturbator
Speaking of Queer
Fifth Columnist
Jeffrey Bernard

Yearly Membership
£25
1980

A Kinder Society

Margaret Thatcher bestrode the 1980s; that pivotal decade that reshaped Britain. 'There is no such thing as society: there are individual men and women, and there are families,' she famously misquoted Oscar Wilde: 'Society exists only as a mental concept; in the real world there are only individuals'. Wilde was talking of fashionable society in the Edwardian sense: of Royalty and its hangers on. You could imagine seeing Wilde in the Colony but never Thatcher, though there was a signed photo of her stuck on the wall. Yet what she preached would eventually fill Soho and the club: the individual more potent than the group on one hand, and the commercialisation of the district on the other.

For Ian Board the 1980s began drearily, dealing with endless solicitors' letters. The first, in August 1980, declared a cheque that he had been bequeathed in Muriel Belcher's will a sum of £2,000. Unfortunately for him, the last few phrases stipulated that the club owed Muriel money and that it would pay it off at £25 a week, supposedly members' debts owed to her.

In December, a second letter also then came from the club's solicitor of thirty years, David Gentle, who instructed Board that Carmel Stewart had been left as the 'landlord' and that Board was the 'tenant'. 'The committee agree to pay Carmel the sum of £3,500 at the rate of £50 per week by way of compensation for her loss of office at the club,' it stated. Though what position she had ever held was unknown, other than Muriel's girlfriend.

Gentle wrote to me in 2011 stating, 'I visited the club fairly regularly over the years and became friendly with Muriel Belcher and Ian Board. In Muriel's will she left the club to her friend Carmel Stewart, a Jamaican lady. It was never thought that Carmel would run the club and which was by that time run by Ian Board. In any event, shortly after Muriel's death Carmel decided to move back to Jamaica where I believe she subsequently died. Although I did not deal with it, it is within my knowledge that prior to Carmel moving back to Jamaica she came to a financial arrangement with Ian Board whereby he bought out her interest in the Colony Room.'

David Edwards, the fellow publican and great friend of Muriel and Ian, put it in a different way. "When Muriel died she left the lease to 'melon nips', aka Carmel, and the club to Ian, knowing they hated one another. How can you leave a club to two people who hated each other so much? But that was Muriel's sense of humour."

Carmel was left in even better financial shape by Francis Bacon who in 1982 bought Muriel's West End flat from Carmel and gave it to Edwards' brother John, who gave it up later when he had Bacon's fortune. "It was a beautiful little two-bedroom place that must be worth a fortune now," says David.

Various people have recorded that Ian was cross about all this, and he was also put out when the rent suddenly doubled in summer 1980 to £3,250 per year. Board negotiated with the landlord, and also began to pay Carmel off as proposed. Some say that he eventually paid the debt with money borrowed from Michael Wojas, who had a victim's settlement after being mugged during the Brixton riots in April 1981, prior to his working at the Colony.

Wojas started working in the Colony in 1982/3 via the Tranin family friends of Boards. Son Ben worked at the club, the mother Mona was a member and Mimi the daughter, dated Wojas. "Michael was for a while the great love of my life," says Mimi. "He moved to Amsterdam, then came back to London. Ian was looking for a new barman when Ben went up to Oxford, so I suggested him. Michael was the only barman who wouldn't allow Ian to cane him over the piano. He said 'You must be bloody joking, no!' And Ian respected him for that." Wojas was given a 'telephone' razor scar (that is, from ear to mouth) when he was mugged, Farson also

FROM LEFT TO RIGHT, BACK TO FRONT:
MIKE MCKENZIE PIANIST, MICHAEL WOJAS,
TOM BAKER, BRUCE BERNARD, LIZ MCKENZIE,
MICHAEL CLARK. CENTRE: FRANCIS BACON,
IAN BOARD, JOHN EDWARDS.
FRONT: JEFFREY BERNARD

had one, after refusing to pay his bar bill in Chinatown. "If somebody marked him like that, it was proper 'crim' activity," ex barmaid at the Colony and writer Pam Hardyment said. "Michael said it was racist but you don't get sliced from mouth to ear for nothing. It's usually if you've undersold drugs." There were a lot of criminals at the Colony, she recalled, although it was not as bad as the Kismet.

Thatcher's Britain was changing, dragging Soho with it. Pornographers and property went well for tycoons like Paul Raymond who bought many properties in Dean, Brewer and Old Compton Streets, always with a briefcase full of cash. Raymond would rent out property to the racket willing to pay most: often clip joints that offered sexual frissons then ripped off the unwary with huge bar bills. By the time Raymond died in 2004 he had 100 buildings and an empire worth £74.5m, and Soho was a less gentle place. As one older Soho resident remembered it on a 1985 television documentary by John Pitman called Just Another Day, "The working girls were naughty but fun on the streets, well-dressed and with kind hearts. What came later was evil, I wouldn't walk around the streets now at night." But at the same time, an exciting new underground culture was emerging in art schools and nightclubs. Fashion designer and editor of Beige Magazine, Dean Bright remembered the lengthy sessions of the early 80s. "We faced a dilemma, either tea and cake, home and bed, or more boozing. The boozing won."

Bright was 22 years old and attending St Martin's School of Art. "Yet here I was learning about the art of living with Molly Parkin. We walked up a dark grim staircase at a godforsaken hour, and fell into a green room. I was introduced to a blossom-nosed host who immediately told me I had bad skin and was a cunt. I was petrified but hid behind Moll's skirts, metaphorically-speaking. As we ventured further into the green crevices of the Colony and I was introduced to a snarly-faced man. "Hello young man, do you fancy a fuck?" Francis Bacon peered into my eyes then reeled backwards into his seat. He shouted many expletives as did the host Ian, and I crumbled like a sacrificial virgin. Moll stood up for me but it was a truly terrifying experience. But I'm glad I had it." Bright was designing with Mark Pullen, Parkin's amazing stage clothes for her touring one woman show that was so shocking she was banned from Dublin for bad language.

More frightening for Private Eye and Spectator cartoonist Michael Heath was the fear of being a bore and Ian's blasé attitude to violence. 'If you didn't come up with the right stuff at the Colony, or the French or the Coach and Horses, you were done, dust. If you weren't hip, sharp or on the ball, and coming in with the odd remark, it would be, 'Out, bore!' I remember one day, no one there except Ian behind the bar, a hot day, and at the end of the bar were two drunk men, not young but crooks, burglars, killers, East End nightmare men, beautiful in their way, but big, drunk, laughing loudly, like the Kray brothers, and saying 'Argh I got this

ALASTAIR FAIRLEY AS WOOD
MOLLY PARKIN AS EARTH
DESIGNED BY DEAN BRIGHT AND
MARK ERSKINE PULLEN FOR
ANDREW LOGAN'S
7TH ALTERNATIVE MISS WORLD
'86 EARTH

bit, I shoved it up her ...' and the other one's saying, 'You never, you cunt, fuck, shit you should see 'er arse, argh fuck!' Ian was at the end of the bar saying, 'Gasp, wheeze, throw 'em aht, oo wants to 'ear about their dicks!'

Ian Board was homosexual, deplored heterosexuality and was offended by the nightmare men. 'I said, Leave 'em alone and calmed him down,' says Heath. 'But suddenly Ian says to these two guys, 'Wheeze. Get the fuck out of here! I don't care who you fuckin' are, get yer fuckin' dreary dicks out of 'ere!' No one had ever spoken to them like that before, and one of them, six foot four, said, 'I think you've made a mistake.' And Ian said, 'Fuck off out of it, I'll cut yer fuckin' and they left with Ian following them, shouting. And I thought, God, any minute now one of them's coming back with a gun, then two regulars came in, started drinking and laughing, then a guy came in, and I knew they'd sent him up to do something awful, but he must've thought it's not worth it with an audience, and one of the others appeared, and said,' Not today, not tomorrow, but it'll happen, you're dead.' And Ian didn't give a fuck. 'Kill me now, who cares about yer dreary dick?'

Ian had shared a flat with another Dick, food writer Richard Whittington in Clare Court, Judd Street in the mid 70's, which explains Board's nonchalance towards violence. 'Ian was partial to a bit of rough trade... occasionally of a morning some heavily tattooed man in leathers would be cleaning his teeth, I made sure my spongebag was kept in my room... He once nearly died when tied up and strangled by some shit that passed in the night... no great respecter of privacy, coitus was interrupted by him crashing through my room with three chums, 'Oh 'ello mate 'ow are yer? This is lovely Dickles and that's one of his trollops. He's what we call, normal.' His friends looked horrified. 'How can you bear it, under the same roof?'

Chairman: Frederick Adam, Treasurer: Merrilyn Thorrold, Bruce Bernard, Michael Dillon, Ian Board, David Gentle (solicitor).

After the rows with Carmel, Ian Board had settled in nicely on the tall chair. In April 1981 at a committee meeting, the minutes report that a new rent had been agreed at £3,000pa with the rates to council at £662 per annum. Membership was up to 1,670 members and an insurance policy or pension scheme for Board's eventual retirement was taken out: rather late as he was 52 by then. By October 1981 members of the Colony committee had agreed to have more regular meetings to help Board in the running of the place.

Michael Wojas yet to appear, Board sat on Muriel's perch at the end of the bar. Both in and out of the club, he leaned heavily on Susan and Michael Clark, spending much time at their home. He also moved into a council flat. David Edwards described a typical dinner party there. "Nice size flat mansion block closer to Soho. Small kitchen, hallway, big living room. One Sunday Ian had this luncheon party and he'd got caterers in, the French Whore was there with Viscount (Viscount David Stuart, the estate agent had found Hintlesham Hall for Robert Carrier -bag as we used to call him). So there was about 12 of us sitting around this huge coffee table on a Sunday. There was a lovely linen tablecloth and silver cutlery and I was talking to Viscount Stuart about where we could go afterwards, because on Sunday's in the 80s nothing was open in London, after Ian might throw us out. Well Ian overheard the conversation and said, 'Look 'ere, if you're bored already you can fuck off now!' And he got the table cloth with twelve settings of plated food and threw it out the window from two storeys up. We went to the French Whore's after. Her pimp was called the dwarf and she was, a proper tart.'

IAN BOARD DISCUSSES SARTORIAL DRESSING WITH MICHAEL PARKIN DEC 1982

John Hurt. Did He?

Out on the town Ian Board could be as big a diva as within the club. He often wore track suits for daily occasions with printed t shirts -sometimes without stains - and outside of the club, he would bedeck his body in finery, large dark glasses, necklaces and Lurex jackets and jewelled fingers. In the outside world, dressing up was all the rage with Princess Diana's wedding dress in 1981, plus pop stars like Steve Strange, Madonna, Spandau Ballet, Wham and Duran Duran.

'Big' was in, movies were blockbusters. In Soho art students were New Romantics and the clubs were Le Beat Route, Club for Heroes, Gaz's Rockin' Blues, The Embassy and Legends. And actor John Hurt was most often seen at the Colony or falling down its staircase.

Hurt was very fond of the Beatles and could be heard by members climbing the battered stairway, singing along to Beatles' songs on the old record player. This didn't happen with Board installed, as he preferred musical soundtracks like South Pacific. One day when he was playing Cabaret, 'Twiggy' aka Michael Peel was there.' Board, aka Ida, immediately turned to Francis Bacon and said: "You were in Berlin at the time this was depicting, weren't you Francis?" Francis' reply was: "Yes, I was caught by my father being fucked by a stable-lad and he sent me to Berlin to make a man of me."

There was a record shop opposite the French pub at that time which sold both second-hand and new LP releases from the musicals, so presents often arrived from friends dropping by to the club. Board was a big Hollywood fan and collected autographs. Deborah Kerr was proudly pinned upon the wall, he had once waited upon Elizabeth Taylor (see pic in the 50's) and he had kept the menu following the premiere of Michael Todd's film and premiere party of Around the World in 80 days in 1957. Muriel and Ian had dined on a ten-course meal at midnight in the pleasure gardens of Battersea Park, snacking on, hamburgers a la Noel Coward and fish & chips a la Lizzie Taylor, jellied eels and whelks a la Soho so the menu read. Still, Board had little patience with the prima donna attitude among his own members.

By 1980, John Hurt was one of Britain's biggest acting talents in America as well as Europe. He had stared in Midnight Express, Alien, The Elephant Man, Crime and Punishment, King Lear and 1984. By the end of the 80's he was playing the part of an ex-member of the Colony, Stephen Ward, in the film 'Scandal', about Christine Keeler.

Matt Cogger, an on-off barman through the 1980s and 90s, tells a story that has become legendary. 'John Hurt had fallen drunkenly asleep on the banquette. Time was called but he slept on. 'Come on Hurt you cunt. Wake up!' Ian Board screamed, pointing a finger at him. At that moment a crack of lightening sounded outside the window, but all who were there swore it came from Ian's fingertip, proof that Ida was close to God.' It probably helped push Hurt towards the wagon.

Writer Irma Kurtz remembered Hurt too. 'One day I was at The Groucho and I introduced Francis Bacon to John Hurt both whom I'd met at the Colony, and they got on. I started to say something when John Hurt said 'Don't interrupt when your betters are speaking.' I was shocked but I got my revenge when the next day I wrote in my column in the Evening Standard. 'Last night I was sandwiched between a Bacon and a ham.' Hurt hasn't spoken to me since, but the next time I saw Bacon he came up to me and said, 'I am so sorry if you were treated with impoliteness the other night'.

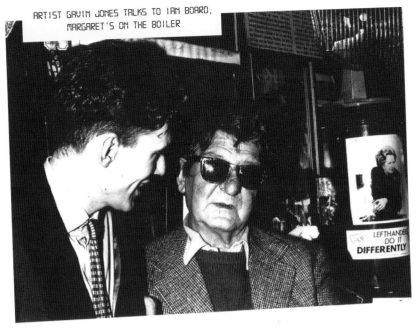

ARTIST GAVIN JONES TALKS TO IAN BOARD,
MARGARET'S ON THE BOILER

To Ian   Harry Diamond

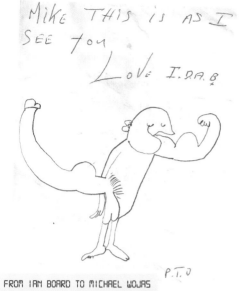

MIKE THIS IS AS I
SEE YOU
LOVE I.D.A.B.

FROM IAN BOARD TO MICHAEL WOJAS   P.T.O

The 'Jewish Piano'

Muriel had died and Bacon might not have been especially fond of Board, but he still went in, not as much as he had, but his visits were seen to convey a Royal Approval. Bacon had become in the intervening decades so much of an art star that people were afraid to speak to him; not so much because of his often sarcastic retorts, but because of his godlike status. Everyone acknowledged, even those in competition with him, that he was at the top of the game. No matter how long people knew him, it seemed they could never be sure of his behaviour towards them. Sometimes outstanding kindness over and above all expectations and at other times Bacon could cut right through the roots of friendship.

He cajoled Farson into believing in their friendship, allowing him to write his authorised biography and then he'd pull out of the deal leaving Farson in a sweat. Farson would have already spent the publisher's advance, Bacon would then give large wads of money as compensation. This happened more than once. He also did this with Bruce Bernard, photographer, picture editor and elder brother to Oliver and Jeff, but then Bruce was also renowned for his quick turn of bad temper. Bacon's company and his champagne made the Colony more attractive to younger artists. Gavin Jones, another good-looking young artist became a little 'too enamoured with the Colony', his dealer Dominic Berning, would later say.

COLONY ROOM CLUB   41, Dean Street,
London W1,
Tel: 01-437 9179.

Dear Member,

Should all go well, if planes don't crash, or any other sort of horror you will have the pleasure of seeing our lovely faces once again when we get back from the school hols on Friday 28th January at 3 pm on the dot. Look forward to seeing you all with handbags overflowing with gelt (that's Jewish for money!).

Love Ian & Mike. XX

'Berning led me up my favourite stairs to the Colony in the 1980s,' says Jones. 'It was like having tea with the elephant man - quite an occasion. The Nose Gay spake first, I was in shock at the sight of the facial flesh. Ian was a complex creature and we all enjoyed the tantrums when just out of range ourselves. I loved the unpredictable mixture... Mad with drink the benchmark for antics was always high. We were all famous in the rooms. The place represented Naughty time. Heavy petting only.' Berning maintains that too much time in the club crucified a very talented artist. Gavin Jones was then being hailed for his painterly talent. 'Ian Board stole his muse. It was terrible timing, a pivotal moment. By the time he'd distanced himself, he had to leave town in order to escape.' Gavin now lives in the Outer Hebridean Islands at the far end of Scotland.

Jones wasn't correct about, 'heavy petting only' under Ian's auspices, because more was going on. Artist Darren Coffield recalled the late 80s. "We'd (he and Joshua Compton) like to go in on Thursdays because it was ladies night and we'd hang out and chat up people like Susie Bardolph (the fan dancer) and people old enough to be our mothers and in some cases our grandmothers. That was sex in Soho."

Mimi Tranin told a story about being one of the girls at Board's bar. "Ian wasn't tolerant of drugs, weed and hash fine, absolutely no needles allowed. Sometime if we were all sitting at the bar he'd pop little lumps of hash into our mouths, and giggle.

I suppose he knew what we were up to, because he'd say, 'Don't forget the Jewish piano (the cash register)' and we were expected to keep out of town members chatting and spending at the bar buying us champagne. The really big spenders we were expected to go out to dinner with and whatever happened after was what we chose to do. In exchange, our bar bills would be paid off. It started with Ian and my mum and when my mum got too old, she did it with me. I guess I was about 20. We didn't think of it as prostitution but it paid for my habit." In Soho this wasn't surprising behaviour in fact Ian could be remarkably tolerant even when shouting abuse. There are different types of rude, and the tongue can be used in both instances as Kate Fawkes, daughter of musician and cartoonist Wally and journalist Sandy reminisced recently. 'As a young girl I went up there one day with Sandy, and there was Peter Langan on his knees, under the Michael Andrews mural, with his head up the skirt of a middle-aged lady. The pleasure she was receiving was apparent to all, thanks to her groans and intermittent shrieks. There weren't many people in the club but the few that were there just kept talking as if nothing was happening. When it was over, Peter Langan continued on his hands and knees for a while, eagerly looking for more takers. When none were found they both returned to the bar as if nothing had happened.'

This was the successful Mayfair restaurateur's party trick in his own restaurant and it was speculated to be the reason why it was so popular with ladies who liked to lunch.

Food writer Richard Whittington concurred with Board's penchant for hash. When they shared a flat, Thursday his cat was 'cheered up... by blowing (marijuana) smoke into a paper bag and putting it over Thursday's head... the brute would go berserk and rake Ian viciously with its claws... he would hug the vile creature grimly. 'Hold on mate you'll be al'right.' After a minute or so, Thursday would visibly relax and the bag would be removed. If you have never seen a cat smile this is how to do it.'

IAN
welcomes you to sip champagne
on
Sunday 21st December, 1980
at
Miss Theo Porters
8 Greek Street
London W1

From   *6.00pm*

The Polish Sausage

Chris Battye, the artist who did a series of paintings of the Colony's interior and its cast, was a long term Chelsea Arts Club member, but became boyfriend of Thea Porter and a Colony member. Famous for his classic Teddy Boy appearance, Battye became part of the newly emerged Soho.

"I started going to Soho because I had a show in Greek St at l'Escargot (the top ticket restaurant in London in 1981)," says Battye. "That's when I started drinking round Soho. It was always Gerry's, French, the Colony, and the Coach and Horses.

"I joined in the early 1980's after a guy called Dick Ward, a graphic designer, took me there. It was in the afternoon, there weren't many people there. I met Francis (Bacon) there and the first thing he told me was how long it took him to get a hard on now he was 70. In the early years, I got on great with Ian. Have you seen that film on Norway TV where I was dancing with Ian Board?" Battye asked but it's sadly lost in time. "He used to keep me back on a Saturday and ask questions. 'How can I get Michael to be a bit more confident?' Don't shout at him so much? I used to advise." Much of the shouting was for show, a sort of entertainment because Board cared for Wojas - aka The Polish Sausage - enormously. He helped him keep away from heavy drugs with a fatherly concern and coaxed him from his shy nervous shell. When Michael first arrived in the early 80s in his mid 20s, he hid behind a long fringe. He

Colony Requiem
Commissioned for the Limited Edition Colony book.

Edition of 125 signed and numbered by the artist.

by Chris Battye

hardly spoke and what he said was almost inaudible. He was extremely polite and very deferential to the members and also to Board, although he had an irritating habit of mumbling.

FRANCIS BACON AND JOHN EDWARDS WERE INSEPARABLY CLOSE

Mimi Tranin explained this was because he was extremely shy. "Mike (Wojas) was fine as long as he was behind the bar and it stood between him and the customers."

Wojas' father had been a terrible bully and gambler and he hated him, just as Muriel had hated her father, and Bacon his. Board had little time for empathy in public and often rallied the cry, 'I escaped from Devon by selling my arse and buying a train ticket. Why can't the African's do the same if they don't like it there.' This, during Live Aid in 1985. He wasn't politically correct but as James Birch commented, "Ian Board was very different outside of the club." Because he was trained as a commis waiter who never lost his knack of serving, much of the rest of his foul mouth was part of the act he thought others expected of him. When he went away with Bacon, John Edwards and Birch, he'd be the one cooking and serving up the food. "Ian reverted to maid. He knew his place," said Birch.

Birch & Bacon to Russia with Love

Art dealer Birch recalled the era. "I suppose it must have been around 1979 when I first went to the Colony. I was with Michael Wishart who was a member, John Maybury, Kevin Whitney and Patrick Proctor. Craigie Aitchinson was in there,

JAMES BIRCH AT THE BAR

as was the infamous Vicky De Lambray" (a transgender prostitute who died in the 1980s in mysterious circumstances but who'd been paid a considerable sum by The Rothschild's after officially changing her name to theirs and putting a sign in the back of a kerb-crawling Rolls Royce stating Vicki de Rothschild- performer). Vicki was a Colony regular.

Liking it, Birch became a member in the early 80s. "Chris Battye would turn up every Friday afternoon to my New Kings Road gallery (opened in 1983) where I was showing The Neo Naturists - Grayson Perry, Wilma and Jennifer Binnie - and we'd go into Soho. There was a ritual of drinking whiskey in those days. You had to have a specific drink. I drank scotch with one cube of ice, I don't know why. It was always busy on a Friday afternoon, with the regulars; Peter Owen (the publisher), Barry Evans(artist), Shakespeare Lane(photographer and Evans' girlfriend).... In 1987 Paul Conran and I opened the Birch & Conran gallery in Dean Street and I would often go in there after work. But then, after 7pm - except for Fridays - it was dead. So I took to taking everybody up there after our openings. It was good for Ian's business and it got them out of the gallery, and after a drink I'd usually slip off to the Groucho leaving everybody there. It was after our Brit Pop Art Show that Bacon came in to look around and that's when I asked him if he'd like to have a show in Moscow, Russia. Two days later in the Colony he gave me a letter saying how much he wanted to have a show. He then took me on a pub crawl including The Toucan and several Wardour Street gay clubs, discussing the ins and outs."

Birch had a contact, Sergei Klokov, who said there were two artists they wanted to show in Moscow, firstly Andy Warhol and secondly Francis Bacon. In these pre-glasnost days dealing with Russia was difficult. Even a phone call had to be booked days beforehand. Everybody was under strict instructions and had to obey orders. Luckily Warhol had just had a show in London at the Anthony d'Offay Gallery and was so exhausted that he didn't want to fly again, so Birch flew Bacon over and the show opened at The Central House of Artists in Sept 1988. Russian writer and Colony member Zinovy Zinik interviewed Bacon on Russian radio and would go on to write the famous story about Board's death in, A Pickled Nose.

Of course the exhibition with Francis Bacon seemed easy to organise but the truth was more complex. Francis Bacon's best friend was artist Denis Worth Miller, whose boyfriend was designer Richard 'Dickie' Chopping who designed Ian Fleming's book jackets. All three had been great friends with Birch's parents when he was small. His grandmother had been a friend of Barbara Hepworth and Anne Dunn, who

RUSSIAN AND BRITISH WRITER ZINOVY ZINIK WITH POLISH WOJAS

had been married first to Michael Wishart and then to Rodrigo Moynihan. Thus Denis, Francis and Dickie used to come and look after Birch and his sister on occasions as kids, and Denis became the cosily-named Nanny Worth Millions. Although Denis and Dickie lived in coastal Essex at Wivenhoe, they had met through the two Roberts, Colquhoun and Macbryde, and formed a strong bond in the late 1940s. Francis even bought a studio and cottage in Wivenhoe, which he eventually sold/gave to Denis, but they would holiday together in the South of France, sometimes with Board and Belcher. In the 1970s Birch was at college in Aix en Provence when Chopping, Miller and Bacon paid him a visit because of the lures of the casino in town. They stayed for several days, taking Birch out to dinner much to his fellow students' amusement.

When Birch was planning the show with Bacon they would go to the Colony two or three times a week before going to one of Bacon's favourite restaurants "He had very strange taste in restaurants. His favourite was The White Tower on Charlotte Street." The White Tower had originally been La Tour de Eiffel and was owned by the famous and much loved Rudolf Stulik. It was Augustus John's favourite restaurant and where William Robert's famous portrait of The Vorticists was painted, featuring Wyndham Lewis leader. It was where successful artists and writers and socialites went to celebrate if they'd had a sell-out show, published or sold a manuscript in the 30s and 40s. It was where Dylan Thomas first seduced Caitlin and where Nina Hamnett sold her book, Naked Torso. It was replete with the glamour of pre-war Fitzrovia.

BACON'S FAVOURITE RESTAURANT

By the 1980's it was a Greek Cypriot restaurant. John Stais, restaurateur had taken it over in 1943 until 1995 and by the 1980s Stulik was long gone from Percy Street along with Charles Laughton (the Hunchback of Notre Dame) and Elsa Lanchester (the Bride of Frankenstein) - Hollywood stars who had once lived around the corner and been regulars.

Worth Miller and Bacon were great friends. In the 20 years before Bacon died they spoke daily on the telephone about philosophy, painting, literature and life, and like so many of their generation, they both loved to gamble. Still, there was a surly competitiveness to their friendship. "We were in the Colony, Francis was sitting up at the bar, Dickie, Denis and I were on a banquette," says Birch. Bacon had decided to ignore them. Denis sensed his friend's annoyance and said to James, "James, please start shouting at me," "What do you mean?" "Just say something nasty call me a name, quick and loudly." He whispered to James. "OK Denis, you're an absolute cunt!" Bacon spun about on his chair in moments and joined in with smiles of enthusiasm. "He's quite right you are a cunt, you've always been a cunt and you always will be." Everything was fine after that, I think we went out to dinner and had a jolly nice time."

Birch thought that Lucian Freud and Francis Bacon had fallen out as something to do with an unknown person called 'Chalkie White' whoever or whatever that means, but there seems to have been many occasions where Bacon was affronted. He had strong moral values, particularly loyalty, that he didn't like crossed. Birch recalls being invited to Freud's retrospective at the Hayward Gallery in 1984. "Bacon invited me out to dinner at l'Escargot and that was instead of going to the opening. He was cross and hurt at Freud for only getting in touch with him when he wanted him to verify him as an artist. Bacon refused to do things like that." In 1976 Christies sold a painting by Freud of John Pope Hennesey (Birch's cousin) for £220. Bacon was already a worldwide star selling for hundreds of thousand pounds.

"The trouble with Lucian's work is that it's realistic without being real", Bacon said and Real was what Bacon was trying to get at. Freud patronised and schmoozed the toffs of the art world and some didn't like that but some loved it. He also went after their daughters and granddaughters, and was renowned for going out to nightclubs. From the Gargoyle he graduated towards Annabel's, Regine's, the Zanzibar and later on Groucho's. The gambling joints and his debts, he was always getting wealthy friends to pay off. Strangely, once his own work started to reach high stakes he stopped gambling the fun of risk had disappeared.

Unlike Freud, Bacon was amazingly generous and helpful to all manner of people, from Muriel's hospital bills to Sonia Orwell's too, Dan Farson, and Mark Boyle and The Boyle Family, he helped in promoting their work. Nonetheless he could be deeply competitive and rude as could many other Colony members, perhaps being an Outsider necessitated it.

BACON LAUGHS AT BEING A WORLDWIDE STAR

APPLICATION FOR MEMBERSHIP   No. 401

The Secretary.
     I request you to place my name before the Committee for Election and, if elected, I agree to be bound by the Rules and Regulations in force or as altered hereafter.

Subscription _____ Date _____ 19 71

Name (BLOCK LETTERS) _____

Address _____

Nationality _____ Occupation _____

Name of Proposer _____ No. _____

Name of Seconder _____ No. _____

Signature of Candidate _____

165

Keith Allen Goes to Jail

Clubland expanded in the 1980s. Prior to the Groucho's launch in 1985, the Zanzibar in Great Queen Street, Covent Garden, was a late-night drinking bar with a glamorous allure, attracting a mixture of pop stars, actors, photographers and many crossover members from the Colony. The bar chef was Alastair Little, on cocktails was Dick Bradsell and front of house myself, author Sophie Parkin. Saturdays were usually deadly until pub closing time, as was the whole of Covent Garden, so jazz was put on, Nick Weldon (son of novelist Fay), pianist Stan Tracey or saxophonist, Lol Coxhill. Lol and Stan would also play along with Barney Bates at the Colony. On this particular Saturday the camp retro duet Biddie and Eve Ferret, were performing the number Peel Me a Grape. A group of people came in from the Comedy Store, the great new comedy venue which was in the premises of The Gargoyle Club on Meard Street, this included an inebriated Keith Allen. Not liking the attention to be on the performers, after twice being told to shut up and sit down, Allen went into the telephone area and stripped off his clothes and paraded naked between bar and tables. On management duty that night, I charged towards him. I will never forget the feeling of my fingers sinking into his doughy belly as I pushed him backwards through the mirrored doors and stood over him like a governess telling him to get dressed and leave. He spent seven weeks in jail for smashing up the Zanzibar.

Allen has said that he busted up the Zanzibar club because he didn't believe in clubs. For someone who disagreed with them, he's spent an awful lot of his life in them in Soho. With his brother Kevin, they spent many afternoons and evenings in the early 80s in the Colony Room. Later, in the 1990s, he graduated to being a regular fixture with model Kate Moss, pop stars Alex James and Damon Albarn of Blur, flitting between the Colony and The Groucho.

Soho wasn't just a destination for clubs, however. In the 1980s two places gave it a sophisticated sheen: L'Escargot in Greek Street and The Soho Brasserie on Old Compton Street where the 21 coffee bar had been. Also of note was Maison Bertaux on Greek Street, rescued by actress Michele Wade in the early 80s. Gourmands had always loved Soho's specialist food shops, but in 1985 along came chef Alastair Little providing a new kind of simple, good quality food which paved the way towards the dining category 'Modern British'. His cookbook would be written by Richard Whittington, Board's one time flatmate who insisted that Board had taught him more about food than anyone else when he threw a piece of liver at him and screamed "Keep it Simple I said".

One of Soho's new tenants was writer Irma Kurtz who loved all that Soho had to offer since her son had left home. "By the time I moved to Soho in 1986-7 I was back in the Colony. Muriel had died. Ian Board was there. It's a lonely job but they both had the ability of pulling in a mix and a bohemian bar is in the mix and communication. There might be a token junkie and there's usually a piano, but it's about the booze and the talk, the conversation being more important than the person you're having the conversation with. Names aren't important in a place like the Colony, so the frustrated or wannabes were never comfortable there."

Masturbator

Photographer Michael 'Surrealist' Woods was taken into the Colony by George Melly, with whom he was collaborating on books. "Ian asked me upon becoming a member of the Colony never to mention to Francis Bacon, about taking his picture because he didn't like all the demands," says Woods. "But I couldn't help myself, and against Ian's advice the first time I saw him in there I went and introduced

ARTIST FELIX TOPLOSKI WITH ARTIST BRUCE LACEY SHOWING AT BIRCH&CONRAN

Photo: Michael Woods

myself and asked if I might take his picture. He turned around really cross, and I could see Ian was really cross behind him and said, 'And that hasn't been done before? I've had my picture taken a thousand times how would it be any different what could you show that others haven't? What would you add?'

There was nothing to say. I went away with my tail between my legs."

"One night I had just finished doing some pictures for Private Eye and I was on my way home and I saw the light was still on upstairs at the Colony, so I went up. My camera was still hanging around my neck. Francis and Ian were alone drinking champagne and they very generously offered me a drink. Francis said, 'Take a picture of me and Ian', he said, with his arms around Board's neck posing.

I refused. 'What can I add that hasn't already been done?'

Francis thought about this for a minute before turning to me and asking

'Do you ever masturbate?'

'Yes sometimes.'

'When is that?'

'I don't know sometimes when I'm feeling anxious or nervous.'

He put his hand upon my knee and asked, 'Are you feeling tense and nervous now?' And smiled.

And then I realised, one of the greatest artists of the 20th century had just called me a wanker. And we burst out laughing and from that moment we became friends because there was no agenda, I didn't want anything from him."

It is a shame that Woods didn't take one photograph, there aren't any pictures of Francis and Ian together alone at the Colony.

In 1988, Farson came out with a book of portraits, Sacred Monsters. Most of them were denizens of the Colony from Noel Coward to Brendan Behan, Ken Tynan to film star Trevor Howard, and most likely Sir Oswald and Diana Moseley as well as Orson Welles (photographed in The French House).

In 1989 a German photographer Florian Denk wrote and produced a pamphlet to celebrate the 40th anniversary, actually the year before. Oddly inaccurate and lacking the Colony's joie de vivre, it was printed black and white and mentioned the earlier inner circle: Andrews, Auerbach, Bacon, Freud and Minton. But the real 40th anniversary memento has to be Farson's 'Soho in the Fifties', dedicated to Muriel and Ian with large photographs and tracts.

Neither Belcher or Board appear in Sacred Monsters, indicating that Farson was reluctant to over-egg the pudding. In the Introduction he describes a Sacred Monster: 'The term is one of approval... more formidable than eccentric and more rare. They are the life-enhancers though they may not enhance their own lives... Indomitable... They are larger than life and FUN. They are the Enfants Terrible that have never grown up.' This could be a description of Muriel and Ian and, as one might observe of Farson, it takes one to know one.

GEORGE MELLY AND DAN FARSON AT MURIEL'S FUNERAL

George Melly   Daniel Farson
But where is the
glass in my hand?

Farson had a talent for turning everything he did into an autobiography, and since he has such a fresh voice, he often got away with the repetition and occasional inaccuracy. As Michael Heath pointed out, 'Dan Farson was just totally breath taking. In the film City Lights by Charlie Chaplin there's a very rich man who's pissed all the time. He keeps meeting Charlie Chaplin as a tramp, buys him drinks and takes him back to his house, gives him more drinks, and in the morning wakes up and throws him out, saying that he'd never seen him in his life before. Farson was like that. Sober, he'd be: "My dear boy how lovely to see you, charming, want to have a drink, another one?" And five hours later he'd be, "I hate you, I loathe you, everything about you I am disgusted by, if ever I can do you harm I will, you're the most revolting fifth-rate cunt I've ever met, you can't draw, I don't know why you don't die."'

Will Self also wrote about Ian Board in the 80s in his book Liver and the novella within it, Foie Humain. Self says that he became a member in the late 70s, but this is more likely to be the early 80s and the membership book indicates 1999 as the year he joined along with his wife journalist Deborah Orr. He sites that the camp code Polari was the language spoken, but as publisher Anthony Blond pointed out in his autobiography Jew Made in England: 'manner, speech, and clothes were homosexual in tone and were dictated by queers'.

The 50s might have passed into the 80s but, 'my dear' and 'get you', were common use at the Colony throughout the time I was St Martin's School of Art around the corner. Ian Board abused it. Kenneth Tynan squandered it throughout the 60s and 70s, along with Anthony Blond and my father, Michael Parkin's generation throughout the 80s. It was more camp mockery than Polari, and didn't always suggest homosexuality.

Actually Blond was a professed bi-sexual. The manners and mores of this particular milieu had one side come from the legacy of the Bloomsbury Set, where 'One's feelings for people should never be cheapened by letting them be seen' as Francis Partridge mother had written to her son Burgo (author of 'A History of Orgies' pub. By Blond) in a letter quoted by Anthony Blond. On the other, was the lewd legacy of Fitzrovia. Hence the mixture of profanity and low camp.

Fifth Columnists

If post-war London was about rebuilding the country and the collective spirit, the 80s was about reinvention of self. The 60s had unravelled the old tie network to an extent, and the 80s crystallised the new order: that it was not about where you came from, but who you knew. Thus the Filofax became a fetish object. This was anathema to Colony members who relied more on bumping into people than the telephone and endless meetings. With Ian comfortably in place, when the big black telephone rang on the bar, he would primly say 'excuse me' before hollering down the phone, 'What the fuck do you want? No, the cunt's not here,' before replacing the phone and hollering to the intended recipient, 'You weren't in, were you?' Younger members howled, laughter ensued whilst older members gave a wry smile. They knew that the Colony nurtured a kind of secret language, nicknames and all.

Michael Peel, known to all as Twiggy, provides a snapshot of this interior world. 'My love affair with the club was based on my preferences for being a fifth columnist: outwardly conventional due to my professional life (I was a pedlar of large ticket computer systems in the City), but otherwise quite the opposite. I adored Ian Board, irascible old sod that he was, and provided he hadn't been on the brandy in the morning, found him most amusing. His wit and charm were, by all accounts, certainly not up to Muriel's standards but he was capable of being utterly outrageous. Many were frightened of him and he drove many away, especially those who were vain, but inside he had a heart of gold.'

Some had to dig fairly deep to find it, while others smiled and it appeared. But one thing was for sure with Board: he never changed his mind about a person once

VIV STANSHALL HAD HIS WAKE HERE

decided. Artist Milree Hughes had a room above Dino's Hairdressers in Dean Street next to Joseph Bennett, who would end up sharing the Queen Elizabeth II boat with her for the Queen's Diamond Jubilee 2012, having designed the whole flotilla. Hughes, now an artist in New York , said: 'I didn't go often, Ian Board would sit at the bar and say things like: "Francis wouldn't think that was funny, Francis is the fucking funniest man in London." One time I was in there with Neneh Cherry, on whom I had an insane crush (Neneh Cherry was a pop star and daughter of jazz giant Don Cherry). He came over and was all like, "Are you members?" We said we weren't but would like to stay for a drink. Anyway he escalated it quite rapidly and said to Neneh, "You're a fucking black bitch." I felt like I should defend her but she came back with, "And you're a miserable drunken arsehole." It came to a face off and we left. Anyway she had the edge on him. She was so fucking cool and he was always just a little creep.'

Mimi Tranin reflects that this racism could have been inspired by Board's hatred of Carmel, who stole the person he most loved away from him. Peel, however, insists it was about strength of character. 'He tried it on only once with me and became sweetness and light the moment I reacted strongly to him. For those more easily intimidated, especially those who tried to hide their weaknesses, Ian was quite exploitative. It is a truism, at least in my view, that those who Ian drove away were weak characters.'

Getting pissed in your own club, as Board relentlessly did, sometimes came with paranoia attached. At the end of the night he'd look about the club for somewhere to hide the cash he'd taken, then the next morning he'd spend hours trying to look for it.

It was a trick he'd learnt from Muriel, the streets of Soho being too dangerous to walk about with a bag full of money and no safety deposit boxes in those days. And since there was no insurance on the place, Board thought he had to outsmart the imagined burglars by ever more inventive hiding places. Occasionally he outwitted himself and the take was never found. David Edwards remembered that this system presented problems earlier on, when Carmel, Muriel and Ian were around, as whoever could find the money first, would pocket it and run off home.

There were also rules and regulations to follow not least with hygiene, and as Peel recollected, 'Westminster Council, in their infinite wisdom, did a health inspection in the early 80s. Their report covered four foolscap pages with short bullet points. One suggested that the carpet was the most disgusting thing they'd ever seen. Allan Hall, then Chairman, was heard to opine: "But we don't drink off the fucking carpet, love." Nonetheless a revamp took place, done by John Payne who always did the club redecoration, and a new carpet laid, which was promptly christened by Francis dowsing it liberally with champagne.' Thus it regained its original stickiness once more.

Its rudeness continued. As Brian Patten, the Liverpool poet wrote to me in 2011, 'I only went to the Colony three or four times in the 80s. The romance of the place passed me by. Felt it was a bit like standing in a small urinal full of fractious old geezers bitching about each other.' Like Will Self, he didn't take to the sticky carpet. It was left to standard bearers like Peel to feel the magic. "At first, I was very content to be more of a voyeur than a contributor, feeling the need to 'learn the ropes' so to speak," says Peel. "One was conscious of the fact that was often in the presence of masters – not just Francis

MIKE MCKENZIE ON PIANO

Bacon but others like Jeff Bernard, George Melly, Molly Parkin, Tom Baker and so many more, often irrespective of fame or fortune. People like Mick Tobin aka Admiral Nelson, a former pugilist who sold the Evening Standard outside the US Embassy, Christopher Howse, a Daily Telegraph obituary writer (obit writers seemed to be drawn to the place perhaps it was the smell of death), Jenny Mortimer, Marsh Dunbar, Barney Bates - literally bashing the hell out of the piano; all evoke very fond memories. So many more memories have been long lost in mists of an alcohol-induced haze.'

Musical Chairs

Barney Bates was a brilliant musician, as George Melly wrote in Punch Magazine of July, 1980: 'Tall, fetchingly nervous, his face with its drooping moustache and curiously formalised haircut resembling the Victorian concept of a noble Arthurian king. Barney has won us all. Nothing he says is ever stupid much is extremely sharp. His opinions on everything, art, jazz, people, is unshrill but definitive, his piano playing imaginative and at times, transcendent.'

Nonetheless, Melly felt it necessary to mention Bates' uncompromising drinking habits. 'His dangerous aspect is that he has an unequivocal passion for alcohol without it having, in his case any apparent effect. At the sight of a bar or bottle his nose and eyes freeze like a pointer, his long sensitive fingers, strike like a cobra. In his presence grog assumes an immense glamour. It glows like the Holy Grail. Only too easily John (Chilton) and I found ourselves part of his Bacchus-like entourage, vine leaves in our hair, our lips wet with the juice of the grape, the hop, the malt, and anything else which can be persuaded to ferment. Yes Barney, despite a faint tendency to vagueness as to what exactly took place in the small hours, emerged at dawn clear of skin, bright of eye and pink of tongue to confront with polite surprise John and me groaning with remorse and as malformed as creatures from the darker reaches of Hieronymus Bosch….We felt we were back in those early days in the band's history when sobriety played little part in our lives and amnesia was our nightly companion.

Dear Barney we don't want to lose you, but perhaps, it's as well you want to go.'

When the gifted Bates played the old Colony upright, he turned the place into the Vanguard in New York. Barney went on to play regularly in the Colony and the Chelsea Arts club in exchange for a room and food. He died drunk in charge of a bicycle, freewheeling across Chelsea one night in the 1990s.

Cunt Struck

The Colony was always about escape. In 1961 Colin MacInnes was the first person to write about and capture the Tardis effect of the place on an afternoon where the blinds would be pulled down against the sun, but it was equally true on rainy days and Mondays too. Twiggy appreciated the Magic Circle disappearing act of the place, 'to escape and for no-one to know where you were.' Twiggy thought himself, 'lucky enough to be the only witness with Ian, to an exchange between Bacon and Bernard one afternoon.

FB: "You know your problem Jeffrey?"

JB: "No Francis."

FB: "You're not gay Jeffrey."

JB: "No Francis"

FB: "Pity..."

JB: "Why's that Francis?"

FB: "Well if you'd been gay, you'd have been a super-star by now."

JB: "I know Francis, the problem is I was cunt struck at the age of 12."

Very occasionally I would take chums there but only after a thorough briefing, endeavouring to explain that, while everyone might seem very camp and therefore gay and, despite the obvious sexuality of Ida, that it was not a gay club – simply that no-one gave one iota. I took a young American colleague one Saturday afternoon after a fairly liquid lunch, having briefed him on the way. He responded by saying: "We have clubs like that in San Francisco."

"No, I don't think you do", I responded. We walked in, his jaw dropped and he

GEORGE MELLY FAMOUS FOR HIS LOUD SUITS

Photo: Michael Woods

never said a word for the entire three hours we were there. Peter Langan was lying on the floor (trying as usual to put his head up women's skirts) kicking his feet in the air in his dirty white suit with 'follow through stains'; your mother Molly was by the fireplace being fondled by what looked like a 17-year old black boxer, George Melly and a transvestite clarinettist were jamming away. Saturday afternoon at the Colony Room's best. Indeed, one of Michael Wojas' first acts of vandalism was to shut the Club on Saturday afternoons, thereby removing at one fell swoop the last vestige of a reason to be in Soho at weekends. My young American chum was still speechless on the aeroplane to Boston the next day.'

Peter Langan was the owner of celebrity restaurants, notably Langan's Brasserie in Mayfair with Michael Caine, the actor. He was a charismatic Irishman and a brilliant businessman who collected Bacon, Freud, Hockney and Patrick Proctor paintings for his walls. Both Chris Corbin and Jeremy King, owners of The Wolsey started there as Maitre'd's, as did Liam Carson who became general manager of The Groucho when it opened in 1985 and would tragically be found dead in the doorway of a hostel for the homeless in 2005 after a downhill battle with drugs at just 51. Langan came to a painful end when, in a fight with his wife, he set light to the house in Essex where they lived and died aged 47. It is believed that drink might have been involved.

Twiggy recounted another anecdote. 'I cannot move on from Francis without retelling a story. We were pissed upstairs one evening and Francis turned to me, as he sometimes did, and said: "Come on Twiggy, let's go and have some fish and chips." By this time, Francis' idea of fish and chips was caviar and lobster at 'Cockroach Wheeler's' (as it was known in Soho) in Old Compton Street, although it was no longer the place it had been 30 years previously. During dinner, I decided that I wasn't going to be Francis' catamite that night and announced that I would pay for dinner. Francis was slightly taken aback, as he was so used to people sponging from him the whole time. He then said to me: "OK Twiggy, and by the way I've sent you an invitation to the opening night of my retrospective at the Tate (it was in 1985)."

"I know Francis, thank you. I got it this morning," I replied. "Well are you coming?"

"No probably not, Francis," I said.

"Why won't you come? Twiggy, there'll be lots of free champagne..."

We slightly went around the houses on this for a few minutes as he queried me as to why I said I wouldn't go. Eventually I could duck it no longer and said: "Well the problem is Francis, I don't really like your paintings."

"That's quite alright dear boy, neither do I, neither do I" was his immortal response. Of course the truth was I had never seen a Bacon painting, only prints and photographs. I did go and there was lots of free champagne but, more importantly, I saw Bacon's painting for the first time and was quite literally gob-smacked and have remained a huge fan ever since. I even went to his studio in Reece Mews on a couple of occasions.'

The end of the 80s saw a remarkable celebration of the Soho world the play Jeffrey Bernard is Unwell, written By Keith Waterhouse from Bernard's weekly Spectator columns and starring Peter O'Toole. This was a triumph for Soho, a celebration of everything that the Colony stood for. Directed by member Ned Sherrin, who quickly fell out of love with both Board and Bacon.

Twiggy recalled the first night: 'There are four bit players, who have atmospheric parts; one of whom depicted Francis and was dressed in a painter's smock and a beret. Francis, sitting in the centre of the dress circle, was so angry he rose up and brought the entire play to a halt. "I don't paint in a fucking beret you cunts, I paint in a Savile Row suit," he shouted and stormed out. Sherrin's retort was that this was a pity because it was only the second play Bacon had ever seen, 'The first being Cats.'

Two days later Jeffrey Bernard was celebrating himself: firstly by trying to set his trousers alight by putting a lit fag into his pocket - easily done - and secondly, with the publishing of Jay Landesman's collection of his and Taki's columns at the Spectator in book form as Low Life and High Life. With his peculiar charm he told an interviewer that as a columnist you knew when you were having a bad day – "When your typewriter was full of last night's curry" - and by describing why Soho was still the place to be. "The pubs have been taken over by arseholes in the blue denim-suited brigade making advertising films. Despite the dirty bookshops Soho is more furtive than it was. But the liberal brigade has taken over Hampstead, and Chelsea's finished. There's nowhere else to go." And so he kept going into the Colony to argue with Board and chatter with Bacon. Sometimes Board would throw him out. On one occasion before his legs were amputated and he couldn't get a wheelchair up the stairs, Bernard was thrown down the stairs but came back with a ladder outside to climb through the front window. Board however was waiting for him with a boiling kettle and a screech: 'I'll bloody well push you off if you don't fuck off.'

Bacon would also be celebrating before the end of the decade with his triumphant show that Birch had put on in Moscow in 1988, then another in Washington in 1989,

LIZ MCKENZIE, KEITH WATERHOUSE AND PETER
O'TOOLE TROUSERS DOWN IN CELEBRATION

PETER O'TOOLE AND IAN BOARD

LEFT TO RIGHT: PETER O'TOOLE,
JEFFREY BERNARD, KEITH WATERHOUSE

Photos: Courtesy of Darren Coffield

cementing the end of the Cold War with Bacon's series of 'screaming Popes'. But without doubt the most important exhibition of the decade for the Colony Room Club was Michael Parkin's, Artists of The Colony Room in Belgravia where he gathered together work from all the major artists of Muriel's day, including Edward Burra (introduced by George Melly in the 1970s when Burra was living in Hastings, where he died in 1976), Auerbach, Barry Driscoll, Keith Vaughan, John Craxton, John Minton, Colquhoun and MacBryde, Buhler and Aitchinson, Bacon, Wirth Miller and Freud, Rodrigo Moynihan and both his wives, Anne Dunn and Elinor Bellingham Smith. It went right back to the early days of Nina Hamnett and Augustus John and forward to the days of Peter Blake, Michael Clark, Martin Fuller and Eduardo Paolozzi. Karl Weshke represents the Cornish contingent but there could have been Terry Frost and Roger Hilton. It is noticeably low on female artists, with neither

Paula Rego, Sheila Fell or Sandra Blow but at least it had Hubert Dalwood's ashtray, and a painting by John Deakin. The opening party was magnificent and Board was dressed like a true reigning queen with only Farson trying to steal his thunder, and the Sri Lankan poet Tambimuttu observing it all from the corner as if it was the 50s again. The 80s might have changed the culture of Soho, but it saw a steep rise in the documentation of the cultural landscape of the area and the Colony – and gave a sense of how important and legion were all the artists with 'Sohoitis'.

ARTISTS OF THE COLONY ROOM EXHIBITION AT PARKIN FINE ART 1982

MICHAEL PARKIN, MICHAEL CLARK, CLAIRE SHENSTONE

CHRISSIE & ARTIST PETER BLAKE

TAMBIMUTTU, JEFFREY BERNARD

DAN FARSON, MICHAEL PARKIN

MOLLY PARKIN, DICK BRADSELL, JOHN MAKEPEACE

Chapter 6

The Naughty 90s

Yearly Membership
1990   £50 - £100

Save the Colony **The Ruling Queen** The New Old French
Death of Francis and Isabel Who Took Who at the Beginning
Board to Death **The Trouble with Wills**
Inheritance Tracks **Half a Century** Love is the Devil
Room of Fairy Tales

The 1990s was a decisive decade. Thatcher was de-throned, John Major took over and Lucian Freud accepted his Order of Merit from the Queen. Francis Bacon was heard to comment, 'How very common'. Many Colony-goers rejected them, including LS Lowry to Graham Greene, Eileen Agar, Henri Moore and Trevor Howard. Economically Britain was volatile while crime, unemployment and the first Gulf War in Iraq decreased the sense of security.

In the clubs meanwhile, there was a different energy. Cocaine had become increasingly prevalent but Ecstasy was ushering in a new consciousness, of sorts. Then there was the 'ladette' culture – women getting as pissed as men. This had been happening for decades at the Colony, gender being no excuse for remaining sober.

Ian Board had more than just his pension to worry about, courtesy of Westminster Council. The landlord, Mr Ibrahim made an application for change of use. He wanted 41 Dean Street as offices, and wanted the Colony out. It was around this time that Mr Ibrahim foolishly decided to visit a not entirely sober Board at his premises. Faced with the possibility of closure, Ian physically and verbally attacked the landlord. As Ibrahim was reported as saying in the Evening Standard, 'I cannot go into the club without Ian being rude. Why should I stand it? They are drunk and rude, his members, and many are homosexual. I have the right to use the building for what I want.'

Thus the decision was to be made by Westminster Planning sub-committee on the 3rd February 1991. Ian Board and Michael Wojas started to galvanise the troops with a petition of the great and good members, such as novelist Beryl Bainbridge, Frank Auerbach, Francis Bacon, George Melly and Lisa Stansfield, and by sending it out as a press release. The Evening Standard's Londoner's Diary was always easy to gain coverage as so many journalists drank at the bar and could tip the section.

In charge of press was member Pam Hardyment, who pleaded: 'Fight the planning application in order to save a little bit of the heart of Soho'. Board was quoted as saying: "I was onto Lord Stuart of Findhorn and will be contacting George Melly. We've despatched someone to stay with Lord Montagu (Pitt Rivers' and Wildeblood's friend) for the weekend to bend his ear. We are not going to lose this club just because some c*** wants to turn us into offices." It was reported in The Times Diary that Board was not only fighting with his huge petition of well-to-do Colony members, but also with the might of its neighbours The Groucho Club and The Soho Society. English Heritage was also sympathetic. How times would change.

Artist and member Darren Coffield, who was introduced by the late curator Joshua Compston (of Factual Nonsense fame) remembers the episode well: "Bacon offered to buy the leasehold so that the club would always be safe. He didn't care how much it cost as he didn't care about money. I don't know why Ian didn't accept it as it would have made the club safe."

David Edwards told me that Bacon offered to buy the Colony for his brother John, Bacon's great friend, so that he would have something to do. "But John told Bacon that he was much happier doing nothing in life and since all Bacon wanted was for John to be happy, he left it." Also, while Bacon undoubtedly picked up the tab for Muriel, he was less predisposed towards Ian Board.

The club was saved, without much ceremony. "When the planning committee came through and it was overturned everybody was very happy and I suppose Ian just thought it wasn't necessary," says Coffield. 'The club was saved, that was it." Yet much of this was due to Michael Wojas' sober organisation and application.

Winning the day; Ian & Michael Celebrate saving the colony with it's members

Photo: Catherine Shakespeare Lane

183

The Ruling Queen

As the 90's began, Board had become rather imperious, leaving much to Wojas, who seemed to be getting the hang of it after 8 years. It was clear to the newish members what was happening, as Coffield recalled. "Ian wasn't very good with money running the place like a museum he wouldn't let any new members join at the end. Ian seconded me as a member which was quite unusual. Joshua and I went there in 1989 on our 18th birthday. It was a strange place to drink, as no-one in there was under the age of 30." He reminisced. "The first nights of going up there I remember Board talking to me about Molly Parkin who was quite a mythical figure: "I hope she hasn't discovered God like they all do when they give up the booze." Everybody was asking, where's Molly?" (Molly Parkin gave up drinking in 1987 prior to her first grandchild Paris' birth and went into recovery, and yes, did rediscover God, to some relief and others disbelief.)

Like Parkin, performer and writer Bob Kingdom, also gave up at the end of the 1980s and remembered the lows and highs of Ian Board's behaviour. 'Not long before he died, I saw Ian Board walking up Dean Street towards me. "Hi, Ian," I said. His brandy nose throbbed as he said: "I heard you stopped drinking." I had to admit it. "Yes," I said. "Cunt," came the response. He walked on.' But when Kingdom and Parkin had been drinking the story was very different. As he recalled,

'One Saturday afternoon in the early 80s, with Molly Parkin, I'd done a matinee at a pub theatre in Hampstead. Molly suggested we call in at the club, "It'll be quiet, if it's open." It was, with just three people standing at the bar: Lucian Freud, Francis Bacon and John Edwards, with Ian behind it. "Oh, it's Miss Parkin and Dame Edith," welcomed Ian. This was sweet, no audience, no showing off, no put-down. Each was allowed a moment in rotation, no one hogging the lime-light. Is that shaft of afternoon sun shining upon us part of a fantasy? No. Ask Moll.'

The ruling queen and favourite of Board's, after Molly Parkin's drinking career stopped, was Rochdale chanteuse Lisa Stansfield, who came with her husband Ian Devaney. They had stormed the music world, sold over five million records by the early 1990s and won bucket-loads of awards. Still they were young, beautiful, talented and millionaires who not only adored Board but would become pivotal in the club's final year. After their first meeting, when Ian asked who the fuck she was, Stansfield replied, "I'm just a little pixie", when to the rest of the world she was an international superstar. Board was bewitched, they became friends and he would go and stay with her family in Rochdale, outraging and charming them equally.

Farson also told a tale of Board's inimitable guest behaviour. He was visiting Exeter where his brother, improbably, was Mayor. They stopped in at Farson's local pub where a couple of old farmers sat silently in the corner. Board had family with him, depositing his wallet on the bar as he instructed the landlord, "Here's my bead bag Miss, doubles all round and buy those lovely gels in the corner a drink too." Farson was warned never to bring Board there again, but the farmers loved him.

Board hadn't always been so flamboyant a character indeed, he was noted as being 'abstemious and efficient' by composer Malcolm Williamson (Master of the Queens Musick) who in the late 1950s was the club's pianist, tinkling out Gershwin, Cole Porter and Rogers. Williamson reflected on Muriel and Ian's 'deep and infrangible friendship, reflecting credit on them both. I feel that Soho of these days, when the Colony Club drew countless people of the arts into an extended family, by no means all heavy drinkers. Ian's faithful unswerving, moderating affection for Muriel and her now vanished world, deserves a salute.' Board never read this in The Times, sadly, as it was part of his obituary.

Affection over Board, Ian and his pixie Lisa

Photo: Catherine Shakespeare Lane

Left to Right: Farson, Board, Botham & Pam Hardyment behind

Gaston Retires. A last drink with Wendy Richards and John Payne

The New Old French

Another important member of both Colony and the wider Soho neighbourhood was journalist and author Noel Botham who, with his fiancé Leslie Lewis, a one-time exotic snake dancer and bar manager, took over The French House in 1989 when Gaston Berlemont retired aged 75. Berlemont's departure was a great loss to the area and many thought that under new ownership, without his paternal eye, it wouldn't survive.

As Leslie Lewis said recently, while Board might have had a foul mouth, he offered a sympathetic ear at this difficult time. "Noel was great friends of Muriel. She collected her 'young men' and he was a young journalist in Fleet Street when he first went. I never met her, though, and went to the Colony for the first time in 1989. Ian Board took me to one side and said, "I have to call you a cunt in public, you understand..." But he was always nice to me and I always liked Ian."

"I was offered The French by the brewery. I'd been at Peppermint Park (an American-themed cocktail bar on St Martin's Lane). The site of the French Pub was about to be condemned by the council. The place had bomb damage from the war and it hadn't ever been properly fixed. Noel and I went in halves with Gaston, but Gaston was 75 and wanted to retire. We spent £200,000 doing it up to look as it used to, but when we opened most people were really horrible. Gaston, I think, wanted us to fail. It's very hard for the person who's built something up to think of themselves as replaceable. So I'd go up to see Ian Board in the afternoons and he was the only person to be really sympathetic. We used to talk properly and he was always kind to me."

In return Leslie was kind to the Colony, and a cordial relationship grew so that when the ice machine broke or the essential champagne had run out, they helped each other out. Meanwhile, the regulars from the French decamped for the time being to Norman Balon's pub The Coach and Horses, partly inspired by its new popularity after Keith Waterhouse's successful play, 'Jeffrey Bernard Is Unwell'. Everybody wanted to try the 50p cheese sandwiches and Norman's scathing looks for themselves.

Fortunately, the revived French was helped by a new source. "I think Ian must have a word with Francis (Bacon) who was giving us a wide berth," says Leslie Lewis. "One day Francis started to come in, then he started to come in everyday for a pre-lunch bottle of champagne and the word got round. He'd always order a bottle of champagne and he'd always pay with a £50 note. It saved the business." Bacon's energy was a natural attraction, and the £50 notes gave the pub an air of prosperity that was sorely lacking.

Although getting older, Bacon was still going to the Colony, and writing letters of apology to Wojas for drunkenness in the early 90s.

Gaston & Norman The Soho Publicans

Dear Michael,

I am so sorry about the other night but thank you so much for getting me home. I must be mad at my age to get so drunk. I would like to get you a present but do not know what to get. Do please get something with the enclosed. Thank you again for all you did for me.

Yours

Francis.

He enclosed a £50 note.

Death of Francis and Isabel

In April 1992, Francis Bacon died. "We got married the day before Francis died and Noel and I went our honeymoon to Spain," Says Lewis. "Nobody went to Francis' funeral, but we sent a wreath of yellow roses saying, 'Love from the French House' and dispatched a photographer friend of Noel's to take it there. Bacon always said he didn't want a funeral, but he was buried in Madrid and a picture was on the front page of the Times with the wreath. He was in love with a young Madrid man, from a good family." Whatever Bacon's romantic arrangements, John Edwards was left the bulk of The Francis Bacon Estate and went to live first in Miami and then Thailand.

Typically brusque, Ian Board was quoted in The Telegraph of 1 May, 1992: "I hope they are not going to make a bloody awful fuss over the funeral. He used to

Daniel Farson shows the picture of a dead Bacon in his coffin

say, 'When I'm dead, put me in a plastic bag and throw me in the gutter.' Bacon's idea of religious ritual was to dispense with the usual and employ an unorthodox use of an alter candle."

Despite Bacon being 82, it was still a shock when he died. Everyone respected his wishes, and as cartoonist Michael Heath said: 'Francis had an enormous power over everybody, he was so successful, and he had this aura, but he was still there among us, and prepared to get drunk with us, and we all kowtowed. We all thought he was a man of huge talent, and he was. You can't knock his stuff you can't knock Charlie Parker, unless you're an idiot. They've done it, and laid it down.'

Bacon and Board might not have been bedfellows although they did holiday together. 'Francis Bacon, Muriel Belcher and I used to go to the South of France. That was before English peasants invented the package tour.' Still, Board found a lot to miss with Bacon's passing, and there was some mutual affection. When art curator James Birch organised

Wojas & Christies Man with Francis Bacon's Portrait of Muriel

an exhibition of Bacon's work in Moscow, an idea developed in the Colony. Bacon arranged a signed photo of President Gorbachev conducting an orchestra, inscribed 'To Dear Ian from Mischa.' But then Bacon was always generous. Three months before Bacon's death, his muse and Muriel's great friend, Isabel Rawsthorne, née Lambert, had died aged 80. She had lived a life full of art: as a painter and set designer herself, and also as a muse to powerful and charismatic men. In the 30s she was sculpted by Jacob Epstein and Giacometti, in Paris she was painted by Derain and Picasso.

One might assume she helped cement the relationship between Bacon and Giacometti who visited the Colony with him several times before he died, though Freud liked to lay claim to it. Isabel was in her 50s when Bacon asked Deakin to photograph her for his paintings. Her husbands were both composers Constant and then Alan Rawsthorne, when Rawsthorne died, she set up a trust to continue to promote his work.

The Colony gang plays away at Hirsts in Devon with Wojas, Maia Norman & Joe Strummer

Photo: Pascal Latra

While Ian Board was still perched like a parrot with a purple beak, in the early years of the 1990s, a new breed of young members, started appearing: not just Darren Coffield and Joshua Compston. Much of this renewed interest was to do with James Birch's gallery, which had been next door but one to the Colony until 1990, when spiralling Soho rents made it impossible to sustain.

Birch first met Damian Hirst at Anthony d'Offay's gallery. "He was a chippy (a carpenter and technician) and blagged along with me to the Colony," he says. "It was the first time Hirst had been there. And in his turn he bought everybody else to the Colony, the roll call of YBAs."

As Birch puts it, "As his (Hirsts) fame progressed, he definitely became nicer." Artist Paul Fryer recalls some typically lairy moments in the club. "The first time I went there was with Damien in 1992," he said. "Ian Board was there, quite animated, saying 'Who the fuck is this cunt, what the fuck are you doing in here?' from his stool. 'Fuck me you're rude', I said. Ian laughed and said, 'Get that man a drink'. I suppose when something like that happens you know you're in the right kind of place. I lived in Leeds so whenever I was coming up from London, that was where I'd go."

Darren Coffield maintains that 'Most of the YBA's didn't start going there until after the 50th anniversary exhibition in 1998, although Tracey (Emin) was going there the year before. They were quite late.' But as Emin wrote to me: 'I went in there with Joshua Compston in 1993. I thought everyone swore a lot. With Ian I was super-impressed by his nose and how much he swore, in fact I was quite shocked. But Michael was my friend and after a few years of me just rolling up at the Colony Room, one night when I was absolutely paralytic he got me to sign the form to become a member which he had actually already filled in on my behalf. I'm really good friends with Hamish McAlpine (film producer and art collector) and it was a regular haunt of his and more and more artists of my generation started going there. But the most important thing about the Colony Room is that it stayed open all afternoon.'

It seems obvious why Coffield and his Slade counterparts enjoyed the place so much. His afternoons were spent between "the Slade, the Colony and passing out at the National Gallery lectures while standing up. People like Bruce McLean, tutors at the Slade, wouldn't drink at the Colony. 'How come the man with the big red nose didn't throw you out or abuse you?' they'd ask. It gave us kudos, but there was a thin line between being witty and really abusive with Ian."

Board's wit or otherwise was often questioned. Favourite Boardisms included: "Shut your cake-hole you dreary boring fart," and "Have you looked at yourself in the mirror, you should put a bag over that face". But then how could he compete with Muriel and her Mu'isms? Ken Thompson recalled taking a new assistant, a nice girl Annabella Courage into the club. "Close the door," Muriel screeched. "That winds going right up my cunt." "I'm so terribly sorry", said Miss Courage closing the door.

Board to Death

Ian Board, surrounded by old friends going sober on him, occasionally tried to give up, swapping vodka for orange juice. It wasn't good for his moods, and his doctor told him to stop as the citric acid was destroying his stomach lining. "It was literally driving him mad being in a room full of people drinking and getting drunk," said Coffield.

Board was certainly venomous as in the story of when a man asked for some peanuts at the bar on a busy afternoon. "Peanuts? Peanuts! You boring dreary little cunt, this is the Colony Room not London fucking zoo."

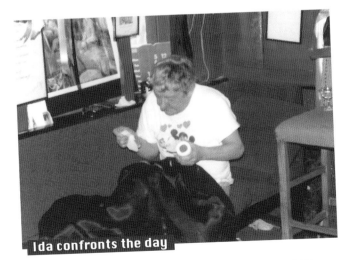

Ida confronts the day

But he could also be courageous, said Richard Whittington, 'At closing time the well rehearsed shout, "My names Ian David Archibald Ian fucking Board, and I'm bored stiff with the sight of the lot of you, so fuck off!" Ian was as brave as he could be nasty.'

Darren Coffield tells the story of the gangster 'baby-faced' Scarlotti. "This bloke Scarlotti appeared and asked for protection money. Well, Ian and Muriel had been asked for protection by The Krays, it was said, and didn't give into them, so Ian wasn't about to now. He came up and pulled a knife on Ian, who picked up a bar stool and was fending him off. The police were called and six months later they went to court and this very well-heeled barrister we called Gleneagles because he liked Scotch (Gleneagles = legal eagles) cross-examined him in court. 'Mister Scarlotti you're well known in the East End aren't you?' ' Yes.' ' Would you call yourself a violent man?' 'No, but in the East End I'm known as baby-faced Scarlotti."

Some might have said Board was close to the edge but perhaps he was just trying to uphold Muriel's morals. As Frank Auerbach wrote to me, 'I was aware of Muriel Belcher's moral stature, her courage, her instinctive assessment of people... against the self-righteous and self-protective, the smug and pretentious'. Ian upheld Muriel's strange beliefs by retaining the Mezuzah in a box above the doorway to the club as a protective talisman. Considering neither of them were Jewish this was a little odd.

Even in 1994 Board was spitting acid at the Council, which tried to impose a proposed fire lobby. 'Dear Mr Sporle... I oppose the proposal in the strongest terms.' It didn't go ahead. Board also had had to fight in 1993 to keep the colour of the door green and different from its neighbours Zilli's. "He wouldn't get rid of that green," Signor Zilli told me with dismay in 2012. Westminster Council had set upon homogenising Soho, an area so wicked in the 1960s it gave people a frisson of excitement.By the 90s Board acknowledged little outside the club. As he was quoted in the Observer he believed–"This is the most royal residence in London (Buckingham Palace... Betty's prize souvenirs, sod that!) This is the holiday of holidays."

In April 1993, there was an incident over a mobile telephone. Board hated mobiles and considered there no need to use them, as the Colony had a pay phone. He grabbed the offending mobile from a dubious looking man and threw it across the room. The man turned violent, threatened Hamish McAlpine, took out a knife and threatened Ian. Michael Wojas cut the cord of Ian's phone on the bar and tried to garrotte him with it. McAlpine said, "I whispered to my girlfriend Emma Harrison, "Call the police" They arrived just in time, as I thought we were going to be killed." Board always created high drama when fearless with drink.

Writer and Colony member Pam Hardyment said that Board provided an almost parental role. "Ian David Archibald Board was a bit like a mother to me but then I didn't have a mother so I didn't know what they should be like." She said. " I was in Greece to dry out, get off the booze and run a restaurant for six months and I said to Ian, because the Colony was my second home: 'Whatever you do, please be here when I come back, when I've grown a new liver. Then he was gone. Sandy (Fawkes, journalist) sent me a postcard and at the end tagged on, 'and by the way Ian Board has died.' I couldn't believe it."

Board went into hospital with a pain, but everyone expected him back, even if it was with breathing apparatus attached. He never returned. A kind David Edwards, bought him a bottle of vodka to ease the pain and bring a party atmosphere to the ward and he died of lung cancer on June 26th 1994 on what would have been Muriel's 94th birthday. Just like Muriel and Bacon, Ian didn't believe in

Young Fearless Hamish McAlpine of Tartan Films

Melly and Farson enjoy Board's Funeral summer '94

an afterlife. "When you're dead you're dead", he would say. He was just 63 but looked ten years older. Russian writer Zinovy Zinik, wrote in a short story A Pickled Nose, how Ian's fabled huge proboscis had miraculously shrunk back into his face on death. Hard to imagine, but look of the photos of Board as a handsome young man. The Colony had not been good for his health.

More obituaries were written about Ian Board than any other club owner, each one of them mentioning his WC Fields-like protuberance of a nose. His funeral was front page news on The Evening Standard West End Extra: 'Soho says Goodbye'. The Times, The Telegraph and The Independent and the Guardian also carried obituaries. Strangely, Muriel Belcher only got two: one anonymous write-up in The Times and a salute by Elizabeth Smart in House and Garden. And while Muriel's December funeral had been cold, Board's was full of June warmth. It peaked with Lisa Stansfield singing 'Bring On The Clowns' and 'They Can't Take That Away From Me,' accompanied by the amazing jazz pianist Michael McKenzie who had played at the Colony before moving up to the Savoy. He had played the same at Muriel's funeral 15 years before.

Long time members George Melly, Peter Fawcett (a businessman known as Peter Foreskin) and editor from the Sunday Times, Allan Hall each read out the address at Golders Green on 4 July 1994. Hall highlighted Board's addiction to the use of sustained invective upon the vulnerable, his love of saying 'hypocritical bollocks' and a belief in never saying anything behind your back: 'He would wait until you came in and hurl the whole vile book straight into your face.'

And with weary inevitability, Board made either a mess of his will, or like Muriel, had mischievously set the cat among the pigeons. Michael and Susan Clark, who had been so kind to Muriel on her deathbed and indeed to Board after she had died, were left his money and belongings including the insurance meant for his retirement. The club was left to Michael Wojas - although there is reason to believe that he might have said different things to different people because of the amount of disgruntled annoyance when the will was read and sides were taken between Wojas and Michael Clark. But as food writer Richard Whittington who had shared Board's flat through the 1970s along with Thursday the cat, pointed out: 'Like Muriel, Ian got almost all his calories from alcohol'. Apart from the occasional salt beef on rye with horseradish and English mustard from Phil Rabin's or The Nosh Bar on Great Windmill Street, and drinking on an empty stomach can often lead to false promises and strange happenings. Did Michael Wojas ever get back the money he had lent Board to pay off Carmel 'the Fox', or was it used as his payment to keep the club? Some Colony facts are impossible to ascertain.

Barney Bates, Ray Natkiel and Angus Forbes

Craigie Aitchinson

Dan Farson, Irma Kurtz, Eddi McPherson

Liz and Mike McKensie with Keith Waterhouse

Michael Clark had painted many pictures of Bacon but he had also painted Muriel on her deathbed. Board had been a frequent visitor at the Clark's family home, and some people have said that Board was a little in love with Clark. However there is no doubt that he was immensely fond in a fatherly way towards Wojas, who he felt he had rescued, the fact that Wojas felt the same way about Board reciprocated the emotion.

"Michael Wojas phoned me up," says Darren Coffield. "He had to go and clean out Ian's stuff and would I help him? Michael Wojas said Michael Clark was going to be there and there might be a confrontation. All the personal stuff Michael wanted of Ian's, he never got. Ian was meant to come out of hospital but he died quickly. Wojas said he started getting letters from Clark's lawyer and I think his attitude was, if you want it come and get it. Clark had stopped drinking so he didn't." A year later in June 1995, Wojas had a letter from Michael Clark to David Gentle, Board and the Colony's Solicitor asking what was happening with dividing up the estate left in Wojas care and 'the matter of a tax rebate owed to Ian's estate.' Wojas wrote over the letter 'Tax rebate due £33.28. £8.32 each to Clark and Susan,' and filed the letter.

By August 1995 Wojas must have been wondering if fighting over the club and running the Colony was worth it. Pubs were no longer required to close in the afternoon, and thus the raison d' être of the afternoon drinking club vanished overnight. Oddly, it seemed to have the opposite effect. Though many clubs in the area did close then, when suddenly people were able to drink anywhere, it drove them into wanting a more select atmosphere. Clubs started to boom, from old fashioned Gentleman's clubs to snooker clubs, to Soho House (which opened in 1995), Gerry's and Groucho's. There was lineage in this boom. Orlando Campbell, who started running fashionable clubs, first the Globe then Green Street had a father, Charlie Campbell, who had been maitre'd of The Neal Street Restaurant. As Darren Coffield recalls: "Orlando first opened the Globe and the lead guitarist of Pink Floyd (David Gilmour who married Polly Sampson the mother of Heathcote Williams son) came in and looked around and said, 'Nothing's changed'. It hadn't. Orlando had taken it over and just bought a few new tea towels. We all played chess with Bjork who wasn't very famous back then."

The old guard noticed, as Coffield points out. "Green Street was the place to go. Ian (Board) was quite nasty at first, but secretly he quite liked what Orlando was doing and had a soft spot for him. So when Orlando lost everything with Green Street, he let him regularly sleep on the banquettes at the Colony."

A previous generation was connecting with a new generation. Orlando Campbell, one of the celebrity barmen with Liam Carson of the Groucho Club and previously of Langan's. Campbell began the Westbourne Hotel after Green Street and bought artists in. "We all had exhibitions there and because every room was themed I had a room, Tracey Emin had a room, I think there was a Damien Hirst room," says Coffield. "He got us all to sign contracts in case it all went wrong, which it did, so we all got our work back. And Wojas and Board loved Orlando Campbell," said Coffield.

'Every now and again I would take Ian out to eat and sometimes took him to my Dad's house for Sunday lunch.' Campbell wrote and told me from France where he now lives. 'He (Board) would actually eat and was immensely polite. He'd reminisce about the old days with Dad who had discovered the Colony aged 18: in fact, they bored me so much I would threaten my father with leaving him there. I was quickly given £20 and told to get a cab (to take Board away). Ian never came to the Globe as it was too far and too late, and Ladbroke Grove was a no go area for him.'

'He did come to a place Fergus Henderson, Piers Thompson and I had at 17 Mercer Street in Covent Garden, because Muriel had lived close by,' says Campbell. 'He knew his limitations and came at lunchtime because he was back at 3pm to open the Colony so he was safe. Ian was a bit apprehensive about Green Street, especially when I told him I had painted the bar the same colour as the Colony, as a homage. Eventually he made it at lunchtime with Michael and was very meek and courteous, a fish out of water. Lots of 'thank-you's' and large tips for the waiting staff, and he even managed to gob in his hanky rather than in a glass and offering up the phlegm result as an oyster, an Ian treat. In France I buy six every Sunday and think of Ian.'

Some of the newer Colony adherents were not driven by the Colony's legend, but by the fun that could be had there. Artist Abigail Lane, who started going to the Colony in the 90s after Sarah Lucas had started working there, loved the club but for Michael Wojas, not for what it had represented in bygone days. "I remember meeting Michael and going there with Tracey (Emin), being there after hours, having a laugh, the usual American Pie being sung. Michael and I absolutely clicked just like that and I became a lifelong member, and the first example of couples behind the bar: Michael and I cooked that up together. I was living with Paul Fryer. We were at our wildest and I just met Vanessa (Fristedt, Swedish Blonde designer) after Joshua died (in 1996 aged 26 from an overdose of ether). Damien (Hirst) and Keith Allen were already going there. I already had an imaginary idea about the Colony that it looked like the 1950s picture, with bamboo and plants, though it didn't. I thought it would be a bit more swish."

"I lived with Michael Landy (the conceptual artist) for years south of the river and we were very homebody and didn't really go out apart from openings and gallery dinners. The night Damien won his Turner prize in 1995 was the first time I stayed out all night. And I remember it very well. I was wearing a pink fluffy dress and was told off for smoking underneath the table in the Tate. I rang Michael in the morning and asked him to come out and meet me."

Sarah Lucas said she thought Damien took her there but "Really can't remember when... I didn't really know or think of the history of it. I didn't understand the look of the place. I mean the green. I wasn't sure what it meant. I'm still not sure I do now actually." But it would become the main place for all these young artists to congregate. Donating art to the walls and drawing Michael into their world when it seemed everything was theirs for the asking.

"Usually people go to college and then split up to do other things, but we were all being invited to do shows, so we travelled together to America after our degree show at Goldsmiths. What luxury, with all your mates, staying in the same hotel having a total laugh. So of course you stayed together like a bad circus, and the more you got up to bad shit, the more people wanted you to behave like that." Which explains why the YBAs gravitated towards the Colony: it was a private space you could be bad in.

"Gary (Hume) and Sarah (Lucas) went there but the Colony wasn't about them. They drifted in and out. My relationship with the Colony was absolutely about Michael. I loved his weird, rocky self, that everyone rocked along with. I went to a Free junior school and the Colony reminded me of it. There were rules and structure but then you could do whatever you wanted, as long as you took responsibility for it. I felt very at home. I wouldn't have liked it earlier on. I couldn't have stood all that 'fuck off cunty' rudeness. Michael wasn't like that: he wasn't aggressive. He'd come and stay for weekends to get away from Soho to south London. I liked him and he liked me and so I think I got the best of him."

Paul Fryer, then with Abigail Lane, remembers the years 1996-97. "My overriding memory is that there was something funny happening all the time, like climbing to the Groucho Club across the roof (the Colony's payphone window led to rooftop access to the Groucho Club's Soho Room, used regularly by Keith Allen, Damien Hirst and Alex James). There are too many stories of embarrassment. Michael would put the record 'Delilah' on. He knew that song made me go mental, so he'd wait until I was at that point in the evening and put it on. I'd start singing, everybody would join in and I jumped up onto the bar and I fell off the bar backwards expecting everyone to be there to catch me, but they weren't and I fucking hurt myself. So I said to everyone: 'Hey you cunts, why didn't you fucking catch me?' and they said, 'We didn't know

you were going to fall.' So I did it again and only two people broke my fall: Karen Selby and Sally Dunbar. I loved it when everyone dressed up behind the bar to assume their alternative inner barman or barmaid, and how they dealt with people in a different way."

Paul Fryer belts out Delilah

Photo: Brian Stevens

199

**Darren Coffield
& Declan Browne**

**Pam Hogg
& Phil Dirtbox**

Justin Mortimer
& Kathy Dalwood

The Wilson Twins

**Alex James
& Jan Kennedy**

**Liam Carson
& Orlando Campbell**

Tilda Swinton
& Tallulah

Suggs and wife Betty

Tracey Emin & Matt Collishaw,

Damien Hirst & Maia Norman

Jay Jopling
& Sam Taylor Wood

Tim Nobel
& Sue Webster

John Maybury
& Troy

Daniel Craig
& Heike Makatsch,

Akim Mogaji
& Julian Cole

"I used to love the outings we used to go on, to someone's birthday party or a house in the country: the Colony Club on tour. We used to go to Damien's place in Devon, everyone would pile into cars, or Tracey's birthday party and we'd all be transported along with Michael there, not behind the bar for once. On one of the freakier outings we all went to Mexico. Michael had wandered off from the airport, we'd lost him. Me and Damien had been there a few days. It was so humid you couldn't do anything. Then Aaron the Red Snapper publisher arrived. We gave him a telephone book with a pencil and a phone and said "Find Wojas. He's got to be in one of these hotels." He spent five hours non-stop calling up people. Meanwhile Damien and I are making Wanted posters and putting them up all around town with a picture of Michael with his scar. Finally, Michael walks in with his girlfriend Pascal, "What do you mean I'm lost. I just went for a fucking drink."

"But Michael, that was three days ago,"

"So fucking what? I'm on my bloody holidays." People came back in a state, two of them in wheelchairs and Michael's girlfriend got thrown off the flight on the way back, or so I heard."

Matt Cogger was a barman at the Colony off and on throughout the 1990s, during which time the celebrity barman notion took off. 'Michael was at a poker tournament at the Groucho,' Cogger remembered. 'It was the time that Keith Allen (actor and director) was still being a notorious bad boy, hanging round with Alex James (from pop band Blur) and Kate Moss (model) in the 90s. They were all sitting around singing to Revolver, The Beatles' album. T P McKenna's son Brethney, the actor and barman at the French and Gerry's, often had bad hangovers. He stumbled up the stairs during his break, as Matt was trying to instruct Miss Moss who wanted to play at bartending. As Brethney fumbled for the change for a beer, Matt said go on to Kate, who said, "can I get you anything?" Brethney looked up but all he could say was, "Becks." Brethney's face looked as if he was hallucinating, with the world's biggest supermodel serving behind the bar.'

Tim Noble, who with Sue Webster is one the of the great YBA double acts, was one of the celebrity barmen in 1999. At Hamish McAlpine's house in Broadstairs in 2012, he recalled the Colony in surreal fashion. "It was me and my friend who first went in there, but since I didn't have a friend it was me. And you walk up the creaky stairs and the first thing is you can't get in, can you? And then the next thing that you're confronted with is Francis fucking Bacon, the bastard! How did that place become like that? I like places like that, places that are five steps ahead and you walk in and somebodies shouting at you – 'fuck off you fucking cunt' - and then you look at them, and have to work out: are they actually saying fuck off you fucking cunt back down the stairs, or are they actually saying on the corner of their lips fuck off you fucking cunt, come in? And then in the corner is the piano with someone banging away on it and the keys are all missing and messed up, it's like the music of your fucking mind, it's like a whole orchestra that's already become set, it's like you've just met your mother and met your father but everything smells bad, and its smells sticky and then outside you discover... it's just another lovely sunshiny day... I hated the place. I tried everything I could to never go back there again... I was lucky I left. Michael (Wojas) was the most surprising person I ever met in there. I kept on trying to tell him to leave and open up a garden centre for tropical plants, but he couldn't..."

Inheritance Tracks

The atmosphere after Ian Board's death had changed, and the descriptions of the place from later members begin to rattle in their cages. Paul Freud is a shy unassuming man, son to Lucian. "So I used to go in 94," he says. "'Would you like a drink?' Ian said. 'You never refuse a drink at the Colony'. I looked up at the mantelpiece and there were 15 glasses of wine. It seemed like 15, it might have been seven. 'There you are, everyone's bought you a drink.' I was seeing double anyway. I thought, very generous. I felt very welcome."

"Later Wojas and I fell out. I usually went there on my own. Damien and his brother was there, the guy in a white suit, Elvis, Gavin Turk. I was always frantically drawing at that time. I showed Michael this drawing I was doing, he was so impressed

Michael Wojas by Paul Freud

and he put it in a frame and hung it behind the bar. I really belonged, I thought. I was really pleased, my drawing on the wall of the Colony. I didn't know how pleased I was until the next time I went there, a few weeks later, and it was gone. Michael was evasive and didn't say where it had gone to. I was fucking fuming. I sat in a corner and talked to Gavin, I said 'what's going on there' and explained the situation. Wojas could have it on display, but I wasn't giving it to him, otherwise he's just taken it. That was my understanding and that was why I was annoyed. I don't know if Gavin was getting me on it, he said, 'Ah that's it, it'll have disappeared into his private collection by now in his office.' And now I'm feeling like I've been duped into giving this really very fine, more than a sketch, intense drawing very much of the moment. My last words rather loudly, were ' You cunt!' And I walked out. I didn't go back for years.

When I did return I was treated like the prodigal fucking son. It was important to me it was on the wall, I like to go back and refer to a piece of work after I've done it. Otherwise it's like taking it out of the orphanage before putting it up for adoption. So Michael seemed to understand and he said 'welcome back'. He was on his knees kissing my hands; but I still never saw the picture again."

At this point, Michael had been given so many pictures by so many artists who all wanted them on the wall, that there simply wasn't enough space. Michael would rotate pictures, storing them upstairs, which was not tidy. As Sebastian Horsley was to say so eloquently, the art collection was a 'direct result of Wojas's work over the years in making the Colony special'. More artists were coming to the Colony because Wojas had directly targeted them. And with them came the art dealers and collectors, although not all could take the club. "I was with quite an important collector coming up the stairs one day to be confronted by Michael sitting on the toilet," remembered

Paul Freud. "I never saw the man again, he was so disgusted. Michael had looked like he was having a pony. I couldn't say what he was doing, admin or drugs.

"He had a list on the wall. 'What's that?' I said. 'It's a list of people who owe money.' I saw my name was on the list. So I said I'd forgotten about it, I paid it off or renegotiated it. 'What's happened to the list?' I asked next time I went there, and he said, 'I had to take it down. People have been deliberately not paying in order to get onto the list. They just want to be part of the legend.'"

Paul's father Lucian Freud was one of the great Colony stalwarts in his day. But Paul never went with him. "I wouldn't repeat the stories about my dad. It's personal and treads into territories of repeating other people's stories, but I'll tell you this. When I went up there once there was a bit of a commotion, everyone taking photographs. Damien Hirst was in there getting his cock out with a cigarette in the end of it. "You don't need to do that sort of thing to get attention," I said. "How long have you been doing this sort of thing?" He said, "Since I had eye teeth," and smiled. It was the first time I'd ever seen that, a cock smoking a cigarette." In the 90's Hirst had said to a journalist, "I can't wait to get into a position to make really bad art and get away with it. At the moment if I did certain things people would look at it, consider it and then say 'f off'. But after a while you can get away with things.' (said in 1990 Spalding, Julian. 'Why it's OK not to like modern art' The Times 8 May 2003.)

Hirst Relaxes with a drink

Damien and partner Maia wearing the Beard

Photos: Clancy Gebler Davis

Remembering what it was that got you to the top can also be hard to want to recall, as Hirst's now ex-partner Maia Norman said in an interview. 'Those vodka-fuelled Soho nights, when she and Hirst painted the Colony Room Club red (Hirst had a habit then, when in his cups, of demonstrating his extendable foreskin), are not to be touched on. 'Damien always gets a little bit squirmy when that turns up,' she says bashfully. 'I just say, "Thank God we all grew up." Although, God forbid we grow up too much, as well.' Norman, who is 47, talks a lot about 'keeping young' - it is one of the driving forces behind her label.' (The Telegraph 23 May 2010) In 2010 Maia Norman was designing fashion having had three children with Hirst, by 2012 she had left Hirst for a 59yr old former mercenary Tim Spicer and Hirst was being photographed in the papers dating a 22yr old.

Millie with an affectionate Hirst

Angus Fairhirst wears Sarah Lucas cigarette breasts with Gavin Turk

Janet St Porter & Sam Taylor Wood compare teeth Jay Jopling behind

All Photos: Clancy Gebler Davis

Pollock's Bones
by Abigail Lane
Edition of 125 signed and numbered by the artist.
Commissioned for the Limited Edition Colony book.

Lack of Proprioception
by Marc Quinn

James Birch remembered 1998 at the Colony, the 50th anniversary and the exhibition he put on to commemorate it. A particular scene amused him. Barry Flanagan the sculptor was sitting in the Colony and Sarah Lucas had come up with the idea of serving behind the bar on Wednesday nights. Michael Wojas thought this a great idea. Not only did it mean all their mates came in, but he didn't have to pay barman costs. Faced with Flanagan, Sarah Lucas laughed back on being introduced,' "I can't take a man called Barry seriously." This struck Birch as particularly funny as Sarah Lucas was going out with a man called Gary, artist Gary Hume.

The celebration of 50 years of the Colony was organised and orchestrated by James Birch. The show was at A22Projects in Farringdon, and Birch contacted members old and young to put together something that was significant to the YBAs as a group: an exhibition not all about the past but more about the future. Wojas was totally involved and excited by the whole project. He commissioned a film crew to interview the participating artists and swing a camera around while the show was being put together. Some of it was easier to get hold of than other pieces and Damien Hirst only put his piece in at the last moment, flying ducks suspended in formaldehyde, which doesn't appear in the catalogue. Still, the most expensive piece to insure then was Patrick Caulfield's at £40,000. The show opened to a full and admiring crowd but only one or two pieces were sold. "We never made any money from the shows and the only people who ever bought anything were other artists," says Birch. This was despite the roll call of exhibiting artists. Chris Battye, Patrick Caulfield, Daniel Chadwick, Darren Coffield, Keith Coventry, Clem Crosby, Barry Driscoll, Barry Flanagan, Tracey Emin, Paul Freud, Damien Hirst (pencil drawing of a skull), Justin Mortimer, James Moores, Ray Natkiel, George Melly's portrait of Barry Flanagan and visa-versa from 1972, Marc Quinn, David Remfry, Jake Paltenghi, Neil Hedger, John Maybury, Ed Winters, Peter Davis and by Kate Braine, a bronze head of Ian Board's that would have a hole drilled into it and a plug for the special opening ceremony where Michael Wojas would syphon Board's ashes into their final

resting place, which would then sit in the bar. Was this coincidental or did Wojas know that one of the main advocates for trepanning (drilling a hole in your skull) was Colony member Lady Neidpath, aka Amanda Charteris, who'd made a film Heart Beat in the Brain, of herself doing this in the 1970s?

Wojas did have the foresight to get one of the celebrity barmen evenings filmed inside the club. This would eventually become the most valuable part of the project and be used to some effect a decade later in Lisa Stanfield and Nick Mead's documentary film Dean Street Shuffle or as it has now been renamed, The Colony.

Meanwhile Wojas paid out an extraordinary amount of money, around £4,000 in dribs and drabs of cash, to two filmmakers Julian Cole and Akim Mogaji for no copyright. Wojas wanted to make a documentary solely about the Colony Room. Maybe the impetus came from Ian's death and the idea of his own oblivion, being sunk into the club in a similar way, that made Wojas pull his finger out. He was always writing down notes in booklets with memories of what Board had once told him. 'Princess Margaret...' is a story which has unfortunately died with them, though undoubtedly she was there. Perhaps it was because of the 40th anniversary when nothing of any consequence had been done that Board had claimed they were going to paint the Colony pink. Most probably the idea of the filming and the documentary came from John Maybury and the BBC.

Kathy Dalwood
Colony Room Ashtray

Cast of Love is The Devil mix with regular members

Photo Courtesy of BFI and John Maybury

Love is the Devil

By 1994 John Maybury had made a film for Channel 4 with Tilda Swinton (and Rupert Everett), an adaptation of a play she'd done at the Royal Court called 'Remembrance of things fast, true stories and visual lies' which won the LA film critics award and the Berlin Film Festival for Maybury as director. "Which was why the BBC came to me with the Bacon project," says Maybury. "It was amazing, the amount of people who went to the Colony Room. I always described it as the exterminating angel: you went in that door and you could not leave, like in the Luis Bunuel film of that name. You'd try to go someone would offer you another, or someone would appear you wanted to talk to, and then it would all kick off again. This is the thing of high functioning alcoholics. Journalists drank from the lunch through to evening, from pub to club, in order to get stories pre computer and mobile phones; the info and invitation exchange was one of the great things about the club."

Maybury made the film about Bacon, called Love is the Devil, for the BBC in 1998. It starred Derek Jacobi as Bacon, Daniel Craig as his lover George Dyson and Muriel was played by Tilda Swinton. Wojas had been alone at the throne for four years by then. Sandy Fawkes was to die in 2005 aged 75, Eddie McPherson, Suggs's mum is still alive and singing in Soho.

"Alan McDonalds Production design was so good at replicating the Colony." Maybury said, "we got Sandy and Eddie as background artists and Sandy got so pissed at the pretend bar before we started filming that when Derek walked in, she ran up to him wailing, "Francis, Francis..." I intervened softly. "Now Sandy, Francis is dead, this is Derek Jacobi who's playing Francis."

It was such a beautiful set you really thought you were in the Colony: It's actually very easy to recreate the space (but not the atmosphere). The weird thing was, with writing these scenes and trying to explain to the BBC that these people were a bunch of drunks, and they all think they are being super witty with each other, but drunks aren't actually that witty, it just seems funny to them because they are drunk. So to hit that nuance is quite difficult to write bad witticisms, banality and plain rudeness. I was furious when recently I heard from George Melly's widow that Francis said to her, "I've never seen the point of you." She wasn't a Colony habitué. I could've used that line. We did film in the French Pub that great line from Bacon – "I can tell by your necktie that you have absolutely no talent at all". We used Gary Hume as the ill fated artist trying to befriend Francis." Extras were pulled from the clubs ranks.

As Love is The Devil was being made, more YBAs were swelling the clubs numbers, pulled by the fame and publicity circus that surrounds any well-marketed film. "It was only really with the YBA celebrity chasing, attention seeking, when that underground notion went astray," says Maybury now. "They were to all intents of purpose ambitious little shits, most of them. I'm not sure if some people would say the same about me."

"That's the difference, between the artists like Terry Frost or Tony Earnshaw in the Colony. I love Andrew(Logan) and Duggie(Fields), who were never and I don't think ever will be properly accepted by the traditional art world. They took the

Derek Jacobi as Bacon shares a ciggie with Daniel Craig as George Dyer in Love is The Devil

Photo: Michael Woods

fashion route and it's interesting that fashion designers like Thea Porter and Jean Muir were members." ("I do have a sweet boyfriend in London, Frank Dickens," Rhodes said. "He's a cartoonist, and his strip is Bristow... but fashion is very taxing... I'd like to be married, but I'm just not sure that would work out.") It didn't. "Thea Porter's shop was just around the corner and I remember a giant Logan Butterfly in the window. I wonder if Logan isn't accepted in conventional art circles because he makes things about light and life, as opposed to the endlessly, Mysterious Death?"

Maybury certainly has a point when you see that over 50% of those listed or winning the Turner Prize which began in 1984, were members or at least frequented the Colony. And far more artists, that haven't been listed for the Turner but would have assumed to have been were - Gary Hume, Sue Webster and Tim Noble, Daniel Chadwick, Clem Crosby, Keith Coventry and Marc Quinn.

"The appeal," as Maybury eloquently points out, "and one of the difficult things to explain to people, was that the Colony was a cocoon. It was protective, and certainly the ballet lot (Helpmann, Ashton, Fonteyn, Nureyev) could go in there and not be recognised and have a drink and nobody would give a shit, that was the quality and the aspect of the place, it wasn't elitist, wasn't snobby, yet it was super elitist.'" A contradiction in terms, an oxymoron, something that Patrick Hughes, Les Colman and Anthony Earnshaw would all appreciate part of the 70's Northern Surrealist set. Earnshaw, 'a scruffy working lad, no money, uneducated' and from Leeds (like Hirst), whom George Melly was to meet in 1964 in Leeds to purchase his first painting.

Along with Gail, his second wife, he would spend many hours enjoying the Colony with Patrick Hughes and Molly Parkin, then married. Perhaps the surreal atmosphere of Edward Burra, Jeff Nuttal and Earnshaw soaked into the walls and attracted artists like Gavin Turk who would have one of his plaques on the wall, the nature of it being like an English Heritage award, robbing him of his final MA degree from the Royal College. His final degree show being a white room with the blue plaque and the immortal wording 'Gavin Turk Sculptor, worked here 1989-1991 Borough of Kensington.' Unbeknown to him Jocelyn Stevens, Rector of the RCA at the time was to be made Chairman of English Heritage 1992-2000, and found the plaque less than amusing. 'Three days before the end of his Degree show, Gavin Turk received a letter from Jocelyn Stevens (not a member of the Colony). Following a meeting of the Academic Board for Concessions and Discipline held on 11 June, the Board decided that you had displayed insufficient work of the standard required for your Final Examination and agreed that you should be required to re-submit to the Final Examination Board on Friday 21 June at 4.00 pm. You will be expected to show a substantial body of work of at least 6 - 8 pieces.'

Turk went to the meeting with a slide-projector. Amongst his own work, he showed additional slides. He felt this was necessary 'to illustrate the lineage and context... It seemed to me that an interest in contemporary debate was absent or even irrelevant.' Frieze magazine reported in Sept1991.

Perhaps worth noting that though not a member, Jeff Koons who has caused his own controversy in the art world (taken in by James Birch) greatly enjoyed the Colony.

Gavin Turk's father was a jeweller who had a shop in Soho, in Dean Street in the 70's so he knew the area well, and he told me in 2012 how he had taken to the Colony in the 90s. "Lots of people had mythologised the place and I think there was an acknowledged sense that you had to go through a humiliation ritual

Gavin Turk and his blue plaque

Photo: Jonathan Root

to be part of it. I went there first with Joshua Compston in 1993: this guy spouting a shock of blond hair from his head and Russian Constructivism from his mouth, and always working on some hare-brained scheme like, how to change the cultural production of the country. He was going to radicalise other people's lives and I think he was a bit ahead of the curve. Before that time, the Colony was the only place where you could be an artist and freely talk about art and not seem abnormal. So the Colony became full of these radical contemporary characters."

There was also The Chelsea Arts Club but for most young artists it was the wrong end of town and what actually drew Turk in was the older part of the club, "watching it work, when Ian went into one of his striding up and down and calling everyone a 'fucking cunt and wished they'd all go away and what did they think they were doing there anyway and they were such arseholes and shits', this crazy guy ranting on whilst everyone else was just quietly getting on. It was a weird performance, a show. A punk 'couldn't give a shit' atmosphere in the air. Some people worked really hard to get their membership. It involved an early meeting which was really frightening: the very thought of being alone with Ian Board at 3pm in the afternoon." And discovered to his amazement that alone or outside the club, Ian was a normal, sweet, softly-spoken and intelligent man.

ABSOLUT VODKA

COLONY ROOM CLUB

50TH ANNIVERSARY ART EXHIBITION

EXHIBITION FROM
19TH OCTOBER – 7TH NOVEMBER
WEDNESDAY – FRIDAY
12 – 6PM

A22 PROJECTS
22 LAYSTALL STREET
LONDON EC1R 4PA

WORKS SELECTED BY GA... ...O AND MICHAEL WOJAS

Invitation to the Colony's 50th Anniversary Show by James Birch

Michael Wojas said in the 90's that what he liked about the Colony was the changing parade of faces, and how people came and went through the decades, how they'd be there three times a week then suddenly they'd disappear into another life, have children or move countries, and return five years later. As ever, some understood the point of the place, while many others could not.

Room of Fairy Tales

Deborah Curtis Turk is now married to Gavin Turk but for years, "I was always just Gavin's girlfriend. When I felt comfortable I could do the humour and the quips but there in the Colony, I'd go back to feeling like my shy

Deborah Curtis and Gavin Turk's fairy tale wedding day

Photo: Sophie Parkin

teenage self. I felt like a fish out of water. I didn't like the competitiveness. People who were friends outside I couldn't cope with inside. And I think there were people there who didn't have a real sense of self, and so would use the wit and interesting people to create an identity for themselves, and a lot of people were being destroyed by it. I think Gavin was attracted to the distilled essence of all those bars and clubs." She was also critical of it from another perspective. "I had small children and I believed that you integrate your children into your life and that if you couldn't take your kids up there, it made me feel excluded. That was my resistance. I was a bit political around children." Since 2007 Curtis has been running the House of Fairy Tales, an art performance charity for children and adults.

Life changed in the club just as it did outside. Some saw it as a disappearing of hours, a mirage, others like a malevolent presence eating them and their time up. Popular mythology saw the end of the 90s as wild days, fuelled by phenomena like Brit brilliance and YBA bravado – everything seemed possible, everybody became famous and everybody came into the Colony. And then as quickly as they arrived, they drifted away. Coffield had been right: in some respect Michael Wojas had alienated the old crowd by bringing in the new. Undeterred, he still had the energy and imagination to begin something else, so Phil Dirtbox, his part time barman, started the Saturday Night cabaret which would become Sunday Night Music Night. Gaz Mayall, of Gaz's Rockin' Blues in the basement of what was The Gargoyle Club in Meard Street, became a more frequent visitor. "Being a boogie woogie pianist,

Emin, Wojas and Collishaw with the Hirst Spot painting still hanging

having an upright real piano in the house was a major attraction."

New visitors felt the magic. When artist Karen Selby first visited in 1999, she felt it was a life changing occasion. 'I first went to the Colony in September 1999 with "Magic Mickey", a short, acne-scarred Irishman who never stopped talking,' she said. 'He believed in the power of spells and he'd fix any problems you had with a theatrical chant. Promoting my exhibition, "Private Keep Out", at Shoreditch Town Hall, he promised to take me to the Colony Room (somewhere I'd vaguely heard of) I wondered aloud what to wear. "Try and impress and you'll be out," he said.

'The place was packed. It gave you the feeling of being in a fish tank whose water needed changing. Sarah Lucas was behind the bar. I recognized her, though not the tall, thinly handsome man that was Angus Fairhurst. Later on I would have such a terrible obsession with him that my GP sentenced me to six months of counselling to recover. I did, recover, thankfully, but for now I was happy to compliment Sarah on her t-shirt, (decorated with tribal looking breast plates in her trade mark fags), and to get her friendly reply along with my vodka and soda.

Mickey then introduced me to Michael (Wojas). He was ghostly pale with a scar slashed across one cheek and in between cackles and wheezes, he rocked back and forth. This was striking at first, in the way that a physical deformity can make you self-conscious but we fell in to easy conversation and after a while I noticed I was rocking back and forth in time with him myself.'

Michael became famous for his rocking. Some thought it a side effect of autism, but it also increased at times when he felt stressed or unwell. At times Wojas barely rocked at all: when the club was fun, full and financially viable.

'There was a newspaper clipping behind the bar (with the headline: Mobiles more dangerous than drink - Judge rules), photos, postcards, pieces of junk, Damien Hirst spot paintings worth hundreds of thousands of pounds (wrapped in cling film and with a sticker that said '99p') along with original photos of Francis Bacon.' Selby continued. 'There were many famous faces, loads of YBAs, even a few I knew. The vodka and sodas went down, the hours slid by. I spent most of my time talking to Tim Noble and Sue Webster. Their star was just in the ascendant, ever since a recent TV appearance, I'd judged obnoxious for tearing up a water colourist's work. Now I thought they were a hoot. I would steal a look around the place. I couldn't believe my luck in discovering this secret, sleazy bit of history. I felt like I'd gone through a green door into a back bar in the Adult Adventures of Alice. As I looked around and read some of the invitations to opening nights at dazzling galleries that I could only dream of (all signed with a personal and jokey remark to Michael) I saw that my own cards were there on the mantelpiece too. Depicting myself and my partner Sal (my wife, I liked to say), naked but for high heels, we were hitting each other over the head with our dildo collection. PMTx2 (squared) it was called, I was accepted.'

Selby was smitten and along with her girlfriend Sal, would spend large amounts of time with Michael. Sal would end up working in the bar and looking after Michael in a relationship that made them look like brother and sister.

Around the same time actress George Sutcliffe (currently in London West End's

Sally Dunbar and Karen Selby were PMT x 2 (squared)

Selby's Paradise Cunty Bar

The Mousetrap) worked as sometime barmaid at the Colony, the French and Gerry's, but the Colony formed her. 'My mother and granny were both members of The Chelsea Arts Club, my father was always a member of Gerry's and Tatty Bogles. But it was Matt Cogger and Simon Crabb who took me to the Colony in about 1999. They'd been DJing in one of the Chelsea Arts Club balls, I was at RADA and I was extremely nervous because Amanda Harris was at the bar (she was a lead at The Royal Shakespeare Company). I ended up doing the odd shift behind the bar and cleaning Eddi's (McPherson) house."

"I remember once being in the club with Alex James, Joe Strummer and Damien Hirst, there were about eight of us and somebody came in that none of us liked, so we all disappeared out of the window when they were at the bar, crossed over the roof and into The Groucho Club.

"Michael was amazingly bright. We often got plastered and I remember once sitting at the bar with Mike as he tried to explain to me how the universe worked and how the planets turned with balls, tin foil and newspaper. He could explain things such as why water goes down the plughole the way it does. I remember staying up all night with him watching Fear and Loathing in Las Vegas, both of us completely off our tits and going out to get sausage sandwiches at 7am." Georgina happily reminisced having finished her five year marriage to film star Sean Bean, yet still having to take out restraining orders on him. In the Colony he was always quiet.

Having been a member since the late 1980s Darren Coffield could see what was happening following Board's death. "We did try to warn Michael that if he became too synonymous with a certain group and then they decide to move the party on, then you're going to be left high and dry. They bought a lot of publicity and other less desirable things to the club. When Ian was alive and protecting his license he put a notice in the toilets: 'Anyone found taking any substances in this club other than drinks or cigarettes will be banned for life.' When Michael started to lose his way he'd be up all night with all these people and the club just wouldn't be clean half the time, as he'd only just got up at 1pm. I'd get there at 3pm, the early afternoon

Black & White Photos: Clancy Gebler

Joe Strummer, Wojas' hero

Sarah Lucas and Damien Hirst,
Living it Up

Phil Dirtbox chats up
Anita Pallenberg

Keith Allen Fists across
George Sutcliffe smoking

Alex James on banned cell phone

Colour Photos: Darren Coffield

drinking culture was dying out, and Michael would hand me a bag and say, "Bank last night's takings for me of whatever's left from the night". You could see how he was losing the plot and some very parasitic people got involved with the club. I suppose that's the nature of drugs." The fantasy of Britain's reinvention as 'Cool Britannia' would also start to collapse, although at times it did seem akin to the The Fun Palace that architect Cedric Price and impresario Joan Littlewood had conceived at the beginning of the 1960s at the bar in the Colony. With the end of the decade, also came the end of the era. Not only had Francis Bacon, Isabel Rawsthorne and Ian Board died but Daniel Farson and Jeffrey Bernard went within months of each other in 1997, by 1999 Henrietta Moraes and Gaston Berlemont would also be gone. The old guard was dying off.

©Berlemont

Santé By Daniel Farson - The End of an Era

Chapter 7
The Final Years 2000-08

Yearly Membership
£100 - £150
2000

Photo: Brian Stevens

Prone to booze? A Research paper by the University of Glasgow in 2008 asked and made a link between children with a high IQ at the age of 10 and drinking problems at the age of 30, it states nothing about the proclivity to drugs. Drugs blossomed into Crack dens and heroine hideouts as Tony Blair was toppled from Labour and Gordon Brown saw in the beginnings of Austerity Britain, America and Europe. Banks crumbled and some MP's were making up their dwindling pension funds with expenses. A scandal was bound to happen.

Back at the Colony life continued as usual –"We used to climb in the toilet, two of us, lock the door, climb out the window and go across the roof and climb in the window of The Groucho. We'd go and put a load of drinks down on somebodies bar bill at the other end of the bar that we didn't like. We stood on the sewage pipe and broke it. Michael wasn't happy." Darren Coffield remembered fondly. But many of the YBA's were becoming part and parcel of the media go round and were more often to be found in Soho House with advertising types, or Groucho's for their new found smart status.

"I always banned myself from Groucho's. It's unreal. Loathsome media types caught up in this whole thing of, 'so, is your film happening or what?'" John Maybury told me, "Exactly the opposite of what the Colony was about. The last thing anyone wanted to know at the Colony was what you were doing. Nobody was interested in what you were doing. And if anyone started talking about what They Were Doing, everybody would start shouting, 'Oh shut up and fuck off you boring cunt, nobody cares!' It was anti-ego. When I got caught up in Natural Nylon production company (began by a group that included Jude Law, Sadie Frost, Jonny Lee Miller, Ewan McGregor, Sean Pertwee), "I took Jude and Sienna(Miller), Ewan, Kiera (Knightly), Johnnie, I was meant to be doing a Christopher Marlowe film with them, and it wouldn't have occurred to me not to take them in there, or whether they would fit, until you got in there and thought, oh dear."

"If your face didn't fit, you were out," Maybury compared it almost to a casting, and that the members would turn and watch as someone came through the door. "The door would open and you were actually walking onto a stage and everybody would turn around, because the place was so small, a HE Bateman cartoon in reverse (the famous cartoon by-line is 'The girl who ordered a glass of milk in the Café Royal' and the waiters and cliental faces are aghast with shock) The person Who dared to walk into the Colony Room Club! The unspoken rules, the nuances of it all."

In a bid to keep the artists from slipping too much towards the Groucho, Wojas staged another art show. This wasn't to commemorate any anniversary but just the art and the artists '2001: A Space Oddity' included many of the artists that had joined after the publicity of the 50th anniversary show at James Birch's. It was also held in the same space.

Maybury proves that it wasn't just an art world but a theatrical one too, though he was very much part of the art world, talking honestly about it. "It's weird I have mixed feelings about the YBA's, love Sarah Lucas, she sensibly got out, moved to the country, and there was sweethearts like Angus Fairhurst (committed suicide in 2008) who were too gentle. There were others, rats up the drainpipe, wouldn't piss on you if you're on fire, naked ambition tattooed upon their foreheads. They were Thatcher's children alright, Michael Craig Martin taught them, more about business than he did about art."

From 2001: A Space Oddity Catalogue
Dan MacMillan's Adolf Hilfiger

Damien Hirst's drawing of ashtray from
Lyon & Turnbull's 2008 Catalogue

223

Artist Gavin Jones, who now lives in the Outer Hebrides, put it another way. "Michael looked after Ian and kept the fridge working... Then the rather daunting task of running the club killed him. They were both genuine."

Simon Crabb was a barman at the Colony in the early part of the new century and proves it wasn't all doom and gloom, though the country might have been going to hell in a handcart, unexpected fun was always just coming up the stairs. He wrote to me; 'It was a Thursday, around seven. People had stumbled through the door as soon as I unlocked it at three. Refugees from the "real world", still on the tear from the night before, some, and although never hectic it had been a busy old afternoon, serving refreshments, sorting out a toothbrush here, a Neurofen there, playing a varied selection of old faves on the knackered cd player to create warmth and set the tone for the evenings voyage.

Phil Dirtbox assumed the role of MC, someone was playing the piano, Cliff Slapper and Phil, was entertaining the troops with a raucous rendition of Sinatroid, when in all his chalk-striped, zoot-suited glory stood George Melly. I hadn't seen him in ages, the steep stairs a challenge but he was obviously delighted finding the beloved haven still vibrant and swinging. Phil, introduced George as a legend and begged him for a song. George declined politely but Phil pressed him. "Let him get a drink down his neck first, for Gawds sake." I said. Phil, added that perhaps George would oblige after a wet and another ditty from himself. George smiled broadly and, waving his hand airily said "We'll, see, we'll see". He sat down taking the weight off his Correspondent shod feet. Phil took up the challenge of performing before the legendary blues-shouter and fellow Scouser, what he lacks in excellence he more than makes up for in enthusiasm and got the Colonials going with, "I've Got You Under My Skin" with his trademark "ad lib", "nothing contagious ladies". After we loudly prevailed upon George to give us a song, delighted, he did.

He had it still, in spades... It was magical and as he finished his last song, a rousing rendition of (Lucille Bogan) filthy blues ditty "Shave 'em Dry", the 15 or so people there stood as one and whooped and hollered like people possessed.'

"I got nipples on my titties, big as the end of my thumb, I got somethin' between my legs'll make a dead man come, Oh daddy, baby won't you shave 'em dry?"

Phil, stepped forward, flung out his arm and said, "Ladies and Gentlemen, the GREAT, Mr. George Melly. And may I say what an honour it was to sing before you." And a twinkle in his eye, George replied "Oh, you know what they say… always the shit before the shovel."'

Photo: Brian David Stevens

Molly Parkin and George Melly turn back time

Neil Fox of Le Gun draws a typical night of Colony Celebs

A Bacon Window

For all the above, its spontaneity and warmth, was the reason why people like actress Georgina Sutcliffe loved it too. "It became like home. I could credit card the main door to get back in, if it had been locked. I feel like I grew up there, and every big thing that happened to me between 18 and it's closure, was celebrated there. I went up there the day I graduated. Peter Brunton took my diploma from me to frame it."

Big Peter was an ex advertising executive for Pearl and Dean. When he retired he looked for a part time job in Soho as an excuse to keep coming back. He got one in Janus the sex shop, famous for its paddles and costumes for spanking enthusiasts. What everyone loved about Brunton aka Big Mouth was his total indiscretion. Film stars and MP's names and their recent purchases were bandied about as common knowledge; well they were in the Colony. He was a generous and much loved character, who called his wife Mrs Hitler. One day when he was telling the Colony, so Hilary from the French House told me, that Janus on Old Compton Street was being made to black up its windows so as not to offend. Francis Bacon said, "Just a minute." Went out to the paint shop and came back with a brush and pot and went with Pete into the shop and painted the window black. "How many people realised when they cleaned that window up that they were destroying a Bacon original?"

Georgina was also a barmaid at Gerry's and would help out at the Colony too, during this period she met Sean who would become her husband. "I loved the bar it was incredible. Everything was under there that anyone could need in an emergency from tampons to blu tac. I remember once going to a premiere with Sean (Bean, now George's ex-husband) and wearing this latex dress. I went into the Colony before and somebody said it wasn't shiny enough, so Michael got out the WD40 from behind the bar to buff it up. Unfortunately I went to the loo and the chemicals ate through the material during the film, and I had to ask a women in the loo for safety pins to try and connect up one side where it had split up to my waist.

The Colony was the last down and dirty club where nobody gave a toss where you were or who you were, but they cared about you, shared in your success and heartbreak but that was why we could always go there to commiserate or to celebrate... many a night I slept on those banquettes; A horrible place to sleep. I loved the afternoons when the sunlit hit the dust and we'd dance, Oh but didn't we just have so much fun?"

As Sebastian Horsley, writer and artist said, "The Club reminded me of an alcoholic Tardis. It was minute on the outside but huge on the inside and you went there for love, which they served by the glassful." Sarah Lucas was good friends with Sebastian and when Maybury refused to go with Horsley to the Philippines to film him being ritually crucified, Lucas went instead. Because Horsley's drug of choice was heroine rather than alcohol, you could often find him in the club upright and sober for a decent conversation and a glass of orange juice. He would go clean for months and regarded the club as his sanctuary from the outside world that mocked at times his extreme attire of Mad Hatters Hat and painted nails.

Matt Cogger recalled Michael hearing the news in 2005 that a rather peculiar member Richard Barnbrook a sculptor trained at The Royal Academy had become the BNP Member of Parliament for Barking & Dagenham, Michael telephoned him from the bar one afternoon: "Hello Richard? It's Michael at the Colony... You're fucking barred!"

Peter Brunton aka Big Pete

227

Isabella Blow & Sue Webster

Photo: Clancy Gebler Davis

Sebastian Horsley & Babette Kulik

Photo: Carla Borel

The Public Prosecutor

But it wasn't only the fashionable and eccentric icons like Horsley and Isabella Blow who were drawn to the club latterly. Unlikely candidates like Clifford Allison 'The Public Prosecutor' remembered it for giving him back his mojo. He became a member just before the end. "It is remarkable how working in a suit, in a town and in an office for 30 years can change you, for you do not realise it yourself..." he said, Michael Wood's had an exhibition that was being filmed for a documentary on George Melly, who took Molly Parkin with him. Melly as guest of honour, spent the evening on the balcony smoking and drinking with Alison and Parkin. "George and those with him displayed huge generosity of spirit which I had forgotten I once had. When the evening was over I left feeling very much that I wanted it back! We met regularly and their company helped hugely with my re-liberation. George had spoken to Molly about me: "Under that grey suit Moll, he's one of us!" is what he reportedly said. We went together to see George at home in his last days. I'll never quite grasp how such an ill man can fill a room with pure force of personality.

"The Colony Room Club What a place! The atmosphere in there was like nothing else. Atmospheres like that cannot be created; they just grow. Molly introduced me to everyone as a 'public prosecutor'. I made so many friends. There was never an unhappy or lonely moment in that club. As a new member I felt it my duty to open conversations with all and sundry and the results were unfailingly friendly and uplifting. Generosity of spirit was there in abundance. I believe I got mine back there. I don't work in an office any more. Life is not a dress rehearsal. I am alive I AM HAPPY! George, Molly and the Colony Room Club literally gave me back my life."

This story of Melly and the Public Prosecutor becomes more surreal when you realise that Melly had stood bail for Neville when prosecuted with Felix Dennis for the School Kids Edition of Oz in 1971 at the Old Bailey. Melly took exception to the lack of bail and from the Press Box shouted, 'You Senile old prick'. Reported in the press as,****. All assumed that Melly had used the C word. Cross examined later by the prosecutor, he was asked, "Do you swear in front of your children?" "Certainly" said Melly. "You would call your daughter a little cunt would you?", "No I don't think she is one. But I might easily refer to a politician as one." Asked to define the word cunnilingus (he referred to it as Gobbling or Yodelling in the Canyon). In 1971 he didn't know of his daughter Pandora's existence, or if he did had no contact with her, but he did have a step daughter, Candy. Candy was the name of a novel by Terry Southern whose fictitious life as a heroine, got up to more sexual exploits, than the fictional Pandora found behind any locked door. When Melly died his spirit seemed to have jumped into his small granddaughter who danced about the coffin and played peekaboo with the audience. Afterwards his son Tom and Candy got into cabs with at least one of George's ex mistresses art critic Louise Buck, Gaz Mayall and leaving the local mortuary pub wake, went to the natural place to celebrate George's life the Colony Room. Where we all sang and wept and danced the night away in July 2007.

The Club filled with music, whether it was Paul Fryer singing, Delilah or Kenny Clayton on Friday nights starting off the cocktail hour by playing and singing his readapted lyrics, the genteel in an English Cunty Garden.

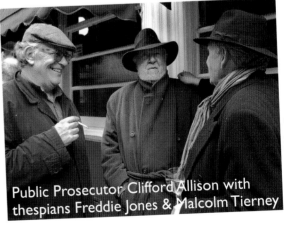

Public Prosecutor Clifford Allison with thespians Freddie Jones & Malcolm Tierney

Photo: Michael Woods

ACORN THEATRE, MARE ST, E2
HACKNEY EMPIRE

COLONY ROOM SHOW TIME

TICKETS £12.00

Box Office:
020 8985 2424
www.spicefestival.com

SPICE FESTIVAL

Rhys Ifans guests on harmonica
for Alabama 3 with Zoe

COLONY ROOM SUNDAYS

MUSIC

DRINKING

POETRY

INVITATION ONLY
6-11PM

Sunday Nights once a month

Musical Poetry Show Time

Whether it was Sunday nights when poetry and music rattled the walls in the last few years, Dick behind the bar in a dress, a wig and childlike makeup, occasionally my son Paris helping out, the place was renowned for its music. In the same way that Wojas had encouraged the younger artists to join the club he then encouraged musicians and their agents and it inspired great loyalty.

Mark Manning aka Zodiac Mindwarp who often played at the club in its last years said, "The psychedelic American war helmet Michael used to wear for kicking people out at the end of the evening, was liberated from a dead Argentinian soldier at Goose Green, it was taken by Gimpo a Falklands veteran and painted by me for my band The Love Reaction."

James Endicott's band The View played in the Colony to celebrate on the night they reached No.1 in the charts. And when Michael's computer packed in, it was

Martin Kelly who gave him 'an old one' from the office of Heavenly Records in Frith Street so that Michael could continue organising and mailing out for the Sunday night events.

Alice Harter was, 'trying to get a band off the ground. I was a band manager still a bar maid. Michael would let me do photo shoots, videos. He just let me have the keys. Michael actively encouraged and supported my musical endeavours, putting The Magic Numbers on at one of the Colony Sunday music nights without having heard them. It's actually how the band got signed. We even presented the Colony Room with a double platinum disc! But I met all sorts there dodgy diamond dealers, Debbi Harry, artists, mainly just drinkers! Seeing a Colony drinker in the French about a year after the closure and realised that although we'd shared many a drink and laugh, neither of us knew what the other did for a living. How refreshing!'

Suddenly everyone wanted to film in there. Whether it was a Vogue fashion shoot with Charlotte Rampling, or the irrepressible Suggs lead singer of Madness with his ITV Show, 'Suggs in the City'. Ian Dury might have loved the Colony as a member and the Blockheads might have played there on a Sunday night, but in Suggs show Paul Weller, the Zombies, Lisa Stansfield, Jools Holland, The Charlatans and Billy Bragg all sang there too.

Nick Meads is a director who had directed the film 'Swing' in 1999 starring Lisa Stansfield and Hugo Speer as the love interest, and was asked to make something out of the 'hundreds of hours of footage as well as the additional stuff we shot' that became The Colony or Dean Street Shuffle. Stansfield and her husband Devaney had stepped in to try and rescue the club when things started getting out of hand with Michael saying he wanted to close the place. With Hamish McAlpine, Twiggy and Ian Freeman they tried to negotiate with the landlord and paid off the rent that was owing. In return they were given by Wojas all the original footage that he had commissioned from Julian Cole and Akim Mogaji 'It wasn't about the gin fuelled evenings and interesting conversations for me it was the acceptance. The film threw me into the heart of this social and brutally honest environment. Midway through filming I found out I had colon cancer. The love and affection I got from members of the Colony was overwhelming. The hugs and kisses I got the day before I was admitted to hospital humbled me. It was the first place I wanted to go when I was well enough.'

Salena Godden is a performance poet and writer 'It was a late summery dusk 2004, when I went into the Colony for the first time and I was with Phil Dirtbox. I knew I was somewhere very special straight away, a dusty boozy dive I wanted to make my home, my local... it felt like climbing into a wonderful secret. I was there regularly from that first introduction, glorious sneaky late afternoon drinks; it felt like playing hooky from school sometimes. I would pop into the Colony after meetings with a BBC producer or some record label bosses and kind of rinse the bollocks off me, clean the starch of those worky meetings away with a stiff drink with Dick. I remember Dick would ask, "What can I get you?" and I would always reply "give me what I deserve!" this would result in a very strong and refreshing cocktail of his invention, followed by laughter, music and a loss of memory.

'The first friend I made in the Colony was Sophie Parkin, a brilliant writer and poet and a great laugh, a contagious laugh coupled with an infectious positive outlook. Many of my earliest Colony memories are spritzers with Sophie Parkin, I recall a first impression of her bright red lipstick smile and her lovable warmth, a true great friend.

'As for Michael Wojas - I admired Michael - but was honestly quite scared of him at first.. We had mutual friends in music, Alabama Three and Peter Doherty. I had a picture of my bum up there, the cover of the Saltpeter EP, and I was proud my ass was up on the Colony wall, I felt included. At first I most often read poems there, but Michael liked my band SaltPeter and so we played many times at the Colony Showtimes too.

'It seemed the Colony was like a secret club house where Soho writers, artists and musicians met to lick their wounds for failed days, gathered to slag off shit reviews or drank to death for glory days and shared the winnings. Ahhh, too many stories they become one summarised memory: losing my shoes and bumbling around Soho in a nightie with a smudged face covered in charcoal from an all-night art lesson session to then loll about on the Colony's ashy carpet with a taste of 'Old Fashioneds' illegal kisses and cigarettes... I truly miss that place!'

Sukie who's band Madame played there too remembered it as a safe house. '...that Michael and Dick looked after me, made me feel so welcome, made me feel that it was important that I was sitting at the bar. Called the cads I brought in with me bastards like nightmarish protective uncles, hoorah... played my album over and over... nights where transsexual leather cat suit lady sang Roy Orbison songs, every one singing along at the tops of their voices... cathartic, gentle, insane, beautiful. I was there for those 3 years as a member (Michael invited me to play first) and then I very humbly asked if I could join... initially I was Sebastian's guest some times and sometimes actor Malcom Tierney's, the rest of Soho/London, the wild west and then this magical place of unusualness... we did the last photo shoot there with photographer Rebecca Miller.'

Left to Right: Hilary Penn, Salena Godden, Elvis McGonagal,
David Brown & Alison Hunter, Carla Borel & guitarist Cobalt Stargazer

Wilma with her Mexican inspired painting

Wilma Johnson Artist said what she liked most was the unexpected, "You never knew what or who you might find behind the door, one evening I came in to find a beautiful poetess passed out on the sofa in a lace dress and one stiletto like a decadent Cinderella. "Shall I try and find her shoe?" I asked her friend. "Don't bother, she lost it a while ago- she hasn't been home for three days".

It was one of the few bars I could walk into without feeling self-conscious as a woman alone, knowing that no one cared if I was wearing a power suit with a sequinned bra, or paint stained jeans and an Iron Maiden tee-shirt. You knew you could order one drink, or twenty without anyone batting an eyelid... There are a lot of 'art bars' where you feel you'd get more respect if you were the guy in a suit who could pay for the vintage Crystal. At the Colony I remember Dick Bradselll calling down the bar one night when I came in broke, "Wilma's an artist who's going to buy her a drink?"

My first Colony phase was in the eighties, I have fond memories of wild nights, most of them a little fragmented. They were the kind of nights you wake up from wondering which bits had really happened and which you had dreamt... the stranger parts were the Colony version of reality.

One night in 2007 I stupidly went to the Colony room in search of normality. I'd been at the England Gallery all day setting up an exhibition of the Neo Naturist Archive. A man from the Tate was coming down, and the stress was focused on Christine Binnie's Marabou trimmed, fuck-me pumps.

'They've had the moth,' she told Jane England, 'what if they hatch out in the night and eat the whole archive...' The whole idea, although quite Damien Hirst was too surreal for me. Having just flown in from Biarritz, the idea of hanging a show, arriving at the private view to find it had turned to dust.

I made my excuses and went into Soho to meet Sophie Parkin. Of course, with hindsight I can see that the Colony was the last place to go in search of the ordinary. I was just thinking it might be less surreal than trying to sell my old underwear to the Tate gallery. I was looking at the shell bra and remembering a crowded Friday afternoon when Ian had said that if I tried it on in the bar and it fit, I could keep it. Of course it didn't, I thanked Sophie for her tip about going to Selfridges to find large cup bras.

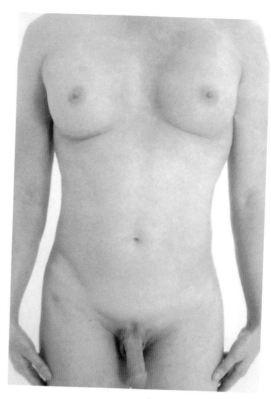

Frances McKevitt,

'I just gave Genesis P-Orridge the same advice, although he's only a double D, so really he could go to Marks and Spencer.'

As far as I remembered Genesis P-Orridge was a man. Apparently he was involved in a project to become a pandrogynous being, turning himself into a physical replica of his girlfriend so they could be two halves of the same person, which involved, among other things, breast implants. He could have gone for a C cup.

I tried to get the conversation back to something more mundane, an antidote to the surreal of the archive but a gorgeous blonde woman came up and asked Sophie 'Are you ready, I just need to find a zip-lock bag and some nail scissors and we can go to the bathroom.'. This sounded dodgy, potentially druggy, 'Rachel, meet Wilma, she might be a perfect person for 'The Project', she's a neo-

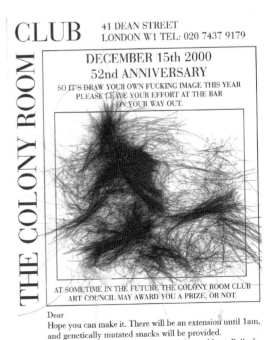

THE COLONY ROOM CLUB   41 DEAN STREET
LONDON W1 TEL: 020 7437 9179

DECEMBER 15th 2000
52nd ANNIVERSARY
SO IT'S DRAW YOUR OWN FUCKING IMAGE THIS YEAR
PLEASE LEAVE YOUR EFFORT AT THE BAR
ON YOUR WAY OUT.

AT SOMETIME IN THE FUTURE THE COLONY ROOM CLUB
ART COUNCIL MAY AWARD YOU A PRIZE, OR NOT.

Dear
Hope you can make it. There will be an extension until 1am,
and genetically mutated snacks will be provided.
We also take this opportunity to wish you a Merry Bollocks
and another New Year.

Rachel Matthews collects
for her pubikini

naturist.' Rachel was making a Pubikini, a bikini woven from samples of different women's body hair. The icing on the cake was that she had been a presenter on Art Attak, my kids favourite programme. I had whole minutes of peace and quiet while they watched her doing magical things with sticky back plastic, before bursting into my studio - 'I know what Art is Mummy, it's sticking things.' I laughed but I started making collages soon after. I owed this woman Rachel a lot − a lock of my hair at least...'

"The night I walked into the Colony I knew I had walked into Michael's house," Said Abigail Lane. "I realised that some of his attitude had been picked up from the past. I liked going in there in the afternoon when the sun was streaming through the windows and I could dump my shopping down and have a drink with Michael and meet some weird solicitor who's bunking off work, and evening coming along and then thinking, I should go home but let's not bother. I know it was the only place I felt comfortable walking into alone. But until the horrible druggy period, it was the one place you could always locate someone. It feels like there's a total hole, I miss it and him still."

Francis had been a vicar in the church, but her life had changed and she began to regularly play American Pie for Colony Sing-a-long's. In those last years Francis could be seen driving into Soho in her pink Cadillac and wearing a black leather cat suit. " One of my own fondest memories was playing a half hour Friday night impro set with David Soul, me on ukulele and harmonies, playing Rock 'n' Roll standards. 'Don't give up on us baby'."

Nick had first gone there with Clarence Clemons a black American saxophonist from Bruce Springsteen's Band and who played with everyone from Lady Gaga to Aretha Franklyn. 'He used to talk about that one club in London every time we ever discussed London. Here is a man who spent his life travelling the world and could go anywhere, but was more taken with that one club than anywhere else in London.'

"One night in 2000, after Joe Strummer's new band The Mescaleros had just performed at the Astoria in Charing Cross Rd, we all piled in for a classic lock in jamming till late." Gaz Mayall relived the memories. "Joe at the bar with a guitar, me and others on piano and a good old fashioned Rock'n'Roll singing session ensued." Matt Cogger was there too and remembered, "An acoustic guitar and about 25 of us improvising percussion - a 10 minute version of White Riot. You had to be there. Unfortunately there was no one in a condition to operate a recorder."

"I almost preferred being there when I was practically the only customer,"Gaz said. "The bar staff, in particular Dick, Simon and Michael were always a magnificent contribution to the intellectual aspect of its Rock'n'Roll, jazzy ARTmosphere. It did get a bit wild towards the end, cocaine in the loo and whatever medication Michael was on influencing the vibes. I finally was given my membership card on my 50th birthday. The expiry date just read 'until further notice'. A few months later the room closed for good. I was absolutely gutted." Gaz Mayall said.

James Birch and the punk poet Jock Scott, a modern day George Barker, father to actress Anna Chancellor (Duckface in 4 weddings and a funeral) daughter Poppy. On her birth certificate he described his occupation as 'Poet and Tragedian' and friend and hero to Irvine Walsh, Joe Strummer and Ian Dury. "We were at the Clerkenwell festival when he called the sculptor Abigail Fallis a 'Fat Slag'. She hit him to the ground and started kicking him. To be fair he was pretty drunk." James said. He took him home to give him somewhere to sleep it off. "The next day I awoke and searched the bedroom and house but couldn't find Jock, I assumed he must have crept off home." James went off to lunch. The builders heard banging and wailing but refused to break down the door to let him out. He'd locked himself into the gallery the basement of James' house. He rung home to Scotland and his mother told him to bugger off. So he rings up the Colony where the reply to his plaintive, 'Where's James, is Birch there?' is answered with, ' I think he's gone to Tangier for three months'. He is locked inside and cannot see his way out. Eventually he rings a friend who brings around mini pizzas, miniature scotch and some water he can drink with straws through the letterbox. At 6pm James eventually returns home to release the caged animal that is Jock Scott into the wilds. The poet's prison, the space

Jock Scott was locked in has now become the private library of Nicholas Serota, head of Tate Britain, London, but it was also the space where both of Birch's Colony exhibitions were held.

"I remember once arriving for talent night and being asked by Wojas to pay," said the performance poet Murray Llachlan Young. "I had entered an exclusive club. The only other person to have paid to play at the Colony was Shane McGowen. The Colony was a smelly room full of dreadful people and I was very proud to be an occasional addition to their number. Usually someone randomly insulted me. 'You know you're a cunt don't you?' was a good one. I remember Suggs from Madness's mother tearing a strip off me, for no apparent reason. I remember, in reply to her hail of expletives I asked, 'You're not violent as well are you?' She replied, 'And you can fuck off with your smart mouth.' The insults and their retorts after a while, felt like a form of exclusive currency; An almost bizarre form of kindness. Edwina had worked at the Kismet as a barmaid but she was also a Jazz singer who had her pick of the Soho crowd of men with her charismatic beauty and quick tongue.

"Michael wasn't my cup of tea," Edwina said to me in 2012, looking back. "But then I knew Muriel and Ian. I went out with them all back then, Auerbach, Freud... but every time I went out with Freud we had a car crash. He was a terrible driver. Enough was enough, when he left me on the side of the road to find my own way to a doctor with a dodgy leg, I said no next time he asked me out. He was a cruel bastard."

Sex for some in Soho was just another way of shaking hands, and for some liaisons that didn't necessarily include an embrace, more of a 'wham bam thank you mam' without the business of money being exchanged. Irma Kurtz pointed out how radical this behaviour was, "The Colony wasn't a pick up joint if you fall in love or into lust that was nice but it was beside the point. Bohemian behaviour meant that you didn't share the same restrictions and morals, now everybody sleeps with anybody from Hendon to Highbury. Sleeping with someone because you want to, doesn't mean anything now."

Writer and comedian Barry Cryer described poignantly how it had been for homosexuals and why Danny La Rue wouldn't come out. "It was a horrible era it was like sexual McCarthyism, full of haunted, hunted people."

Dick Bradsell the famous cocktail barman who invented the Espresso Martini, The Bramble and a Russian Spring Punch, began working at the Colony in 2004 ; an antidote to the cocktail world. "The first day I was there Mandana Ruane (the manager of The Academy Club above Andrew Edmunds), her dog, writer Michael Smith and an Italian concert pianist came in. The pianist started to play the piano, against Wojas' wishes and Mandana began to dance with her dog around the room."

Writer Michael Smith came from Hartlepool where Peter Mandelson was MP . On telling Smith that Mandelson's 'first taste of London bohemian life was at the Colony Room' when taken there by Thea Porter he replied , "Oh Aye! When on a PR visit to the local chippy Mandy remarked "what lovely guacamole" after tasting the mushy peas."

The way life collided at the Colony was the reason why people went there. Abigail Lane noticed it. "The wonderful thing about the Colony was the total disinterest in age groups, sometimes you'd see a bunch of 19 year old models in sparkly clothes, and an old bloke being helped up the stairs by his driver, forced in on each other because of the size of it."

Lane remained a good friend to Wojas. She put on the Colony Room Bar at

Dick worked at the Colony for the last 4 years

239

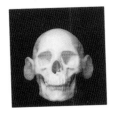  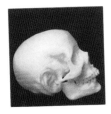

Abigail Lane got everybody doing
skulls with Showroom Dummies

  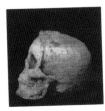

 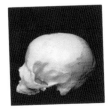 

exhibitions of YBA's in The Showroom Dummies' and Bone Idle in Charing Cross and Selfridges. At the Selfridges show they even had The New York Dolls play live. "I asked Michael to represent the Colony running the bar. I think we all liked the jaunts away and in those days he wanted it to continue. I wish the end could just be cut out of the story, it is just such a horrible mess and everyone took sides and got nasty. My attitude to all that at the end was that I was in quite a mess and was going through Eric's dad leaving and all that. So I wasn't much involved I'd stopped going to the club because it just seemed really druggie and I found it upsetting, the state he was in the whole place had a different feel it wasn't right, it had lost its smell. I've never been a drug taker so I really backed off from it. I always saw Michael personally he came up here to Suffolk. I found it devastatingly upsetting, Vanessa Fristedt, me and Sarah Lucas, we all agreed, 'let's go there and sort it out', and we really lectured him, but it didn't make any difference. He was never there and the club felt like he'd already died and he seemed distracted. I think it was after Jake had his operation, and then I started to get bullshit emails from people seeming to suggest that Michael

couldn't run the club, and I only ever believed Michael. Of course he was a mess doing the tax returns on the floor, his office, the toilet, but no sane person could run the Colony otherwise it wouldn't have been how it was. It was the drugs without a doubt. But it seemed to go from a point where everybody's doing it together and it's just a little bit of coke or weed, to the crack and a few people started to go there and got in a bad way. Because I didn't do it I was less aware but then I'd also be told that I wouldn't feel comfortable. Some had got into something more serious. People were going to crack houses from the Colony, we dropped him off once; it was horrible.

Abigail even took her new baby boy Eric into the club. "I would love Eric to know Michael, he rocked and others rocked with him, take the medication to fit in with life and he got out of his depths with the drug. I thought, he's going to have another phase. I know he lost the will at a certain point, all that back stabbing. He'd sorted enough people out, he was a father figure to Damien and the boys, but there was no compassion left for him."

Save The Colony? Again?

Darren Coffield thought at a point, "The art crowd stopped going up there who'd had substance problems and were trying to give it up. Too many dealers trying to give you coke and get you back onto the stuff. People were trying to exchange wraps for artworks. I didn't want it on me. I mean I had a wife back home and I wanted to go home and go to bed, not up all night running around like an idiot."

'Move over Damien Hirst: the Colony Room Club in Soho is this week auctioning

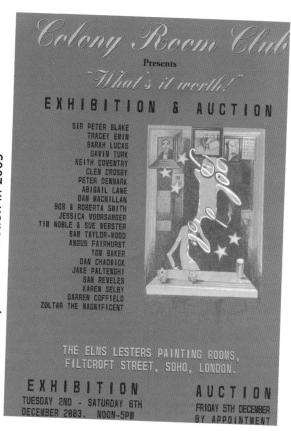

off its art memorabilia. Or is it? Some members are so dismayed that the current owner, Michael Wojas, plans to sell irreplaceable modern art, photographs and cartoons worth an estimated £150,000 that they are threatening a legal injunction. They say the work belongs to the club and not Wojas, who has been running the Dean Street establishment for the past 14 years. Saleroom Lyon and Turnbull has been given until mid-day tomorrow to withdraw the items. There are rumours that Hirst, once a regular at the Colony along with Francis Bacon and Lucian Freud has been approached to use some of the £111 million he netted from last week's sale, to rescue the ailing club. Those against the sell-off include singer Lisa Stansfield and film producer Hamish McAlpine, who want to see the club preserved.' Evening Standard, The (London, England) September 22, 2008

The drugs had become less of a party more of a habit for Wojas and he found others to take them with and buy them off. It has been said by someone who was complicit, that at one point as much as £700 a day was the cost of this habit. Art works began to disappear off to salerooms or were sold back to their original owners. He organised for the Michael Andrews mural to be taken off the wall and told everyone it was being cleaned. Lying became easier than the truth on occasion. Dick was covering for him, whilst the wine and spirits being bought was from Summerfield's cheapest because he couldn't get credit any more from the usual Soho Supplies. "It really offended me the cheap vodka," Dick said, "and when Sarah Lucas asked me to sit and talk to her, he told me that if I sat down with the customers I was sacked... God I hated working for him sometimes and then I'd get an awful feeling, I might turn into him. I'm glad I didn't." Some days he sat slumped in the toilet. Other days he'd rage at people chasing them down the stairs with a baseball bat. Even people who had been members all their grownup lives and who's parents had been founding members, like Charlotte Skene-Catling who optimistically took some clients of her

Glasses by Didier Avignon

Photo: William Corbett

architectural practise for a drink. Attacked by Michael she was so shocked she burst into tears. People took the destruction of the club they held dear very personally. Hamish McAlpine was one of these because as a daily regular customer from the mid 70s until near the end, he loved the place and was a friend of both Muriel and Ian. In 2012 he talked for the first time about the end.

"I guess a few of us are guilty, that we should have looked after Michael," said Hamish. "I had put up money to stop it being closed 10 years earlier. Lisa (Stansfield) and Ian (Devaney) put up money I don't know what the figure was. When suddenly this rumour came out through James Birch, pissed as a rat that Michael had surrendered the lcase of the club causing the members to ask if it was true. He said he wasn't prepared to discuss it. We then started a campaign to get him to tell us, the landlord wouldn't speak to us either. It was a members club he didn't own it; we forced an AGM. What people misunderstood was, It was never a fight against Michael, it was about us wanting to keep the club going and that was seen as being anti-Michael. We thought Michael had been left the club by Ian, we would've been happy to raise money and give him a six figure pay off. Happy to have Dick who was working there carry it on. But suddenly the new junkies of Michael crystallised the fight but why would people enjoy the destruction of seeing what was so much part of each other's lives? And then there was the whole saga of the possessions

A genuine Barry Flanagan for sale

243

of the club, everything in the club was owned by the members. I understand that Damien was close to Michael and I believe he brought back his spot painting but where is the till? I think he'd decided to help out Michael who had already given up. I was told Michael got £25,000 so the Landlord could get back possession of the Colony. There was no other reason why that should have happened, no one ever asked the members. The original fight was about the lease and David Gentle refused to furnish anyone with a copy of the clubs lease. The members launched a legal action to stop Michael then Michael attempted to sell all the art in the Colony, not only had he closed the club but he thought it was all his personal possession, others like Horsley refused."

"We got an injunction against the proceeds which to this day remains in limbo, all the money raised from the auction is in Escro because David Gentle won't agree to a settlement. And now Michael's dead it's frozen until David Gentle is prepared to make a settlement. For the moment it's locked in the auctioneer's bank account. In my mind its crystal clear the contents of the colony are owned by the members of the Colony. Some people took Michael's side and said it was for him. Most artists who gave a piece gave it to the Colony to be on the wall. It's a tragedy I did go to the closing night Dec 16th 2008 where I proposed a toast to Michael the gentleman who closed the Colony. Were you there at the AGM where I started chanting 'Mugabe'. The one thing I'd like to establish is that I never had a vendetta against Michael I just wanted to keep the Colony going, I didn't get annoyed with him when we discovered it was a done deal. Drugs do bad things to people he should have come clean instead of the stress that caused the infighting, and the fight to keep it going; it was a fair equivocal account. I was told there was no money left but it's in Lyon and Turnbull's account. David Gentle sued me personally, the whole thing's a mess, I'm out of pocket in the mistaken belief that the lease hadn't already been signed away. Horsley and others became great allies in our fight to keep it going there was a story planted round Sebastian's death, that he'd died out of regret to the harm he caused Michael but Sebastian's last words to me were, 'my mother told me to never say anything but good about the dead, Michael's dead, good.'

"I am a useless dandy. I am almost bankrupt," Horsley told me in 2007." I will either commit suicide or die at the age of 50 because I will have said all there is to say... will you marry me?" He repeated this in his blog in January 2008, by then he was fully entrenched with promoting The Save the Colony.

"I first went to the Colony in the late 70s The first people I remember there were Peter Brunton (who was to become a best friend over the years), 'Bookshop' Billy O'Connor, Big Tom O'Keefe (Sailor Tom). Beverley Storey who worked at the French, and has been my wife for 30 years." Said Ian Freeman a writer for film magazines. Ian was also part of the Save the Colony with McAlpine and Co. "Of course we tried desperately to save the club, attempting to find alternative premises, trying to get the club listed and seeking investment. All was to no avail."

Dick maintains, "Michael wanted to move the club to another premises, the upstairs of the Coach and Horses was even considered...He had also signed all the artwork on the back, 'this belongs to Michael Wojas'."

As it was, the Colony cnded on 15th December 2008. It was neither a wild party of anger but a sad party of dissolution. Not many people were there Salena, Rachel, Dick, David, Sal, John. All the bottles were taken off the bar. We all took turns in pouring drinks for others, not really believing it was for the last time. It felt as surreal as an adult's disco in a junior school hall. Nobody even took mementos, well I didn't. And then the door was locked and the key put away.

Hamish McAlpine now
by Sophie Parkin

'Friends and members are gathering together to raise our glasses to the maverick King of Soho, our mutual friend, the Polish Prince of the little green room, Mr Michael Wojas,' the £25-a-head bash read. Raffle prizes include a distinctly unbohemian Armani goodie bag and there will be an auction of rare Colony items (including a Blow Job).'

"If Michael Wojas had been as good at running the Colony as he is at organising benefits for himself we would still have a place to drink in," said Horsley. The New Sheridan Club described Wojas as 'looking like a blade of grass growing under a bucket', towards the end of his life, but Soho from the residents point of view didn't seem to be fairing too well either.

"I don't think that Soho becoming more openly gay helped Bohemia – a pink wall went up separating the gay and the straight, stopping the mix. And Damian and Tracey didn't help. Art stopped being art for art sake, and that's all real art should be for. And now it's the monied and the class thing. Something that once was so obviously understood." Irma Kurtz observed. "The Colony was the essence of bohemian Soho. Soho now? Hey It's too brassy." She added.

Horsley was moaning to the papers that "Soho has lost its heart. The music has gone. The bars are being shut down like they are malaria joints. The brothels are being closed down. You don't see pimps and whores, the flowers of the earth. When you clean up the city, you kill it. It stinks of death. The puritans have won. The Christians have dried it up so no rose will ever grow there again." He sounds rather similar to Jeffrey Bernard two decades earlier wailing over denim clad advertising men taking over Soho in the same paper The Evening Standard.

Even if the Auction didn't raise any money for Michael the gigs at the 100 club Oxford Street did. People performed and met up, gulped at Michael's state, and enjoyed the bands. Maggie Hambling insisted upon getting onto the stage and serenading Michael as part of the old school appreciating what the club had meant in the past, now there was no future.

Abigail Lane helped out Michael, "The last auction they did, it had a tall room with stage sets and he asked me to help him with it and it was a sad way of selling things off, he didn't do his research. He'd joined in with the Cocaine; Damien had the wherewithal to get out. But the way that Michael had turned round and said, all you rich artists are in your country houses now well I'm going to do something else, and he did. It was mad, but incredibly successful. Michael found a niche where he could be accepted.

"Michael had this fantasy that Amanda and him were going to get married. Michael always had these girlfriends I think the big love was princess and daddy relationship. I think he was even going to go straight, I think he would have been a great dad. I think we thought there would be another chapter. How sad it should end as an ingrowing toenail." Abigail ended.

"I think the influence of that place, the Colony, whenever people had parties or dinners, Wojas would come along. Everything was a slightly greenish tinge, it wasn't just about influence for me it was about a validation." Said Paul Fryer who was adamant, "Wojas was the Colony Room, for others I know it was Ian Board and earlier Muriel Belcher, but for me it was always Michael. The pictures of Michael on the cross were hilarious, Michael Wojas died for our sins. But what else was he going to do? I mean once he got it handed over to him, he had no choice but to carry on. Once you'd become the owner or the priest of the Colony. Dick could have done it but my question would be, why would he have it? It's a vocational calling, a bit like being Jesus; not everyone's idea of a great career move."

Paul Freud thought it should have kept going. "It was just ready to evolve the challenge to move it on without it turning into some sort of flocked velvet brothel. A proper person who understood art and you could have had a membership list of

Final Benefit for Wojas
Photo originally by Oli Maxwell

247

thousands." He said. "Why wouldn't it be the smallest art club in London? London is stupid and greedy not having it. I have good memories from there on the whole, I've got some good pictures out of it."

Amongst the Colony's effects I found a piece of writing by Michael undated, but obviously before the clubs end, and in a moment of lucidity.

One more lesson From Ian!

To Close the Colony on 15th December 2008! 60 years to the day that it opened.

A)   Sell lease and leave personally. It can continue in name.
B)   Sell lease and let someone open their Colony in different premises.
        Happy to assist and advise but not to run
C)   End it completely – Perfect. Top and tail 60 years.

There are both business and personal reasons.

Having seen the parallels between Ian's tenure and mine, I realise that Ian chose to stay and die running the club, convincing himself that he was fulfilling a promise to Muriel – but not fulfilling himself. Also didn't think he could do anything else – scared to change.
I choose not to! Have fulfilled(and some) any perceived obligations and owe it to myself to use my energy in other ways and not end up in a cul de sac that leaves no outlets for progress/challenge because all ones energy is taken up in combat bureaucratic assault.

I find that the calibre of the members has slowly fallen, in line with the general dumbing down of society as a whole I make members of people I would have turned away 10 years ago. Simply to survive. There is no scope to increase or expand income and all the good ideas (CuntyLife/films/outside bars) are left dormant through lack of time while inhouse policy is continually battling against smoking ban(1st July 2007) and music.

Whilst my brain and energy are intact it would be criminal not to try and use them.
In a more expansive efficient and beneficial way. Not that I suddenly think I am a genius but what is the point of everything I have learnt from the Colony if I can't use it.
All creativity is locked up staying in the room, the womb, the safe… And eventually to the grave, thinking what if I had...?

That's not good enough. I know I have abilities, capabilities and can't let a smokescreen of drink and drugs blind me. The Colony would become my excuse rather than my inspiration, my quicksand not my broadband, not my green and pleasant land.

Damien Hirst revamped the cash register into an art work

Wojas signed believing his reasons to close the place would be his opportunity to a new life, he had made up his mind long before the members had.

Carla Borel

Phil Dirtbox

John Moore

Photos: John Dunbar

The Green Fingernail

In December 2008 with the Colony closed, everyone was left a little bewildered, dazed and confused. The Save the Colony lot moved with Dick Bradsell into a basement of a decidedly odd building. 22 Romilly Street had been done up to become the reconstituted actor's club the Green Room from John Adam Street, but it hadn't really worked. It was in a word too plush and then when someone ran off with all the money, it was left abandoned. Picked up by another entrepreneur that offered his downstairs as a meanwhile Colony home, Dick moved in and wallpapered the walls with song sheets and called it The Green Fingernail club. Salena Godden launched her Book Club Boutique on Friday nights where poetry, writers and singing was celebrated, there were folk evenings, and there were transvestite evenings where great big blokes put on small skirts, high heels and a lot of lipstick. Dick managed with a wig and fake freckles staying behind the bar serving the perfect Espresso Martini that he had originally invented 25 years before at the Zanzibar. His daughter Beatrice and mine Carson, helped out wearing eye pencil moustaches. In short it

was nothing like the Colony, but people who were at the Colony went there and people like Peter Brunton, Dutch, Martin and Twiggy who had no other place to feel at home other than Gerry's, leant on the bar upstairs. Finally Romilly Street closed and everybody dispersed

Colony Girls at Karen Ashton's Art Car Boot Fair
Amanda, Geraldine, Sal, Alice, Vanessa , Millie & Sophie.

249

until the call to arms. There was to be a Wojas Benefit and everybody stepped up and sang and performed and spoke and laughed at the 100 Club. A year later there was Michael's funeral to attend.

'Wormwood Scrubs is now listed' The Guardian proclaimed on March 11th 2009 'but there is disappointing news about the Colony Room Club in Soho's Dean Street, which is officially not part of our heritage. An application to "list" the club, one time home-from-home to Francis Bacon, Lucian Freud, George Melly, Jeffrey Bernard and many other creative types has been turned down by culture minister Barbara Follett on the advice of an English Heritage inspector. Despite noting that Muriel Belcher, the original owner, "deliberately nurtured an ambience suited to artists, Bohemians, gays and all those on the fringes of 1950s society", the inspector sadly concludes that, once the pictures and bric-a-brac are taken away, all that was left was "a sparse room with a functional bar counter". '

The Evening Standard quoted in better detail -

'The 60-year-old club even had the support of London Mayor Boris Johnson, who wrote a letter to the chairman of English Heritage, pledging his unequivocal support for the preservation of the drinking dive. Last year, the club's secretary and head barman, Michael Wojas, suddenly announced he was retiring and closing the club.

The verdict from English Heritage looks pretty definitive. It states that 41 Dean Street simply does not meet national criteria: "We know that, historically, the Colony Club, which is situated on the first floor of the building, was frequented by important and influential figures with huge stature in modern British cultural life, but it is not where they lived or produced their works of art, which may have increased the historic interest...The only fixture of artistic importance, a Michael Andrews mural — once the Colony Club's centrepiece — has gone, and the club's character and ambience derive heavily from the various paintings and bric-a-brac that cover the walls, but these are not fixtures and would not form part of the building if listed. Indeed, many of them post-date the club's 1950s and 60s heyday. Otherwise, this is simply a sparse room with a functional bar counter." 13 March 2009

Self Portrait with Cigarettes
by Sarah Lucas
Commissioned for the Limited Edition Colony book
Edition of 125 prints signed and numbered by the artist

Rachel Sinclair
and Kelly Ann Davitt

Photos: Dutch Michaels

The Funeral

Michael Wojas died on the 6th June 2010. Some said he died of a broken heart, after all that betrayal, he died of alcohol and drugs, others said. Technically he died of cancer of the liver. He never got the money, still frozen from the sale. The funeral on 16th June 2010 was a surreal riot of weeping, laughter and rock. A double decker green bus arrived from Soho to the crematorium in West London where a beautifully decorated made coffin by assembled artists including Abigail Lane and Sarah Lucas, could not fit through the established doors for the burn up. Much laughter, everything had to be different with Wojas, Alabama 3 his favourite band sang over his body, electric guitars wailed and everybody stuffed into the chapel standing, sitting on each other's laps, tears rolling, mouths shouting, as if it was another Sunday Night Showtime at the Colony. Afterwards we drove in the bus back to Soho, singing and drinking vodka and lemonade in plastic cups. I sat with Dick Bradsell and Keith Coventry to the Groucho, where everybody bought their own drinks and performed and looked at the pictures projected across the wall like an old school movie. Salena Godden read out her specially written poem and then I read out mine but couldn't, because my tears kept closing up my throat and splashing onto the words.

Poem for Michael Wojas by Salena Godden

I don't know what to wear

to your funeral today

something black

something pinstripe

something green

something gay

a bottle of vodka breath

and my knickers the wrong way

I don't know what to wear

to your funeral today

an ashtray around my neck

paint my nails lime

a pair of mirrored shades

to hide the tears of tearing time

a magpie on my shoulder

a bacon on my back

a skull and cross bones flag

leopard skin sling backs

because

whenever you were nice to me

it meant the fucking world to me

and when you gave me vodka free

it meant the fucking world to me

and when you gave me money for a taxi

to make sure I'd get home safely

it meant the fucking world to me

it meant the fucking world to me

and when you listened to my CD

and pressed play whenever you saw me

it meant the fucking world to me

that meant the fucking world to me

and when you put my posters in the lavatory

and my fliers on the bar for all to see

it meant the fucking world to me

and that you did this complimentary

it was not obligatory

and it meant the fucking world to me

it meant the fucking world to me

recognise your generosity

michael of the colony

because

it meant the fucking world to me

it meant the fucking world to me

and I don't know what to wear

to your funeral today

something black

something pinstripe

something green

something gay

bottle of vodka breath

and my knickers the wrong way

and all tomorrows parties

raise a glass to yesterday

to all the good times

good people

at your funeral

today.

The Colony Room Club 1948-2008 Dean St Soho
Poem for Michael Wojas, June 2010 by Sophie Parkin

They say,

One door closes and another opens.

But some doors remain close

And none open in exchange.

We are not all Pandora.

There will be no brief glimpse through a keyhole,

No return to, or reinvention of.

Instead, lock the door

Paint it a different colour,

Look away when you pass.

The pavement will remain grey,

The bottle of vodka tipped empty on its side,

The record player, un-played,

The dirty glass, carpet sticky, bar fruit-fly ripe.

But remember that time on a Sunday night

When everything was green and red and gold,

And all the lost squashed into the royal box.

Transformed for one night only,

This Colony of misanthropes.

We were so happy – The laughter crackled,

The microphone screeched, the drum thumped,

The glasses cheered, And Michael shouted,

Even the spoons pinged…

And the evening went in a blink of an eye

And all that remains is the Polaroid, shuttered inside.

The next day on the way back to Rotterdam to my husband Jan, who I had first met at the Colony on Thursday 24 July 2008 with Martin Smetsers, his best friend who lived in Dean street, I got a phone call from artist Lucy Parker, Colony member, to say did I know, Sebastian Horsley had been found dead. As we had waved towards Sebastian's flat in Meard Street shouting come over to Wojas' wake, forget about the animosities, he was dying of a heroin overdose. The coincidence was too poignant, all the remembered times Sebastian had said, without the Colony to go to, one might as well die. All the times I had seen him with his editor, sitting on the banquettes trying to argue sense into his book Dandy in the Underworld. It is a lesson to be careful of what you say in newspapers –'I'm not going to move, I'm going to stay here till I die, which hopefully will be the end of next week. I'm going to finish my book and then commit suicide. The only stylish end to an autobiography is a suicide note. Mine will be: "I've decided to stop living on account of the cost."' April 2006 The Independent.

So much was created in the Colony Room, impromptu musical evenings with world class musicians, poetry performed and written, entire novels, plays, ideas bandied about, drawings made and exhibitions planned. The relationships of wit, humour and spite sealed the room in love. And though people didn't cook in the club, there being no kitchen, people did indeed live, sleep, eat and dream there. It was as many have said a home from home that many never wanted to leave because of its sense of freedom. And as Bertrand Russell said "Freedom in general may be defined as the absence of obstacles to the realization of desires." He also noted that though Britain was a more democratic society post War, this also meant there was less freedom for, 'Freedom of opinion can only exist when the government thinks itself secure.' And no government has post war.

How strange that English Heritage could only see the Colony's worth as being on the walls and not feel it, for the atmosphere throbbed out of the walls and ceilings, laughter vibrated out of the floors; the ambience in its very fibre. As artist Sally Dunbar who occasionally helped out behind the bar wrote to me saying 'At night, once everyone had gone and you were clearing up, you never felt alone. You could feel

Muriel's strong presence looking down on you and you could see the ghosts moving round in the mirrors that lined the walls. To me it felt as though the room was the one constant that never really changed and all of us members through the years were merely ghosts moving through it.' The Colony was quite clearly an embassy in a foreign land, a safe harbour for the unusual, the outsider, the unacceptable, the bohemian. But perhaps you have to be one to recognise it. As Oscar Wilde so perceptively wrote in The Picture of Dorian Gray, 'Nowadays people know the price of everything and the value of nothing.' And if there is one thing that can be said about bohemians is that they have an utter disregard for money.

In May 1992, Mick Brown asked in The Daily Telegraph, what constituted Bohemia? 'a disregard for money. Nobody bothered whether you were rich or not... or how you looked... the thing was to be your own person', said writer Joan Wyndham who had been there. 'But it doesn't exist anymore. The Gargoyles gone and the Colony was more tolerant under Muriel, it admitted hetrosexuals...' I spoke to Joan's husband Shura Shivrag in 2012, he said 'I always liked Muriel, She once did me a great kindness and threw Joan's lover John down The Colony's stairs. I thanked her profusely.' Who was John? 'Oh just some dreadful gay, that Joan had decided to have an affair with.' Her daughter sculptor Camilla Shivrag added, 'her boyfriend was kicked down the stairs by Muriel shouting 'Fuck off cunt features'... he deserved it most likely!'

Perhaps the point about Bohemianism is that it is a phase or a state of mind. You can be a bohemian, like Arthur Ransome and then stop to write bestselling children's adventures, Swallows and Amazon, and become rather grand. Or like Augustus John, Nina Hamnett and Paul Potts remain one all your long days, or like Molly Parkin, no matter how your habits change to include god and exclude alcohol, remain potty mouthed and forever inappropriate in suburbia. 'To me' said Michael Luke, author of The Gargoyle Club. 'It meant spontaneity Impulsiveness. Generosity of heart. With Lucien Freud for example, it was an experience just to walk down the street with him, and often a very unpleasant one. He liked throwing pennies at people

Wojas pours Boards ashes into his head watched by Birch 1998

and he did it with unerring accuracy... it was his way to bring people to higher consciousness you see.' To some this might seem eccentric or anti-social behaviour, to others who gathered in the Colony, totally understandable. Even outsiders like to be included somewhere.

In 2012 Ivo Denay director of National Trust London said he would have saved it. I explained that people had contacted not only English Heritage but also the National Trust who had told us there was no way that they could keep it because how could anyone pay to go in there? It is always in the aftermath that people regret what has been lost, whether it be the green spaces of the countryside or the green space of a small room in Soho. When they are gone there is no resurrection that will return them to how they were if they had continued unabated.

It was a glorious sixty years for those who were there and found the succour and strength of mutual associates and friends, all who had a love of life, humour and joy to share. It was a magical room of energy, creative life force and spectacular deaths. But how can anyone sleep at night in what is now three flats, is beyond me; there must be a hell of a racket going on in those walls from all the arguments, fights and good times that never made it out of the door and back into, Soho.

Kenny Clayton on Piano plays 'In An English Cunty Garden'

Post Script

As I was finishing editing this book I got an email from a friend who had a friend who had been given a Francis Bacon which could not be verified by the Bacon Estate, though Brian Sewell and Edward Lucie Smith art critics, both thought it to be the real thing. John Mullarkey asked if he could bring it to me to see what I thought seeing I might know something of the history. The painting is of Mick Tobin, founder member of the Colony, legendary in Soho. An ex-boxer, seaman and carpenter he appears in Jeffrey Bernard's book by Graham Lord and was undoubtedly in the Soho mix. Born and bred Soho he went to the same school as Danny La Rue, St Patricks in Soho Square. Both went into the Navy, post war Danny was on stage with Barbara Windsor, Mick worked backstage. Known as the Admiral, he was often in the position to give work to struggling artists and got both Freud and Bacon in as set painters, as well as Jeffrey Bernard on the ropes. They enjoyed other pursuits besides drinking together, notably conversation and gambling on the horses. Lucian Freud painted him and a triptych of three heads that Bacon painted in 1968, '3 Studies for a Portrait', they could be Mick. When Ken Thompson and Mary Swann, long time Colony members and friends to all, saw the painting they exclaimed, 'My god its Mick by Bacon!'.

The story of how John Malarkey got to have a Bacon, that he can't get verified is typically Soho typically the Colony. John had an afternoon drinking club, Wilde's in Little Portland Street which he gave up when the licensing laws changed in 1995. Mick was a regular at the Colony, and John's place, during his career at Covent Garden Royal Opera House where he was close to Maria Callas. Once that ended, he sold newspapers outside of the American Embassy. He had his portrait by Freud and reputedly sold it for £400. He got into debt to the tune of 2grand through court cases for possession of marihuana. John and two mates helped him out as a gift but Mick insisted he give them something in return; the portrait that Bacon had given him. Since none of them knew about art, they didn't ask him any questions like when was it painted? And, when did Bacon give it to him? Money other than for a pint and a flutter, was of no concern to Mick, who was famous for being one of the good guys of Soho.

I certainly think it looks and strongly feels like a Francis Bacon and there is no doubting their friendship, but just like with so much else that came out of Soho, believing in how much it is worth is another thing. Art after all, is only worth what somebody is willing to pay for it, whether it was a painting or a man in a frock; the international celebrity that became Danny La Rue.

I like to imagine the serendipity in writing this book has led me to uncover a wonderful history and hopefully an unknown portrait of Mick Tobin by Francis Bacon, that secretly hung on my wall in Deal, whilst I tried to uncover the truth.

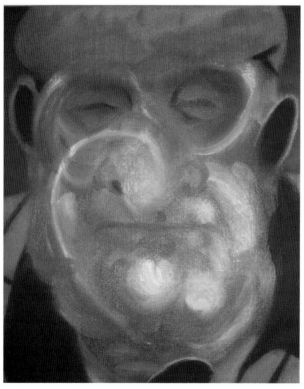

Portrait of Mick Tobin by his friend
Francis Bacon

Francis Bacon

Index

Bibliography

George Barker	Collected Poems	Faber 1987
Jeffrey Bernard	Reach for the Ground: The Downhill Struggle of Jeffrey Bernard	Duckworth 1996.
Jeffrey Bernard & Taki	High Life, Low life	Jay Landesman 1981
Oliver Bernard	Getting Over it	Peter Owen 1992
Caroline Blackwood	For All That I found There	G. Braziller NY 1974
Anthony Blond	Jew Made in England	Timewell Press 2004
Gordon Burn	Sex& Violence, Death & Silence	Faber2009
Jeremy Cooper	No Fun Without U: The Art of Factual Nonsense	Ellipses 2000
Tom Cross	Artists and Bohemians	Quiller Press 1992
Dan Davin	Closing Times	Oxford University Press 1975
Tom Driberg	Ruling Passions: Autobiography	Jonathan Cape 1977
Daniel Farson	Out of Step	Michael Joseph 1974
Daniel Farson	Soho in the Fifties	Michael Joseph 1987
Daniel Farson	Sacred Monsters	Bloomsbury 1988
Daniel Farson	Never a Normal Man	Harper Collins 1997
Daniel Farson	The Gilded Gutter Life of Francis Bacon	Century 1993
Constantine Fitzgibbon	The Life of Dylan Thomas	JM Dent&sons 1965
Geoffrey Fletcher	London After dark	Hutchinson 1969
Sean French	Patrick Hamilton A Life	Faber&Faber 1993
Laura K Jones	Art A hedonist Guide	Filmer Lt 2010
Graham Greene	Night and Day (ed. Christopher Hawtree)	Chatto & Windus 1985
Robert Hewison	Under Seige, Literary Life in London 1939 - 45	Weidenfeld&Nicholson 1977
Nina Hamnett	The Laughing Torso: An Autobiography	Constable 1932
Nina Hamnett	Is She a lady? A problem in Autobiography	Allan Wingate 1955
Denise Hooker	Nina Hamnett: Queen of Bohemia	Constable 1986
Sebastian Horsley	Dandy in the Underworld	Sceptre 2007
Viva King	The Weeping and the Laughter	MacDonald 1976
Clayton Littlewood	Dirty White Boy: Tales of Soho	Cleis Press 2008
Graham Lord	Just the One: The Wife and Times of Jeffrey Bernard	Sinclair-Stephenson 1992
Michael Luke	David Tenant and The Gargoyle Years	Weidenfeld & Nicholson 1991
Humphrey Lyttleton	It Just Occurred to Me	Portico 2007
Betty May	Tiger Woman	Duckworth 1929
Julian Maclaren–Ross	Memoirs of the Forties	Alan Ross 1965
Julian Maclaren-Ross	Collected Memoirs	Black Spring press 2004
Colin McInnes	England Half English At Mabels	McGibbon & Kee ltd 1961
Arthur Calder Marshall	The Magic of My Youth	Rupert Hart Davis 1951
George Melly	Owning Up: The Trilogy	Penguin Books 2000
Compton Miller	Who's Really Who?	Blond & Briggs 1983
Henrietta Moraes	Henrietta	Hamish Hamilton 1994
John Moynihan	Restless Lives	Samson and Co 2002
Robin Muir	John Deakin Photographs	NPG/Schirmer/Mosel 1996
Virginia Nicholson	Among The Bohemians: Experiments in Living 1900-1939	Viking, Penguin 2002
David Niven	The Moons a Balloon	Hamish Hamilton 1971
Frank Norman & Jeffrey Bernard	Soho Night and Day	Secker & Warburg 1966
Phillip O'Connor	Memoirs of a Public Baby	Faber & Faber 1958
Francis Partridge	Everything to Lose	Gollancz 1985
Anthony Powell	Afternoon Men	Mandarin 1992 first 1931
Marsha Rowe & Mike Pentelowe	Characters of Fitzrovia	Felix Dennis / Pimlico 2002
Michael Peppiatt	Francis Bacon: Anatomy of an Enigma	Constable 2008
Paul Potts	Dante Called You Beatrice	Eyre & Spottiswood 1961
Barbara Skelton	Tears Before Bedtime and Weep No More	Pimlico 1993
Nigel Richardson	Dog Days in Soho: One Man's Adventures in Bohemia	Victor Gollancz 2000
Alan Ross	The Forties	George Weidenfeld 1950
Nancy Schoenberger	Dangerous Muse: A Life Of Caroline Blackwood	W&N 2001
Will Self	Liver: Foie Humaine	Viking 2008
Andrew Sinclair	War Like a Wasp: The Lost Decade of the Forties	Hamish Hamilton 1989
Elizabeth Smart	At Grand Central Station I Sat Down and Wept	Jay Landesman 1977
Elizabeth Smart's Journals	On the Side of the Angels (ed. Alice Wan Wart)	Harper Collins 1994
Francis Spalding	Dance 'til the Stars Come Down: Johnny Minton	Curtis/Hodder & Stoughton 1991
Douglas Sutherland	Portrait of a Decade	Harrap 1988
Derek Stanford	Inside the Forties: Literary Memoirs 1937-57	Sidgwick & Jackson 1977
Richard Tames	Soho Past	Historical Pub. 1994
Caitlin Thomas & George Tremlett	Caitlin: Life with Dylan Thomas	Secker & Warburg 1986
Caitlin Thomas	Left Over Life to Kill	Putnam 1957
Ruthven Todd	Fitzrovia and the Road to York Minster	Parkin Fine Art Ltd Cat 1973
Ruthven Todd	Unpublished Autobiography Manuscript	
Harriet Vyner	Groovy Bob: Robert Fraser Art Dealer	Faber 1999
Geoffrey Wheatcroft	Absent Friends	Hamish Hamilton 1989
Paul Willets	Fear and Loathing in Fitzrovia: TheLife of Julian Maclaren-Ross	Dewi Lewis Publishing 2003
Paul Willets	Members Only: Paul Raymond	Serpents Tail 2010
Michael Wishart	High Diver	Blond & Briggs 1977
Joan Wyndham	Love is Blue	William Heinemann 1986
Zinovy Zinik	Mind The Doors	Context Books, New York 2001

Acknowledgements

My huge thanks and love go to primarily Jan Vink my husband and publisher for agreeing to do this book. Then appreciation alphabetically; Michael Andrews Family, Ros Archer, Frank Auerbach, Susie Bardolph, The Barker Family, Chris Battye, Phillipa Beale, Oliver Bennett, Oliver Bernard, Dominic Berning, James Birch, Carla Borel, Dick Bradsell, Gyles Brandreth, Winston Branch, Dean Bright, Craig Brown, Orlando Campbell, Tommy Candler, Harold Chapman, Michael Clark, Darren Coffield, Matt Cogger, Simon Crabb, John Dunbar, Sally Dunbar, Michael Dylan, David Edwards, Kate Fawkes, Ian Freeman, Paul Freud, Neil Fox , Tracey Emin, Barry Evans, Paul Fryer, Christopher Gibb, Salena Godden, Maggi Hambling, Pam Hardyment, John Hart, Alice Harter, Michael Horovitz, Milree Hughes, Patrick Hughes, Paul Johnson, Wilma Johnson, David Jones, Gavin Jones, Mary Kenny, Bob Kingdom, Hanja Kochansky, Irma Kurtz, Abigail Lane, Murray Llachlan Young, Graham Lord, Sarah Lucas, Gaz Mayall, John Maybury, Hamish McAlpine, Dutch Michaels, Barry Miles, John Moore, Tim Noble, Geraldine Norman OBE, Victor Oliver, Michael& Diana Parkin, Molly Parkin, Paris and Carson Parkin Fairley, Brian Patten, Michael Peel, Hilary Penn, Clifford Rowan, Karen Selby, Catherine Shakespeare Lane, Victor Spinetti, Tory Stroud, George Sutcliffe, John Tanner, Mimi Tranin, Ken Thompson, Deborah and Gavin Turk, Candy Upton, Anne Valery, Dick West, Geoffrey Wheatcroft, Dudley Winterbottom, Michael Woods, Sir Peregrine Worsthorne, Zinovy Zinik... And finally, Muriel, Ian and Michael of the Colony Room, all its members and their hangers ons, without which the culture of Britain would be decidedly barren and this book couldn't exist.

A special thank you to Giselle Berlemont, who so generously lent me her father Gaston's incredible archive (all old pics of The French and Dean Street.) Amanda Harris for the Colony archive, Darren Coffield for his archive and Michael Parkin, for his Artists of the Colony archive of letters, manuscripts and pictures by Farson and Diamond but his copyright. And for photographs reproduced:Peter Golding for Harold Chapman's, Michael Woods, Brian David Stevens, Clancy Gebler Davis, Pascal Latra, Dutch Michaels , Olivia Rutherford & William Corbett p233 and Frank Dickens for the cartoons left at the Colony and anyone else I may have missed out, who's work photographic or otherwise has been reproduced via the Colony archive. I must also include RBKC Library, Deal Library and the British Library. Thank you.

In Memory of Jessie Lieberson1987-2012
who will now be surrounded forever by books and stories.

Second Edition
Copyright © 2012 Sophie Parkin
Sophie Parkin. All rights reserved.

Second hardback edition printed 2013 in Belgium.

A catalogue record for this book is available from the British Library.

ISBN 978-0-9574354-1-4

Published by
Palmtree Publishers
For more copies of this book, please email: info@thecolonyroom.co.uk
www.thecolonyroom.co.uk
Tel: 01304377030

Cover designed by Swedish Blonde
Edited by Oliver Bennett

Printed and bound in Belgium, Albe De Coker NV